KB088473

Decoding the TOEFL® iBT

Intermediate

READING

INTRODUCTION

For many learners of English, the TOEFL® iBT will be the most important standardized test they ever take. Unfortunately for a large number of these individuals, the material covered on the TOEFL® iBT remains a mystery to them, so they are unable to do well on the test. We hope that by using the *Decoding the TOEFL® iBT series*, individuals who take the TOEFL® iBT will be able to excel on the test and, in the process of using the book, may unravel the mysteries of the test and therefore make the material covered on the TOEFL® iBT more familiar to themselves.

The TOEFL® iBT covers the four main skills that a person must learn when studying any foreign language: reading, listening, speaking, and writing. The *Decoding the TOEFL® iBT* series contains books that cover all four of these skills. The *Decoding the TOEFL® iBT* series contains books with three separate levels for all four of the topics as well as the *Decoding the TOEFL® iBT Actual Test* books. These books are all designed to enable learners to utilize them to become better prepared to take the TOEFL® iBT. This book, *Decoding the TOEFL® iBT Reading Intermediate*, covers the reading aspect of the test. It is designed to help learners prepare for the Reading section of the TOEFL® iBT. Finally, the TOEFL® iBT underwent a number of changes in August 2019. This book—and the others in the series—takes those changes into account and incorporates them in the texts and questions, so readers of this second edition can be assured that they have up-to-date knowledge of the test.

Decoding the TOEFL® iBT Reading Intermediate can be used by learners who are taking classes and also by individuals who are studying by themselves. It contains ten chapters, each of which focuses on a different reading question, and one actual test at the end of the book. Each chapter contains explanations of the questions and how to answer them correctly. It also contains passages of varying lengths, and it focuses on the types of questions that are covered in the chapter. The passages and question types in *Decoding the TOEFL® iBT Reading Intermediate* are slightly less difficult levels than those found on the TOEFL® iBT. Individuals who use *Decoding the TOEFL® iBT Reading Intermediate* will therefore be able to prepare themselves not only to take the TOEFL® iBT but also to perform well on the test.

We hope that everyone who uses *Decoding the TOEFL® iBT Reading Intermediate* will be able to become more familiar with the TOEFL® iBT and will additionally improve his or her score on the test. As the title of the book implies, we hope that learners can use it to crack the code on the TOEFL® iBT, to make the test itself less mysterious and confusing, and to get the highest grade possible. Finally, we hope that both learners and instructors can use this book to its full potential. We wish all of you the best of luck as you study English and prepare for the TOEFL® iBT, and we hope that *Decoding the TOEFL® iBT Reading Intermediate* can provide you with assistance during the course of your studies.

Michael A. Putlack
Stephen Poirier
Allen C. Jacobs

TABLE
OF
CONTENTS

ABOUT THE TOEFL® iBT READING SECTION

Changes in the Reading Section

TOEFL® underwent many changes in August of 2019. The following is an explanation of the changes that have been made to the Reading section.

Format

The number of passages that appear in the Reading section is either 3 or 4. The time given for the Reading section is either 54 (3 passages) or 72 (4 passages) minutes.

Passages

The length of each passage has been slightly shortened. A typical Reading passage is between 690 and 710 words. However, there are some passages with as few as 670 words.

In addition, there is a heavier emphasis on science topics. This includes topics such as biology, zoology, and astronomy.

There are sometimes pictures accompanying the text. They are used to provide visual evidence of various objects discussed in the passage. On occasion, there are also pictures used for glossary words.

The glossary typically defines 0-2 words or phrases.

Questions

There are only 10 questions per Reading passage now. This is a decrease from the 12-14 questions that were asked on previous tests.

Question Types

TYPE 1 Vocabulary Questions

Vocabulary questions require the test taker to understand specific words and phrases that are used in the passage. Each of these questions asks the test taker to select another word or phrase that is the most similar in meaning to a word or phrase that is highlighted. The vocabulary words that are highlighted are often important words, so knowing what these words mean can be critical for understanding the entire passage. The highlighted words typically have several different meanings, so test takers need to be careful to avoid selecting an answer choice simply because it is the most common meaning of the word or phrase.

- There are 1-3 Vocabulary questions per passage.
- Passages typically have 2 Vocabulary questions.

TYPE 2 Reference Questions

Reference questions require the test taker to understand the relationships between words and their referents in the passage. These questions most frequently ask the test taker to identify the antecedent of a pronoun. In many instances, the pronouns are words such as *he*, *she*, or *they* or *its*, *his*, *hers*, or *theirs*. However, in other instances, relative pronouns such as *which* or demonstrative pronouns such as *this* or *that* may be asked about instead.

- There are 0-1 Reference questions per passage. However, these questions rarely appear anymore.

TYPE 3 Factual Information Questions

Factual Information questions require the test taker to understand and be able to recognize facts that are mentioned in the passage. These questions may be about any facts or information that is explicitly covered in the passage. They may appear in the form of details, definitions, explanations, or other kinds of data. The facts which the questions ask about are typically found only in one part of the passage—often just in a sentence or two in one paragraph—and do not require a comprehensive understanding of the passage as a whole.

- There are 1-3 Factual Information questions per passage. There is an average of 2 of these questions per passage.
- Some Factual Information questions require test takers to understand the entire paragraph, not just one part of it, to find the correct answer.

TYPE 4 Negative Factual Information Questions

Negative Factual Information questions require the test taker to understand and be able to recognize facts that are mentioned in the passage. These questions may be about any facts or information that is explicitly covered in the passage. However, these questions ask the test taker to identify the incorrect information in the answer choices. Three of the four answer choices therefore contain correct information that is found in the passage. The answer the test taker must choose therefore either has incorrect information or information that is not mentioned in the passage.

- There are 0-2 Negative Factual Information questions per passage.

TYPE 5 Sentence Simplification Questions

Sentence Simplification questions require the test taker to select a sentence that best restates one that has been highlighted in the passage. These questions ask the test taker to recognize the main points in the sentence and to make sure that they are mentioned in the rewritten sentence. These rewritten sentences use words, phrases, and grammar that are different from the highlighted sentence. Sentence Simplification questions do not always appear in a passage. When they are asked, there is only one Sentence Simplification question per passage.

- There are 0-1 Sentence Simplification questions per passage.
- The answer choices for these questions are approximately half the length of the sentences being asked about.

TYPE 6 Inference Questions

Inference questions require the test taker to understand the argument that the passage is attempting to make. These questions ask the test taker to consider the information that is presented and then to come to a logical conclusion about it. The answers to these questions are never explicitly stated in the passage. Instead, the test taker must infer what the author means. These questions often deal with cause and effect or comparisons between two different things, ideas, events, or people.

- There are 0-2 Inference questions per passage. Most passages have at least 1 Inference question though.
- The difficulty level of these questions has increased. In some cases, test takers must be able to understand an entire paragraph rather than only a part of it.

TYPE 7 Rhetorical Purpose Questions

Rhetorical Purpose questions require the test taker to understand why the author mentioned or wrote about something in the passage. These questions ask the test taker to consider the reasoning behind the information being presented in the passage. For these questions, the function—not the meaning—of the material is the most important aspect for the test taker to be aware of. The questions often focus on the relationship between the information mentioned or covered either in paragraphs or individual sentences in the passage and the purpose or intention of the information that is given.

- There are 1-2 Rhetorical Purpose questions per passage.
- There is a special emphasis on these questions. Some questions ask about entire sentences, not just words or phrases.

TYPE 8 Insert Text Questions

Insert Text questions require the test taker to determine where in the passage another sentence should be placed. These questions ask the test taker to consider various aspects, including grammar, logic, connecting words, and flow, when deciding where the new sentence best belongs. Insert Text questions do not always appear in a passage. When they are asked, there is only one Insert Text question per passage. This question always appears right before the last question.

* There are 0-1 Insert Text questions per passage.
* There is a special emphasis on these questions. Almost every passage now has 1 Insert Text question.

TYPE 9 Prose Summary Questions

Prose Summary questions require the test taker to understand the main point of the passage and then to select sentences which emphasize the main point. These questions present a sentence which is essentially a thesis statement for the entire passage. The sentence synthesizes the main points of the passage. The test taker must then choose three out of six sentences that most closely describe points mentioned in the introductory sentence. As for the other three choices, they describe minor points, have incorrect information, or contain information that does not appear in the passage, so they are all therefore incorrect. This is always the last question asked about a Reading passage, but it does not always appear. Instead, a Fill in a Table question may appear in its place.

* There are 0-1 Prose Summary questions per passage.
* There is a special emphasis on these questions. Almost every passage now has 1 Prose Summary question.

TYPE 10 Fill in a Table Questions

Fill in a Table questions require the test taker to have a comprehensive understanding of the entire passage. These questions typically break the passage down into two—or sometimes three—main points or themes. The test taker must then read a number of sentences or phrases and determine which of the points or themes the sentences or phrases refer to. These questions may ask the test taker to consider cause and effect, to compare and contrast, or to understand various theories or ideas covered. This is always the last question asked about a Reading passage, but it does not always appear. Instead, a Prose Summary question may appear in its place.

* There are 0-1 Fill in a Table questions per passage.
* These questions rarely appear anymore. Prose Summary questions are much more common than Fill in a Table questions.

HOW TO USE THIS BOOK

Decoding the TOEFL® iBT Reading Intermediate is designed to be used either as a textbook in a classroom environment or as a study guide for individual learners. There are 10 chapters in this book. Each chapter provides comprehensive information about one type of reading question. There are 5 sections in each chapter, which enable you to build up your skills on a particular reading question. At the end of the book, there is one actual test of the Reading section of the TOEFL® iBT.

▮ Question Type

This section provides a short explanation of the question type. It contains examples of typical questions so that you can identify them more easily and hints on how to answer the questions. There is also a short reading passage with one sample question and explanation.

▮ Practice with Short Passages

This part contains three reading passages that are between 200 and 250 words long. Each reading passage contains one or two questions of the type covered in the chapter and has a short vocabulary section.

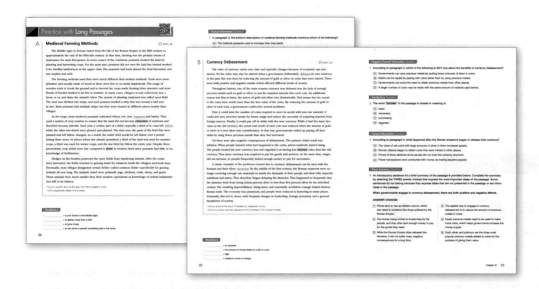

Practice with Long Passages

This section has two reading passages that are between 400 and 450 words long. Each reading passage contains four questions. There is one question about the type of question covered in the chapter. The other three questions are of various types. There is also a short vocabulary section after each passage to test your knowledge.

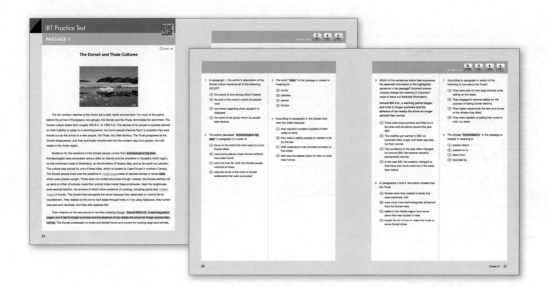

iBT Practice Test

This part has two reading passages that are between 500 and 600 words long with 9 questions each.

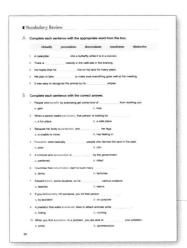

◼ Vocabulary Review

This section has two vocabulary exercises using words that appear in the passages in the chapter.

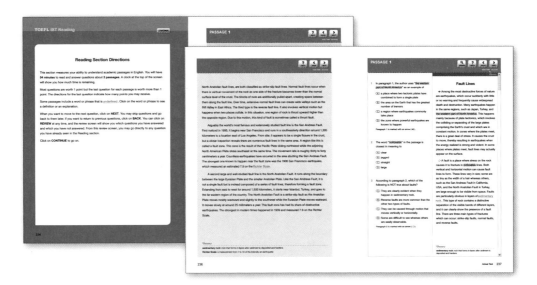

◼ Actual Test (at the end of the book)

This section has three full-length reading passages with 10 questions each.

Chapter **01**

Vocabulary

◢ About the Question

Vocabulary questions focus on words or phrases that appear in the passage. You are asked to select a word or phrase that has a meaning similar to that of the highlighted word or phrase in the passage. These questions require you to know the meanings of words or phrases that are necessary to having an overall understanding of the passage. There are 1-3 Vocabulary questions for each passage. Passages typically have two Vocabulary questions.

Recognizing Vocabulary questions:

- The word "X" in the passage is closest in meaning to

- In stating "X," the author means that

- The phrase "X" in the passage is closest in meaning to

Helpful hints for answering the questions correctly:

- You should be able to substitute the correct word or phrase in place of the highlighted word in the passage, and the passage will read grammatically correctly. Read the relevant sentence and substitute each answer choice to help determine the answer.

- Most of the words or phrases that are highlighted have more than one meaning in English. In many cases, the correct meaning of the word or phrase in the passage is not the most common one, so be careful of answer choices that appear too obvious.

- Look for context clues in the passage. Context clues frequently appear in the sentences immediately preceding or following the one with the highlighted word or phrase. They can provide hints that can make determining the meaning of the word or phrase easier.

The Gunpowder Plot

After King Henry VIII of England split with the Catholic Church, there were numerous conflicts between Catholics and Protestants. One such event took place in 1605. Upset with the rule of King James I, a Protestant, a group of Catholics decided to blow up some buildings in London. Led by Robert Catesby, the men put thirty-six barrels of gunpowder in the basement of Parliament building. Before the gunpowder could be ignited, it was discovered being guarded by Guy Fawkes, one of the conspirators. What came to be known as the Gunpowder Plot failed to destroy Parliament and to kill the king. After it was exposed, the conspirators were all either killed in battle or were captured and then executed. Since then, November 5 has been known as Guy Fawkes Day, and effigies of Guy Fawkes are burned in bonfires lit by the English to celebrate the foiling of the plot.

The word "ignited" in the passage is closest in meaning to

Ⓐ installed

Ⓑ armed

Ⓒ exploded

Ⓓ purchased

I Answer Explanation I

Choice Ⓒ is the correct answer. When gunpowder is ignited, it explodes. A context clue in the passage is the mentioning that the conspirators wanted to "blow up some buildings in London." Blowing up something is the same as exploding it.

A | The Komodo Dragon

CH01_2A

Native to Indonesia, the Komodo dragon is the largest lizard in the world. It grows to about three meters in length and weighs up to 150 kilograms. The Komodo dragon is a predator that hunts and eats virtually anything it finds. Its most common prey are pigs, deer, and large water buffalo, but it also devours dead animals if the opportunity arises.

When it hunts, the Komodo dragon typically lies in ambush as it uses its dull greenish-gray skin coloring to **camouflage** itself in grass or brush. When an animal walks close by where the lizard is hiding, it attacks. The Komodo dragon uses its powerful legs to knock its prey down and then viciously bites the animal to **incapacitate** it. This enables the Komodo dragon to eat at its own leisure.

In some instances, the animal that is attacked manages to survive the initial **onslaught**. Nevertheless, it soon dies because a single bite by the Komodo dragon is fatal. Its saliva contains up to fifty different types of bacteria, several of which are deadly toxins. These toxins cause the bitten animal to go into shock and also prevent its blood from clotting. The result is that any animal which escapes after being bitten will still die anywhere between a few hours to several days afterward. Interestingly enough, the toxins do not harm the Komodo dragon. When two lizards fight, they often bite each other, yet their saliva appears to have no **adverse** effects on them.

*camouflage: to hide oneself from others, often for the purpose of hunting
*onslaught: a vicious assault

1 The word "incapacitate" in the passage is closest in meaning to

Ⓐ kill

Ⓑ threaten

Ⓒ injure

Ⓓ intimidate

2 The word "adverse" in the passage is closest in meaning to

Ⓐ negative

Ⓑ major

Ⓒ obvious

Ⓓ permanent

Vocabulary

- _____ = nearly; almost
- _____ = the act of attacking without being seen
- _____ = spit
- _____ = to become solid, as in blood hardening

B | André-Marie Ampère

André-Marie Ampère (1775-1836) was a French scientist who specialized in physics and math and is best known for his work with electricity. Born into a wealthy family, he was educated at home with his family's large library used as a resource. Upon reaching his teen years, Ampère matriculated at a college in Lyon to study math and physics. The French Revolution soon began, and it not only interrupted his studies but also led to the loss of his father, who was executed during that time.

Ampère survived the revolution and began tutoring students in math. By 1809, he was a full professor of math at the famed École Polytechnique in Paris. It was while he was teaching that electricity became his obsession. In 1820, he made his first great discovery when he realized that if an electric current flows in the same direction in two parallel lines, they become attracted to each other. Conversely, if the current flows in opposite directions, they repel each other. He called his discovery electrodynamics. Today, it is known as electromagnetism.

Ampère later devised a mathematical formula called Ampère's Law. It is used to measure the size of a magnetic field based upon the electric current which made it. He further proposed the existence of the electron, which was later discovered by scientists. He is also credited with discovering the element fluorine. On account of his groundbreaking work in the field, the electric current unit was named the amp in his honor.

*matriculate: to enter a school
*repel: to push against; to drive away

---

1 In stating that electricity "became his obsession," the author means that he

Ⓐ wrote about it

Ⓑ focused on it

Ⓒ asked people about it

Ⓓ taught it

2 The word "groundbreaking" in the passage is closest in meaning to

Ⓐ individual

Ⓑ persistent

Ⓒ sponsored

Ⓓ innovative

▌ Vocabulary

· _____ = to kill a person by order of a government   · _____ = to create; to think of

· _____ = to teach someone one on one   · _____ = to suggest

C | Khmer Architecture

The Khmer Empire existed in the land occupied by the modern-day nation Cambodia from the eighth to the fifteenth century. While most of the buildings constructed during that time are gone, some structures still exist. Most of the extant buildings are temples, which were among the only structures made of brick and stone. Buildings that were built of wood failed to last long in the region's rainy, humid environment. Despite the lack of variety of structures, those that remain showcase various aspects of Khmer architecture.

The Khmer people mostly employed sandstone for the temples, but they also used bricks and a type of hardened clay called laterite, which is reddish in color. Each temple was dedicated either to a Hindu god or to Buddha. Thus each temple had a central sanctuary in which a statue of a Hindu deity or Buddha was placed. These sanctuaries were not large, having only enough space for the statue. Surrounding that central area were long covered galleries. The temples also had elaborately carved entrances and long spire-like toppings called prangs.

Many Khmer temples were decorated with bas-relief sculptures. They had religious motifs based upon the Hindu or Buddhist beliefs of the people who erected them. Perhaps the most distinctive feature of Khmer temples is the temple mountain. This is a multilevel tower meant to represent Mount Meru, which is sacred in Hinduism. The famed temple at Angkor Wat has several temple mountains reaching high about the surrounding complex.

*showcase: to highlight; to display
*bas-relief: a type of art in which a figure projects slightly from the background

---

1 The word "extant" in the passage is closest in meaning to

Ⓐ premier

Ⓑ surviving

Ⓒ designed

Ⓓ sturdiest

2 The word "elaborately" in the passage is closest in meaning to

Ⓐ cautiously

Ⓑ specially

Ⓒ physically

Ⓓ ornately

Vocabulary

- _____ = to use
- _____ = a holy place
- _____ = a god or goddess
- _____ = clear; obvious

18

◢ Mapping

The following chart shows the structure of the passage. Fill in the blanks with the appropriate words.

Khmer Architecture

Khmer Empire lasted in ❶ _____ from eighth to fifteenth century

– some buildings from then still exist

– mostly ❷ _____ and other buildings made of brick and stone

Used sandstone, bricks, and laterite for temples

– each temple was ❸ _____ to Hindu god or Buddha

– had central ❹ _____ with statue

– had long covered ❺ _____

– had elaborately carved ❻ _____ and prangs

Decorated with ❼ _____ sculptures

– had ❽ _____ motifs

– distinctive feature was temple ❾ _____ (multi-level tower representing Mount ❿ _____)

– ⓫ _____ has numerous temple mountains

◢ Summary

The following is a summary of the passage. Fill in the blanks with the appropriate words.

The Cambodian Khmer Empire lasted from the eighth to the ❶ _____ century. Some of the structures built then still exist. They were made of ❷ _____ and stone, not wood. The Khmer people used ❸ _____ and laterite to make their temples. Each temple had a central ❹ _____ with a Hindu or Buddhist statue. Covered ❺ _____ surrounded the sanctuary, and there were elaborately carved entrances and prangs. Bas-relief sculptures with religious ❻ _____ decorated Khmer temples. They also had temple mountains, which were ❼ _____ towers. Angkor Wat has several temple mountains.

A | **Medieval Farming Methods**

🎧 CH01_3A

The Middle Ages in Europe lasted from the fall of the Roman Empire in the fifth century to approximately the end of the fifteenth century. At that time, farming was the primary means of sustenance for most Europeans. In every corner of the continent, peasants worked the land by planting and harvesting crops. For the most part, peasants did not own the land but instead worked it for wealthy landowners in the upper class. The peasants and lords shared the food harvested, and any surplus was sold.

The farming methods used then were much different than modern methods. Tools were more primitive and usually made of wood as there were few or no metal implements. The usage of wooden tools to break the ground and to harvest the crops made farming labor intensive and slow. Beasts of burden tended to be few in number. In many cases, villagers would collectively buy a horse or ox and share the animal's labor. The system of planting employed was called open field. The land was divided into strips, and each peasant worked a strip that was around a half acre in size. Most peasants had multiple strips, but they were located in different places nearby their villages.

As for crops, most medieval peasants cultivated wheat, rye, oats, <u>legumes</u>, and barley. They used a system of crop rotation to ensure that the land did not become exhausted of nutrients and therefore become infertile. Each year, a certain part of a field—typically a third of it—was left <u>fallow</u> while the other two-thirds were plowed and planted. The next year, the parts of the field that were planted and left fallow changed. As a result, the entire field would be left fallow over a period lasting three years. In places where the climate permitted, a third of the land was used for summer crops, a third was used for winter crops, and the last third lay fallow the entire year. Despite these precautions, crop yields were low compared to those in modern times since peasants had little or no knowledge of fertilization.

Hedges on the borders protected the open fields from wandering animals. After the crops were harvested, the fields reverted to grazing lands for whatever herds the villagers and lords kept. Eventually, most villages designated certain fields—called common fields—specifically for grazing animals all year long. The animals raised were primarily pigs, chickens, cattle, sheep, and goats. These animals were much smaller than their modern equivalents as knowledge of animal husbandry was still in its infancy.

*legume: a plant, such as the pea, that has its seeds in pods
*fallow: unplanted; empty of any crops

Vocabulary

- _____ = a poor farmer in the Middle Ages
- _____ = to gather crops from a field
- _____ = to grow crops
- _____ = an act done to prevent something bad in the future

1 In paragraph 2, the author's description of medieval farming methods mentions which of the following?

   Ⓐ The methods peasants used to increase their crop yields

   Ⓑ The names of the tools that were used to plow the ground

   Ⓒ The types of crops that were planted in peasants' strips

   Ⓓ The manner in which animals were utilized by peasants

2 The word "exhausted" in the passage is closest in meaning to

   Ⓐ stricken

   Ⓑ tired

   Ⓒ destroyed

   Ⓓ depleted

3 The word "those" in the passage refers to

   Ⓐ summer crops

   Ⓑ winter crops

   Ⓒ precautions

   Ⓓ crop yields

4 An introductory sentence for a brief summary of the passage is provided below. Complete the summary by selecting the THREE answer choices that express the most important ideas of the passage. Some sentences do not belong because they express ideas that are not presented in the passage or are minor ideas in the passage.

   Peasants in the Middle Ages used a variety of methods when they farmed the land, but they were not able to grow many crops.

   ANSWER CHOICES

   ☐1 The land that the peasants farmed was divided into small strips that individual peasants grew crops on.

   ☐2 Most peasants did not own any animals because they could not afford to buy them.

   ☐3 Peasants often left parts of their fields fallow to reduce the chances that all of the nutrients would be removed from them.

   ☐4 The people who farmed the land had to expend a lot of energy because they had poor tools and rarely had access to animals.

   ☐5 Most of the tools that were used by peasants were made of wood rather than of iron or other types of metal.

   ☐6 If there was any surplus left from the yearly harvest, then the extra food was sold to others.

B | Currency Debasement

The value of currency varies over time and typically changes because of economic ups and downs. Yet the value may also be altered when a government deliberately debases its own currency. In the past, this was done by reducing the amount of gold or silver in coins that were minted. There were both positive and negative results which affected different levels of society.

Throughout history, one of the main reasons currency was debased was the lack of enough precious metals such as gold or silver to put the required amount into each coin. An additional reason was that at times, the prices of gold and silver rose dramatically. This meant that the metals in the coins were worth more than the face value of the coins. By reducing the amount of gold or silver in each coin, a government could solve several problems.

First, it could mint the number of coins required to meet its needs with less raw material. It could also save precious metals for future usage and reduce the necessity of acquiring material from foreign sources. Finally, it could pay off its debts with the new currency. While it had the same face value as the old currency, the actual real worth of each coin was reduced when the amount of gold or silver in it was taken into consideration. In that way, governments ended up paying off their debts by using fewer precious metals than they had borrowed.

Yet there were also negative consequences of debasement. The primary initial result was inflation. When people learned what had happened to the coins, prices suddenly started rising. The people trusted the new currency less and regarded it as having less intrinsic value than the old currency. Thus more currency was required to pay for goods and services. At the same time, wages did not increase, so people frequently lacked enough money to pay for necessities.

A classic example of the problems created due to currency debasement can be seen with the Romans and their silver denarius. By the middle of the first century, the Roman emperors were no longer receiving enough raw materials to satisfy the demands of their people and their lofty imperial ambitions and tastes. They therefore began debasing the denarius. This happened so frequently that the denarius went from being ninety-percent silver to less than five-percent silver by the mid-third century. The resulting hyperinflation, rising taxes, and essentially worthless coinage helped destroy Roman trade. The economy was paralyzed, and people were reduced to bartering in many places. Eventually, this led to chaos, with frequent changes in leadership, foreign invasions, and a general breakdown of society.

*debase: to lower the value of something, especially money
*denarius: a silver coin that was the primary monetary unit of ancient Rome

Vocabulary

- _____ = on purpose
- _____ = the amount of money listed on a bill or a coin
- _____ = high
- _____ = unable to move or change

1 According to paragraph 3, which of the following is NOT true about the benefits of currency debasement?

    (A) Governments can save precious metals by putting lower amounts of them in coins.

    (B) Debts can be repaid by paying with coins rather than by using precious metals.

    (C) Governments can avoid the need to obtain precious metals from other places.

    (D) A larger number of coins may be made with the same amount of material used before.

2 The word "intrinsic" in the passage is closest in meaning to

    (A) basic

    (B) necessary

    (C) purchasing

    (D) regarded

3 According to paragraph 5, what happened after the Roman emperors began to debase their currency?

    (A) The value of old coins with large amounts of silver in them increased greatly.

    (B) Roman citizens began to obtain coins that were minted in other places.

    (C) Prices of items declined since people did not trust the currency anymore.

    (D) Fewer transactions were conducted with money as trading became popular.

4 An introductory sentence for a brief summary of the passage is provided below. Complete the summary by selecting the THREE answer choices that express the most important ideas of the passage. Some sentences do not belong because they express ideas that are not presented in the passage or are minor ideas in the passage.

When governments engage in currency debasement, there are both positive and negative effects.

ANSWER CHOICES

    [1] Prices tend to rise as inflation occurs, which can result in problems like those suffered by the Roman Empire.

    [2] The money being minted is trusted less by the people, and they often lack enough money to pay for the goods they need.

    [3] While the Roman Empire often debased the denarius, it did not suffer many negative consequences for a long time.

    [4] The easiest way to engage in currency debasement is to reduce the amount of precious metals in coins.

    [5] Fewer precious metals need to be used to make more coins, which helps governments increase the money supply.

    [6] Gold, silver, and platinum are the three most popular precious metals added to coins for the purpose of giving them value.

The Dorset and Thule Cultures

The far northern reaches of the Arctic are a cold, harsh environment. For most of the period before the arrival of Europeans, two groups, the Dorset and the Thule, dominated the land there. The Dorset culture lasted from roughly 500 B.C. to 1500 A.D. The demise of its people is typically blamed on their inability to adapt to a warming period, but some people theorize that it is possible they were forced out by the arrival of a new people, the Thule, into their territory. The Thule prospered as the Dorset disappeared, and they eventually transformed into the modern-day Inuit people, who still reside in the Arctic region.

Evidence for the existence of the Dorset people comes from archaeological dig sites. Archaeologists have excavated various sites on islands and the shoreline in Canada's Arctic region, on the northwest coast of Greenland, on the shoreline of Hudson Bay, and as far south as Labrador. The culture was named for one of these sites, which is located at Cape Dorset in northern Canada. The Dorset people lived near the seashore in longhouses made of stacked stones or stone slabs which were placed upright. These were not roofed structures though. Instead, the Dorset perhaps set up tents or other structures made from animal hides inside these enclosures. Near the longhouses were several hearths, the remains of which show evidence of cooking, including ashes and midden heaps of bones. The Dorset lived alongside the shore because they depended on marine life for nourishment. They walked on the ice to hunt seals through holes in it by using harpoons, they hunted walruses and narwhals, and they also speared fish.

Their reliance on the sea proved to be their undoing though. Around 800 A.D., a warming period began, and it led to longer summers and the absence of ice nearby the shore for longer periods than normal. The Dorset possessed no boats and lacked bows and arrows for hunting large land animals, so they tried to survive by migrating farther north to colder regions. There is some evidence that some Dorset people managed to survive for a few more centuries, but, by 1500, all traces of them had vanished.

One question concerning the extinction of the Dorset is whether the Thule had anything to do with it. The Thule came from the Alaska region and, by around 1100, had moved eastward into lands once dominated by the Dorset. They possessed iron tools and used large boats on open water. They developed tools and methods which helped them hunt whales from their boats. In fact, many of their homes' frames were built from whalebones covered in skins. Hunting whales from boats enabled them to survive in regions where the Dorset could not during the warming period.

It is possible that the Thule played a role in the demise of the Dorset. Thule legends, which were transmitted to the Inuit people, feature stories of conflict between the two groups. The Thule were more warlike than the Dorset and had better weapons, so they may have driven them away after some brief conflicts. That, however, is mere conjecture. As yet, archaeologists have discovered no direct evidence of any conflicts. There is evidence at Dorset sites that they were also occupied by the Thule, but there is nothing suggesting battles took place. What is certain is that no interrelations occurred. Modern studies of DNA collected from Dorset and Thule remains show a marked distinction in their DNA. Additionally, there is no evidence of Dorset DNA in modern Inuit people, who are descendants of the Thule.

*Glossary

longhouse: a communal dwelling that can be very long and in which two or more families reside

midden heap: a pile of garbage

1   In paragraph 1, the author's description of the Dorset culture mentions all of the following EXCEPT:

   Ⓐ the period of time during which it lasted

   Ⓑ the area of the world in which its people lived

   Ⓒ one theory regarding what caused it to disappear

   Ⓓ the name of the group whom its people later became

2   The author discusses "archaeological dig sites" in paragraph 2 in order to

   Ⓐ focus on the tools that were used by some Dorset tribes

   Ⓑ name some places where Dorset artifacts have been found

   Ⓒ point out how far north the Dorset people ventured at times

   Ⓓ describe some of the ruins of Dorset settlements that were excavated

3   The word "slabs" in the passage is closest in meaning to

   Ⓐ bricks

   Ⓑ pebbles

   Ⓒ pieces

   Ⓓ blocks

4   According to paragraph 2, the Dorset lived near the water because

   Ⓐ they required constant supplies of fresh water to drink

   Ⓑ they were a sailing people so needed to be by the sea

   Ⓒ their sustenance was provided primarily by the ocean

   Ⓓ that was the easiest place for them to build their homes

5 Which of the sentences below best expresses the essential information in the highlighted sentence in the passage? Incorrect answer choices change the meaning in important ways or leave out essential information.

Around 800 A.D., a warming period began, and it led to longer summers and the absence of ice nearby the shore for longer periods than normal.

Ⓐ There were long summers and little ice in the area until sometime around the year 800.

Ⓑ The weather got warmer in 800, so summers were longer, and there was less ice than normal.

Ⓒ The conditions in the area often changed, but around 800, the weather became permanently warmer.

Ⓓ In the year 800, the weather changed so that there was much more ice in the water than before.

6 In paragraphs 3 and 4, the author implies that the Thule

Ⓐ thrived when they resided in lands that were extremely cold

Ⓑ were much more technologically advanced than the Dorset were

Ⓒ sailed to the Alaska region from some place that was located in Asia

Ⓓ taught the art of how to make iron tools to some Dorset tribes

7 According to paragraph 4, which of the following is true about the Thule?

Ⓐ They were able to hunt large animals while sailing on the water.

Ⓑ They engaged in several battles for the purpose of taking Dorset territory.

Ⓒ They highly valued both the skin and bones of the whales they killed.

Ⓓ They were capable of sailing their boats in cold, icy water.

8 The phrase "transmitted to" in the passage is closest in meaning to

Ⓐ spoken about

Ⓑ passed on to

Ⓒ taken from

Ⓓ recorded by

9 **Directions:** Select the appropriate statements from the answer choices and match them to the Arctic culture to which they relate. TWO of the answer choices will NOT be used. **This question is worth 3 points.**

Drag your answer choices to the spaces where they belong. To remove an answer choice, click on it. To review the passage, click on VIEW TEXT.

STATEMENTS

1 Met some groups of Europeans who visited the Arctic

2 Built homes that were made from the bones of animals

3 Managed to exist as a people for around two millennia

4 Lived in large longhouses that had stone roofs

5 Were the ancestors of the modern-day Inuit people

6 Hunted by walking out onto ice frozen on the sea

7 Moved northward when a warming period began

ARCTIC CULTURE

Dorset (Select 3)

-
-
-

Thule (Select 2)

-
-

Coal in the Industrial Revolution

A replica of the 1712 engine built by Thomas Newcomen © Tony Hisgett

For much of human history, people used wood or charcoal made from wood to produce heat. In rare areas where coal could be obtained from the surface or from underground places close to the surface, nearby settlements had an additional source of heat. It was not until the eighteenth century, which marked the onset of the Industrial Revolution, that coal took on a prominent place in human life though. In fact, during that time, coal and industrialization essentially developed a symbiotic relationship where each benefitted from the other. Some major effects of the onset of coal mining were the rise of steam-powered machines, the construction of factories, the growth of urban centers, and the development of railway systems.

Prior to the 1700s, coal was dug up in limited quantities and almost always from open-pit mines. Dirty, heavy, and difficult to transport, coal was used only locally; however, around that time, many places, Britain in particular, began suffering from the loss of forested regions. Around London, for example, extensive deforestation occurred because of people cutting wood for fuel and for construction. As a result, wood had to be transported from distant places, thereby making it more expensive than coal. This, in turn, increased the appeal of coal.

As demand increased, the primary problem was reaching large coal deposits underground. Attempts to dig deep coal mines almost always resulted in them being flooded by groundwater. At that time, there was no easy way to pump water out of mines. But in Britain, several engineers were designing engines that could run on steam. To power the engines, they needed coal to heat water to create steam. Because of mine flooding though, coal was in short supply. So some engineers dedicated themselves to producing steam-powered pumps to eliminate this problem. The first of these engines was created by Thomas Newcomen in 1712. His design was later improved by James Watt in 1776. All throughout the 1700s, hundreds of steam pumps were built to pump water out of deep mines across Britain.

In turn, the rise of steam-powered engines would become a key component of industrialization and urban growth. As more sophisticated steam engines were designed and built, they acquired the ability to operate machinery to spin and weave cotton and wool fibers into yarn to make textiles. ■ Textile factories needed workers, and workers needed homes, so new urban centers arose. ■ Later, processes for making stronger iron and steel required the use of greater amounts of coal. ■ Coal would swiftly become the backbone of industrialized nations across the globe. ■ The production of coal increased by fifty percent between 1700 and 1750, by nearly 100 percent by 1800s, and by 500 percent by 1850.

There was still a problem though. Coal was not located everywhere, and moving it was difficult because road systems in most places were substandard. The solution was the building of canals and railway systems. In the eighteenth century, numerous canals were built solely to move coal from mines to urban centers. This method was slow and could not meet demand, so the solution was railways. Wooden track systems were typically utilized to move coal in large crates from mineshafts. Some mines near rivers and canals used short rail spurs to move coal to boats. Eventually, engineers came upon the idea of using iron rails and steam engines to haul coal. By the mid-nineteenth century, railways had become the main means of quickly transporting goods, including coal, and people across countries.

*Glossary

mineshaft: an underground passageway made for the purpose of finding ore or minerals

short rail spur: a secondary railroad track that lets railroad cars be loaded or unloaded without interfering with other railway traffic

10 Which of the sentences below best expresses the essential information in the highlighted sentence in the passage? Incorrect answer choices change the meaning in important ways or leave out essential information.

It was not until the eighteenth century, which marked the onset of the Industrial Revolution, that coal took on a prominent place in human life though.

- (A) People were unable to make any use of coal until the eighteenth century, which was when the Industrial Revolution began.
- (B) Coal was important all throughout human history until the start of the Industrial Revolution in the 1700s.
- (C) Because the Industrial Revolution started in the eighteenth century, people thought about using coal then.
- (D) It was in the 1700s when the Industrial Revolution began that coal became important to humans.

11 The word "symbiotic" in the passage is closest in meaning to

- (A) reciprocal
- (B) parasitic
- (C) independent
- (D) complex

12 The author discusses "deforestation" in paragraph 2 in order to

- (A) complain about the harm done to the environment in Britain
- (B) point out that there were no more trees left anywhere in London
- (C) explain why people became more interested in coal than in wood
- (D) argue that new policies were needed in Britain to reverse its effects

13 According to paragraph 3, people had a hard time mining coal underground because

- (A) steam produced by engines often got trapped in underground mines
- (B) nobody knew how to remove poisonous gases from mines
- (C) the existing equipment was unable to dig very deep underground
- (D) water that flooded underground mines could not be pumped out easily

14 Which of the following can be inferred from paragraph 3 about Thomas Newcomen?

  Ⓐ The steam engine which he invented was used in coal mines in Britain.

  Ⓑ He worked together with James Watt in order to make a steam engine.

  Ⓒ His invention marked the beginning of the Industrial Revolution in Britain.

  Ⓓ He became a wealthy man thanks to the steam engine that he developed.

15 In stating that road systems in most places were "substandard," the author means that road systems

  Ⓐ had been repaired

  Ⓑ looked like regular roads

  Ⓒ were in poor condition

  Ⓓ went to few places

16 According to paragraph 5, railways were built because

  Ⓐ they were able to transport large amounts of coal faster than canals

  Ⓑ they allowed trains to travel on city streets in large urban centers

  Ⓒ they were capable of being built much quicker than canals and roads were

  Ⓓ they cost much less to make than roadways and canals did

17 Look at the four squares [■] that indicate where the following sentence could be added to the passage.

This made the production of cloth very efficient, which then lowered the prices that people had to pay for clothes.

Where would the sentence best fit?

Click on a square [■] to add the sentence to the passage.

18 **Directions**: An introductory sentence for a brief summary of the passage is provided below. Complete the summary by selecting the THREE answer choices that express the most important ideas of the passage. Some sentences do not belong because they express ideas that are not presented in the passage or are minor ideas in the passage. **This question is worth 2 points.**

Coal played a major role in the development of the Industrial Revolution.

-
-
-

ANSWER CHOICES

1. Groundwater often seeped into coal mines, so it was difficult to mine coal underneath the Earth's surface.

2. Coal usage increased in the 1700s and 1800s as it was used in textile factories and to make steel and iron.

3. People burned a great deal of wood before they used coal, so deforestation became a major problem in places.

4. Once steam engines were developed, it became possible to mine coal underground.

5. Both canals and railways were built in order to move coal to places across countries.

6. In the past, people were able to heat coal that they found lying on top of the ground.

◼ Vocabulary Review

A Complete each sentence with the appropriate word from the box.

virtually	precautions	descendants	transforms	distinctive

1 A caterpillar _____ into a butterfly while it is in a cocoon.

2 There is _____ nobody in the café late in the evening.

3 He hopes that his _____ live on his land for many years.

4 We plan to take _____ to make sure everything goes well at the meeting.

5 It was easy to recognize the animal by its _____ stripes.

B Complete each sentence with the correct answer.

1 People who **benefit** by exercising get some kind of _____ from working out.

   a. gain   b. loss

2 When a person seeks **sanctuary**, that person is looking for _____.

   a. a fun place   b. a safe place

3 Because her body is **paralyzed**, she _____ her legs.

   a. is unable to move   b. has feeling in

4 **Peasants** were basically _____ people who farmed the land in the past.

   a. poor   b. rich

5 A criminal who is **executed** is _____ by the government.

   a. pardoned   b. killed

6 Countries that **industrialize** start to build many _____.

   a. farms   b. factories

7 Edward **tutors** some students, so he _____ various subjects.

   a. teaches   b. learns

8 If you **deliberately** hit someone, you hit that person _____.

   a. by accident   b. on purpose

9 A predator that waits in **ambush** likes to attack animals while _____.

   a. hiding   b. running

10 When you find a **solution** to a problem, you are able to _____ your problem.

   a. solve   b. ignore

Chapter **02**

Reference

Question Type | Reference

◢ About the Question

Reference questions focus on the relationships between words and their referents in the passage. You are asked to identify what the antecedent of a pronoun is. There are often questions with subject pronouns such as *he, she, it,* and *they* and object pronouns such as *him, her,* and *them*. There are also questions with relative pronouns such as *which* and demonstrative pronouns such as *this, that, these,* and *those*. There are 0-1 Reference questions for each passage. However, these questions rarely appear anymore. There may be 1 Reference question in an entire Reading section, or there may be none.

Recognizing Reference questions:

• The word "X" in the passage refers to

Helpful hints for answering the questions correctly:

• The correct answer choice can always fit into the sentence. So try inserting each answer choice into the sentence to see which one reads the best.

• All four of the answer choices always appear in the same order as they are written in the passage. They are also the exact words or phrases that appear in the passage.

• On rare occasions, the correct answer appears in the passage after the highlighted word. Most of the time, however, it can be found before the highlighted word.

Early Human Migrations

Anthropologists generally agree that the first humans lived somewhere in Africa. Tens of thousands of years ago, they began migrating from their homeland. Sometime between 90,000 and 30,000 years ago, humans traveled from Africa to the Middle East. Then, they went to southern parts of Asia and eventually made it to Australia. Later, around 40,000 to 12,000 years ago, a second migration took place. These humans moved northward into Europe and settled parts of the continent that were not covered by ice. It was in Europe that modern humans came into contact with Neanderthals, who were another type of hominoid. They, however, went extinct after making contact with humans. As for the Americas, there is some dispute regarding when they were settled. Many anthropologists claim the first humans arrived in the Americas around 12,000 to 15,000 years ago. But some believe humans may have gone there 30,000 years ago.

The word "They" in the passage refers to

Ⓐ These humans

Ⓑ Parts of the continent

Ⓒ Modern humans

Ⓓ Neanderthals

| **Answer Explanation** |

Choice Ⓓ is the correct answer. The "they" that went extinct after making contact with humans were Neanderthals. Note that only three of the answer choices could possibly go extinct, and two of them refer to humans. Since "they" went extinct after meeting humans, then you should be able to use the process of elimination to find the correct answer.

A | The Design of Washington, D.C.

CH02_2A

In 1791, the United States was a new country and therefore required a capital. The American Congress selected the site of **it** to be on the banks of the Potomac River in Maryland. This location was ideally suited between the northern and southern states and, being on a river, provided access to the interior of the nation. George Washington himself asked French architect Pierre L'Enfant to **survey** the site and to make recommendations for the layout of the city.

L'Enfant designed the city with wide avenues, public squares, and impressive government buildings. He placed the building for Congress atop a high hill, which became known as Capitol Hill. It then became the center of a radial design of wide avenues that cut across a more grid-like pattern of smaller streets. L'Enfant put the home of the president, the future White House, on a street with easy access to Capitol Hill. The grand **centerpiece** of his plan was the Mall, a wide grassy strip stretching from the Potomac to Capitol Hill.

While L'Enfant's plans were ambitious, not everyone approved of them. After clashing with some powerful local landowners, L'Enfant found himself dismissed from the project. Nevertheless, the builders of the city used most of his ideas when **they** constructed Washington. L'Enfant, however, never received official credit or payment for his work. He was recognized by later generations though, and his contributions to the city are recognized today.

*survey: to view an area in detail
*centerpiece: a cornerstone; a focal point

---

1 The word "**it**" in the passage refers to

Ⓐ a new country

Ⓑ a capital

Ⓒ the American Congress

Ⓓ the site

2 The word "**they**" in the passage refers to

Ⓐ L'Enfant's plans

Ⓑ some powerful local landowners

Ⓒ the builders of the city

Ⓓ his ideas

Vocabulary

- _____ = the legislative body of the American government
- _____ = land that borders a river or stream
- _____ = having spokes or rays
- _____ = to fight; to argue

B | Desert Flora

Despite being dry, most deserts have an abundance of plants growing in various places in them. Some are cacti, palm trees, Joshua trees, mesquite trees, desert sage, and yucca in addition to numerous types of grasses, shrubs, and wildflowers. Over time, these desert plants have adapted to their harsh environments in order to survive.

There are various ways in which they accomplish this. Many species of cacti, for examples, have shallow root systems which spread out widely underneath the ground. This enables their roots to gather as much water as possible in the brief instances when there is precipitation. Additionally, the waxy outer skin of cacti enables them to store water longer than other plants. There are no leaves on them, so they also lose little water to transpiration, as is common with leafy plants. Thanks to their numerous adaptations, cacti can survive off the water amassed from a single rainfall for several years.

Among the many wildflowers in deserts are perennials, which are capable of living for more than two growing seasons. These flowers survive by going dormant during extensive periods of dryness and then coming to life whenever rain falls. Perennials complete their reproduction cycles in short periods of time and become dormant again until there is water once again. Some perennials may repeat this process several times a year. The Ocotillo plant is one such example. It can bloom and become dormant up to five times in a single year.

*precipitation: water in liquid or frozen form, such as rain, snow, or ice, that falls from the sky
*transpiration: the process through which water leaves the insides of plants and enters the atmosphere

---

1 The word "them" in the passage refers to

Ⓐ cacti

Ⓑ other plants

Ⓒ leaves

Ⓓ leafy plants

2 The word "which" in the passage refers to

Ⓐ the many wildflowers

Ⓑ deserts

Ⓒ perennials

Ⓓ two growing seasons

Vocabulary

• _____ = plenty of; a large number of

• _____ = to collect; to gather

• _____ = inactive

• _____ = to produce flowers or blossoms

C | Ur

The ancient Mesopotamian city of Ur was among the world's first **urban** settlements. Its ruins have been found by archaeologists in Iraq near the city of Nasiriya not far from the Persian Gulf. The Mesopotamians constructed Ur along the banks of the Euphrates River, but its course has changed over thousands of years. It is widely believed that the coastline of the Persian Gulf was much further inland than it is at present and that Ur was thus a port city.

There is evidence that Ur was settled as far back as 6000 B.C. At its height, which happened around 3000 B.C., the city covered an area of approximately sixty acres and was surrounded by a wall. It consisted primarily of densely packed residences on narrow streets as well as large buildings for worship, trade, and government. The Ziggurat of Ur, a center of worship in the city, is the major building **whose** ruins have been found.

Thanks to the continuous building and rebuilding which happened in Ur, there exists a wealth of archaeological evidence on early Mesopotamian life. Archaeologists have unearthed numerous tombs and thousands of tablets with **cuneiform** writing. After being translated, **these** have revealed a great deal about the history of Ur and the lives of its people. As an example, it has been learned that Ur was controlled by various people in the region, including Assyrians, Babylonians, and Persians and that it declined over time and stopped being inhabited around the fifth century B.C.

*urban: relating to a city
*cuneiform: a type of writing using triangular and wedge-shaped figures used in the Middle East thousands of years ago

1 The word "whose" in the passage refers to

(A) worship, trade, and government

(B) the Ziggurat of Ur

(C) worship

(D) the city

2 The word "these" in the passage refers to

(A) archaeologists

(B) numerous tombs

(C) thousands

(D) tablets with cuneiform writing

Vocabulary

• _____ = the area where the land meets a large body of water

• _____ = heavily

• _____ = crowded

• _____ = a place where a person is buried

◼ Mapping

The following chart shows the structure of the passage. Fill in the blanks with the appropriate words.

Ur

Was ancient city in ❶ _____

– was one of world's first urban settlements

– was once on the banks of the ❷ _____ Gulf alongside the Euphrates River

---

Was settled around ❸ _____ B.C.

– reached its ❹ _____ around 3000 B.C.

– was sixty acres and surrounded by a ❺ _____

– had ❻ _____ streets with residences and other buildings

– Ziggurat of Ur was located there

Much ❼ _____ evidence on early Mesopotamian life there

– numerous ❽ _____ and tablets unearthed

– ❾ _____ of writing on tablets had revealed information about history of Ur and life there

– stopped being ❿ _____ around fifth century B.C.

◼ Summary

The following is a summary of the passage. Fill in the blanks with the appropriate words.

Ur was an ❶ _____ Mesopotamian city built alongside the ❷ _____ River. Archaeologists found it by Nasiriya, Iraq, which is near the Persian Gulf. It was once a ❸ _____ city when the Persian Gulf's coastline was further inland. Ur was settled around 6000 B.C. and reached its ❹ _____ in 3000 B.C. There was a wall around it, and ❺ _____ and other buildings, including the Ziggurat of Ur, were in it. Archaeologists have learned about Ur by studying its tombs and tablets with ❻ _____ writing. For example, it was ❼ _____ by various people and was no longer inhabited after the ❽ _____ century B.C.

A | The Development of the Trumpet

🎧 CH02_3A

The ancient Egyptians, Greeks, and Romans, as well as people in other societies, all played instruments resembling trumpets thousands of years ago. They did not typically use these instruments to make music though. Instead, they were utilized to signal soldiers during battles and to provide sounds during various ceremonies. Over the centuries, these instruments changed to become ones used mostly for playing music. As for the modern trumpet, it evolved from instruments which were played in the fourteenth and fifteenth centuries.

The trumpets during that time were simple instruments. They consisted of a long, coiled tube which had no valves like modern instruments do. This fact limited the range of musical tones the instruments could play. Today, musicologists call the trumpets of that era natural trumpets because the instruments did not mechanically manipulate the tones they produced in any way. In the sixteenth century, improvements in metalworking led to improved trumpets. The best trumpet craftsmen of that time were found in Nuremberg, Germany. The metalworkers there made some trumpets with a simple slide device that slightly increased the tonal range of the trumpet.

In the late sixteenth century, composers began including parts for trumpets in their works. As the trumpet began to improve in quality, it increased in popularity. By the seventeenth century, it was commonly included in musical compositions. At first, it could only play low tones. But musicians gradually began to make higher tones by controlling the shapes of their lips as they played. To make more tones possible, trumpet makers experimented with keys like those found on the clarinet. This instrument was known as the keyed trumpet.

It was not until German musician Heinrich Stolzel developed the first musical valves for brass instruments in 1814 that the modern trumpet was born. The valves he created diverted the flow of air, which enabled it to go through a longer stretch of the instrument's tubing and thus produce different sounds. Stolzel's valves were not perfect, but later inventers created the improved double piston valve, which is commonly used today.

By the mid-nineteenth century, the trumpet had two or three valves and was designed for the key of F. It was a longer and quieter instrument than the ones used today. By the turn of the twentieth century, the three-valve, short modern trumpet was being used. It produced a louder, clearer series of sounds in the keys of B and C. By the 1920s, it was being used as the primary instrument in modern dance and jazz bands. This enabled Louis Armstrong, Miles Davis, and other musicians to show their audiences the beauty and power of the trumpet.

*valve: a device that can control the flow of air through a pipe or other similar structure
*musicologist: a person who studies the history of music

Vocabulary

- _____ = to give a sign to; to alert
- _____ = a sound, often one musical in nature
- _____ = to change; to control
- _____ = main; most important

1 In paragraph 1, the author's description of ancient trumpets mentions which of the following?

    Ⓐ The materials which they were made of

    Ⓑ The type of music which they were able to play

    Ⓒ The society in which they were first invented

    Ⓓ The manner in which people made use of them

2 The word "**they**" in the passage refers to

    Ⓐ musical tones

    Ⓑ musicologists

    Ⓒ natural trumpets

    Ⓓ the tones

3 The author discusses "German musician Heinrich Stolzel" in paragraph 4 in order to

    Ⓐ discuss what inspired him to add valves to the trumpets he made

    Ⓑ explain the invention that allowed him to make the modern trumpet

    Ⓒ describe the importance of the trumpet during the time he lived

    Ⓓ compare the valves he made with those created in earlier times

4 An introductory sentence for a brief summary of the passage is provided below. Complete the summary by selecting the THREE answer choices that express the most important ideas of the passage. Some sentences do not belong because they express ideas that are not presented in the passage or are minor ideas in the passage.

The modern trumpet was developed over a period of time starting in the fourteenth century and extending to the twentieth century.

ANSWER CHOICES

1 The addition of a third valve to the trumpet in the 1900s led to the making of the instrument many musicians play in modern times.

2 Jazz musicians such as Miles Davis and Louis Armstrong preferred to play the trumpet when they performed for audiences.

3 Because many people wanted to hear the trumpet, composers in the seventeenth century often wrote music for it.

4 The trumpets that were played in ancient times were typically utilized by militaries to provide instructions for soldiers.

5 In the 1500s, the adding of a slide device to the trumpet enabled it to increase the tonal range of sounds it could make.

6 Valves that could control the movement of air through the instrument permitted the first modern trumpet to be made.

B | The Effects of Vitamins on the Body

🎧 CH02_3B

Vitamins are compounds the body requires but which it cannot usually produce on its own. There are thirteen of them: vitamins A, C, D, E, K, and a group of eight more that are collectively called the B vitamins. They consist of thiamine, riboflavin, niacin, biotin, folic acid, pantothenic acid, vitamin B-6, and vitamin B-12. Each of these vitamins has different effects on the body.

Vitamin A plays a role in ensuring good vision, bone growth, reproduction, and cellular functions and also enhances the body's immune system. This vitamin is obtained primarily from colorful fruits and vegetables, dairy products, eggs, and liver. Vitamin C, on the other hand, is vital for skin and bone growth, enhances the connective tissues in the body, and helps heal the body during times of illness. Its main sources are fruits and vegetables, particularly citrus fruits and peppers. Vitamin D's main role is to help the body absorb calcium, which is necessary for bone growth. The body creates a natural form of vitamin D when the skin is exposed to sunlight, and it is also found in eggs, liver, and fish.

Vitamin E helps improve the body's immune system and metabolic processes. It comes from vegetable oils, nuts, and leafy green vegetables. Vitamin K assists the body in making proteins necessary for bone and tissue health. In addition, it manufactures the proteins necessary to enable blood clotting. Vitamin K is mostly absorbed by the body from leafy green vegetables. The B vitamin group's primary function is to help produce energy in the body. But these vitamins also contribute to the body's metabolism and promote the production of DNA, RNA, and red blood cells. Fish, poultry, red meat, eggs, and leafy green vegetables are where they mostly come from.

Many people boost their vitamin intake with supplements by consuming vitamin pills, which can be helpful yet are harmful at times. For instance, some individuals, such as the elderly, pregnant women, and people with adverse health conditions, should take supplemental vitamins. Other people, however, take more vitamin pills than necessary. There are even some who regularly consume large amounts of vitamins in the hope that they will prevent or even cure diseases. 1 However, the human body only needs a small amount of each vitamin to function properly, so taking enormous quantities of them is unnecessary. 2 In fact, taking too many vitamins can result in negative side effects. 3 Among these are heart problems, nausea, and nerve damage. 4

*immune system: the part of the body that protects it from diseases
*blood clotting: the process through which blood thickens and forms thick lumps

---

Vocabulary

- _____ = to improve; to make better
- _____ = to stimulate; to cause something to happen
- _____ = something added to make up for a deficiency
- _____ = a feeling of sickness in the stomach

1 According to paragraph 2, which of the following is NOT true about vitamin C?

   Ⓐ It has positive effects on the body's immune system.

   Ⓑ It promotes the growing of skin and bones in the body.

   Ⓒ It can be obtained from various types of fruits and vegetables.

   Ⓓ Its presence can be beneficial to individuals who are sick.

2 The word "they" in the passage refers to

   Ⓐ proteins

   Ⓑ these vitamins

   Ⓒ DNA, RNA, and red blood cells

   Ⓓ fish, poultry, red meat, eggs, and leafy green vegetables

3 Look at the four squares [■] that indicate where the following sentence could be added to the passage.

In addition to those problems, the excess contents are not absorbed by the body but are instead flushed from it and depart as waste.

4 An introductory sentence for a brief summary of the passage is provided below. Complete the summary by selecting the THREE answer choices that express the most important ideas of the passage. Some sentences do not belong because they express ideas that are not presented in the passage or are minor ideas in the passage.

Vitamins have a wide variety of beneficial effects on the human body but need to be taken in moderation.

ANSWER CHOICES

1 It is possible to obtain one of the vitamins that the body requires simply by spending time in the sun.

2 The overconsuming of vitamins can sometimes result in problems for the people taking too many of them.

3 Among the benefits of some vitamins are making the body stronger and better able to prevent illnesses.

4 A large number of vitamins, such as those in the B vitamin group, provide the body with more energy.

5 It is possible to take vitamin supplements in the form of pills rather than simply consuming foods with vitamins.

6 People should regulate their diets to make sure the foods they eat have the proper vitamins in them.

Scottish Brochs

Dotting the countryside in Scotland's northern reaches and on many of its neighboring islands are the remains of tall stone towers called brochs. They were built and used during Britain's Iron Age, which lasted from approximately 800 B.C. to 200 A.D. They stand alone or, in rare instances, exist as parts of larger groups of ruins. Around 500 sites contain the remains of brochs. Since the nineteenth century, archaeologists have puzzled over the reasons that the brochs were built, yet they have managed to come up with several reasonable theories attempting to explain their purpose.

Individual brochs were not identical, but they shared some common design features, such as being round in shape with a slight tapering toward the top. Their builders additionally utilized the drystone method when creating them, so their stones were stacked and fitted together with no bonding agent, such as mortar, to seal them tightly. Each broch had two walls—an inner wall and an outer one—and there were wide spaces between them called galleries. Brochs were up to fifteen meters wide on the inside, and their enormous bottom walls were three to four meters thick. Today, few remain entirely intact, so determining their height is virtually impossible, but the best-preserved one, which is at Mousa on the Shetland Islands, is thirteen meters high. Most broch remains, however, merely stand a meter or two high.

At the bottom of each broch was a single door which served as an entrance. Most entrances had a small cell right on the inside. This is believed to have been a guard cell. The space between the inner and outer walls contained some stone slabs linking them to each other, and many brochs had a set of spiral staircases between their walls. Floors in the center of the structure were constructed of wood, which was fitted into ledges built into the interior of the inner wall. Many brochs had at least two floors, and there is evidence that some had wooden rooftops. A central hearth was also

common. The walls of each broch were completely enclosed with stone, so they lacked openings for windows.

Archaeologists have long debated the purpose of brochs. When investigations on them began in the nineteenth century, it was believed that they were fortresses employed to protect locals against invaders. The theory was supported by the fact that most brochs were located at strategic points, such as near sea passages and at valley entrances. ■ There are also clusters of broch ruins in some areas, suggesting that they were utilized for mutual support. ■ In modern times, this theory has largely been abandoned though. ■ Firstly, many brochs were constructed in wilderness regions which were located nowhere near any human settlements. ■ Additionally, the lack of windows and other openings in the brochs makes it unlikely that they could have been used for defensive purposes.

This has given rise to the theory that brochs served as symbols of power and prestige for their owners. The ruins of other buildings and nearby arable land surround at least twenty broch sites, which implies that the leader and his people lived side by side. A third theory posits that each broch served an individual purpose, be it for defense, prestige, or something else, such as serving as a domicile for a family. According to this theory, the builders made similar-looking structures, each of which had a different purpose. Whatever the case, by the year 200 A.D., the building of brochs had fallen out of favor, so they were no longer constructed.

*Glossary

mortar: a mixture that is used to bond stone, bricks, or other similar substances

ledge: a narrow horizontal projection on a wall

1 In paragraph 1, why does the author mention "Britain's Iron Age"?

Ⓐ To argue that brochs were used as defensive platforms then

Ⓑ To note that it started before iron ages in other regions

Ⓒ To claim that few brochs were built during that era

Ⓓ To give the time period in which brochs were constructed

2 Select the TWO answer choices from paragraph 2 that identify common features of brochs. *To receive credit, you must select TWO answers.*

Ⓐ They were circular and became smaller in size toward the top.

Ⓑ They were tightly constructed thanks to the usage of mortar

Ⓒ They featured both a wall on the inside and one on the outside.

Ⓓ They contained defensive fortifications standing fifteen meters high.

3 The word "This" in the passage refers to

Ⓐ Each broch

Ⓑ A single door

Ⓒ An entrance

Ⓓ A small cell

4 The word "they" in the passage refers to

Ⓐ many brochs

Ⓑ wooden rooftops

Ⓒ the walls of each broch

Ⓓ windows

5　The word "clusters" in the passage is closest in meaning to

    Ⓐ piles

    Ⓑ blocks

    Ⓒ clues

    Ⓓ bunches

6　In stating that the building of brochs "had fallen out of favor," the author means that brochs

    Ⓐ were hard to construct

    Ⓑ became ruined

    Ⓒ were not being made

    Ⓓ had no use to people

7　According to paragraphs 4 and 5, which of the following is NOT true about the purposes of brochs?

    Ⓐ It is thought that they were symbols of power for some leaders.

    Ⓑ Many people today believe they were not utilized to protect areas.

    Ⓒ The majority of them were used by nobles like they were castles.

    Ⓓ It is possible that they could have had a wide variety of purposes.

8　Look at the four squares [■] that indicate where the following sentence could be added to the passage.

Therefore, it is highly doubtful that they were constructed to provide protection for anyone.

Where would the sentence best fit?

Click on a square [■] to add the sentence to the passage.

9 **Directions:** An introductory sentence for a brief summary of the passage is provided below. Complete the summary by selecting the THREE answer choices that express the most important ideas of the passage. Some sentences do not belong because they express ideas that are not presented in the passage or are minor ideas in the passage. **This question is worth 2 points.**

Drag your answer choices to the spaces where they belong. To remove an answer choice, click on it. To review the passage, click on VIEW TEXT.

Brochs were built in Scotland in the past and shared many similarities, but their true purpose remains a mystery.

-
-
-

ANSWER CHOICES

1. The method of stonework that was used to create brochs is considered highly advanced for its time.

2. The strong walls that brochs had made them ideal defensive fortifications for people protecting strategic areas.

3. It is known that brochs had two walls, were circular in shape, and were often built several meters high.

4. Brochs were constructed during the Iron Age in Britain, and they often looked very similar to one another.

5. Hypotheses on the uses of brochs range from them being fortresses to serving as homes for individuals.

6. Some brochs have been found in unpopulated areas while many others were built close to one another.

Geological Tools

The study of geology involves researching the Earth and its inner workings. To accomplish this, geologists utilize various tools. Some are simple whereas others are rather sophisticated pieces of machinery; however, for basic field studies, geologists tend to use four simple tools: the geological compass, the rock hammer, the hand lens, and the field book. Employing those four tools, geologists can make preliminary studies of areas before bringing in more advanced machines and instruments to map surface details and the inner structures of specific locations.

Magnetic compasses have been in existence for centuries and have assisted travelers in navigating from place to place by using the Earth's magnetic field. Geological compasses, however, are used differently. The primary function of a geological compass is to measure folds in the surface of the land a geologist is examining. A geological compass provides the ability to measure the degree of the folds in land being analyzed by comparing them to stable vertical and horizontal planes. It is often used to measure the repetitive folds that stress produces in metamorphic rock formations. A geological compass can additionally measure lineations in rock formations. Those are stress lines cut into a rock by the movement of the rock against other rocks, which are often found near fault lines, where the land is greatly stressed. Although most modern geological compasses use analog principles, digital ones are also available.

The rock hammer is the simplest tool a geologist can use. As its name suggests, it is a hammer for rocks. Geologists use it to collect samples of rocks by striking off pieces from larger ones. They also use it to split rocks in two to examine their inner structures. A rock hammer is normally small enough to fit in one hand. It has a head and a handle with the head having two striking parts, such as a flat head on one side and a sharper pick on the other. ■ Rock hammers come in different weights, ranging from a few hundred grams to half a kilogram. **2** Lighter hammers are employed on soft rocks such as sedimentary formations. **3** The heavier ones are necessary when dealing with harder igneous and metamorphic rocks. **4**

As for the hand lens, it is a small magnifying glass that is similar to what jewelers use to examine gems. Most geologists wear it on a cord which they hang around their necks. It lacks a handle, so it is normally attached to a sturdy housing made of metal that allows the hand lens to slide in and out when in use. Geologists use the hand lens to examine the mineral structures of rocks. Hand lenses vary in magnification, and cheaper, lower-powered lenses can have optical aberrations, causing distortions. More sophisticated devices have multiple lenses and may even have prisms.

The final basic tool required by most geologists is the field book, which is a journal in which they record the information they gather while in the field. Geologists refer to this information as field notes. In the past, a field book was almost always a common paper notebook in which information was written with a pen or pencil. Nowadays, most field books are made of water-resistant paper and coverings. In addition, geologists are turning to more modern methods, among them being tape recorders, laptops, and smartphones, which they use to record their notes.

*Glossary

aberration: a disturbance in rays of light so that they are unable to focus or produce clear images
prism: a transparent body with a triangular base that can reflect rays of light

10 The word "preliminary" in the passage is closest in meaning to

   (A) simple

   (B) coherent

   (C) initial

   (D) in-depth

11 According to paragraph 1, which of the following is true about geologists?

   (A) They typically make use of basic tools when they are working in the field.

   (B) They rely upon advanced machinery in their laboratories to learn information.

   (C) They prefer to utilize sophisticated tools rather than work with simple instruments.

   (D) They must travel to specific locations in order to learn more about them.

12 Which of the following can be inferred from paragraph 2 about fault lines?

   (A) They are found only in certain places where the land has sedimentary rocks.

   (B) They are places where geologists commonly employ geological compasses.

   (C) They are comprised almost entirely of lineations in different kinds of rocks.

   (D) They are responsible for the majority of the earthquakes that happen on the Earth.

13 According to paragraph 3, which of the following is NOT true about the rock hammer?

   (A) There is no standard amount for each rock hammer to weigh.

   (B) It can be utilized to collect samples from rocks by hitting them.

   (C) Its head has two different sides that can be used to hit rocks with.

   (D) There are some geological tools that are less complicated than it is.

14 Which of the sentences below best expresses the essential information in the highlighted sentence in the passage? Incorrect answer choices change the meaning in important ways or leave out essential information.

It lacks a handle, so it is normally attached to a sturdy housing made of metal that allows the hand lens to slide in and out when in use.

(A) The housing that a hand lens is kept in prevents it from suffering any harm when it is not being used.

(B) There is a strong housing for the hand lens, so geologists can slide it in and out without any problems.

(C) The lack of a handle makes using a hand lens difficult at times because it can slide in an out of a person's hand.

(D) A hand lens has no handle, so it is connected to a housing that allows it easily to be moved out to be used.

15 The word "they" in the passage refers to

(A) geologists

(B) modern methods

(C) tape recorders, laptops, and smartphones

(D) their notes

16 According to paragraph 5, geologists use field books to

(A) record information about places that they hope to research later

(B) draw maps of the places that they visit while they are out in the field

(C) take notes on the facts that they learn while investigating something

(D) write down questions about information that they need answers to

17 Look at the four squares [■] that indicate where the following sentence could be added to the passage.

The extra weight enables geologists more easily to cut off pieces of or to crack open these strong rocks.

Where would the sentence best fit?

Click on a square [■] to add the sentence to the passage.

18 **Directions**: Select the appropriate statements from the answer choices and match them to the geological tool to which they relate. TWO of the answer choices will NOT be used. **This question is worth 4 points.**

Drag your answer choices to the spaces where they belong. To remove an answer choice, click on it. To review the passage, click on VIEW TEXT.

STATEMENTS	GEOLOGICAL TOOL

STATEMENTS

1. Can be attached to a cord and then worn around a person's neck

2. Allows the folds in the land being studied to be measured

3. Is used to record information when a geologist is in the field

4. May have a flat end in addition to a sharp end

5. Can provide results that are not as good as possible when a cheap one is used

6. Relies upon the Earth's magnetic field in order to work properly

7. Can produce results in both digital and analog formats

8. Is used to study lines that have been cut into rock formations

9. Can be heavy or light depending upon how a geologist will use it

GEOLOGICAL TOOL

Geological Compass (Select 3)

-
-
-

Rock Hammer (Select 2)

-
-

Hand Lens (Select 2)

-
-

Vocabulary Review

A Complete each sentence with the appropriate word from the box.

distortion	supplements	signal	Congress	defensive

1 The castle was built for _____ purposes to protect the king.

2 The police are trying to _____ drivers to get them to slow down.

3 Susan started taking vitamin _____ to improve her health.

4 There are two separate houses in the American _____.

5 The _____ in the lens made it difficult for John to see well.

B Complete each sentence with the correct answer.

1 Animals that become **dormant** in winter are _____.

a. very active   b. not very active

2 To **utilize** a piece of equipment is to _____ it properly.

a. use   b. build

3 It is possible to find many **tombs** at a _____.

a. cemetery   b. park

4 If a person has an **abundance** of time, that individual is _____.

a. busy   b. not busy

5 By **enhancing** the quality of an item, a person _____ it.

a. improves   b. destroys

6 **Densely** populated urban areas are _____.

a. green zones   b. full of people

7 When a problem **puzzles** a person, that individual cannot _____.

a. write about it   b. figure it out

8 When two armies **clash**, they _____ each other.

a. fight   b. avoid

9 Someone able to **manipulate** things is able to _____ them well.

a. change   b. sell

10 A sailor who can **navigate** a river can _____.

a. see far on it   b. sail on it

Chapter 03

Factual Information

Question Type | Factual Information

◢ About the Question

Factual Information questions focus on the facts that are included in the passage. You are asked to answer a question asking about the facts or information that are covered in the passage. These questions may ask about details, definitions, explanations, or other kinds of information. The information asked about in these questions is always included in a small section of the passage. There are 1-3 Factual Information questions for each passage. There is an average of 2 of these questions per passage.

Recognizing Factual Information questions:

- According to paragraph 1, which of the following is true about X?

- The author's description of X mentions which of the following? (much less common than before)

- According to paragraph 1, X occurred because . . .

- According to paragraph 1, X did Y because . . .

- According to paragraph 1, why did X do Y?

- Select the TWO answer choices from paragraph 1 that identify X. *To receive credit, you must select TWO answers.* (seldom asked)

Helpful hints for answering the questions correctly:

- Most of these questions indicate the paragraph in which the correct answer is found. When trying to answer one of these questions, only look for the information in the paragraph mentioned in the question itself.

- Read carefully so that you understand what the facts are and what the author's opinions or thoughts are.

- Make sure that the entire answer choice is accurate. Be especially careful of absolute words such as *always* and *never*.

- Some answer choices may contain accurate information that does not appear in the passage. Do not select these answer choices. Make sure the answer choice you select has information that appears in the passage.

- Some Factual Information questions require test takers to understand the entire paragraph, not just one part of it, to find the correct answer.

The Louisiana Purchase

➡ As the 1700s ended, the United States mostly only occupied land by the Atlantic Ocean. However, settlers began crossing the Appalachian Mountains and moving westward. This was something of a problem because most of the land west of the Mississippi River had been claimed by France. President Thomas Jefferson sent an envoy to France to discuss the matter with Napoleon, the emperor of France then. The end result was that in 1803, the United States purchased an enormous amount of land from France. This became known as the Louisiana Purchase. It cost the United States $15 million, but it doubled the size of the country. It would be decades before many parts of the region were settled. Nevertheless, the purchase inspired Americans to move west. It also ended Napoleon's ambitions of having an empire on the western side of the Atlantic in addition to one on the eastern side.

In paragraph 2, the author's description of the Louisiana Purchase mentions which of the following?

Ⓐ How far west the land that was bought extended

Ⓑ Its long-term effects on the United States

Ⓒ The boundaries of the land that it included

Ⓓ The name of the American envoy who negotiated its purchase

Paragraph 2 is marked with an arrow (➡).

| Answer Explanation |

Choice Ⓑ is the correct answer. The passage reads, "It would be decades before many parts of the region were settled. Nevertheless, the purchase inspired Americans to move west. It also ended Napoleon's ambitions of having an empire on the western side of the Atlantic in addition to one on the eastern side." Thus the author mentions how the United States was affected by the Louisiana Purchase for a period of many years.

A | Max Ernst

🎧 CH03_2A

One of the major members of the Dada and Surrealist movements was Max Ernst. He was a German artist who lived during the twentieth century. As a young man, Ernst attended university to study philosophy and psychology. During that time, he also began to exhibit an interest in becoming an artist. His studies, however, were interrupted by combat service in the German army during World War I. The violence he witnessed left him **disillusioned** and caused

him to believe the world was irrational. This influenced his art tremendously as many of his works reflected an absurd quality with no basis in reality.

After the war ended, Ernst helped establish an artists' group in Cologne that became part of the Dada Movement. At first, he created **collages** and made works that were dreamlike and futuristic. He mostly used illustrated catalogs for his material by cutting them up and pasting the clippings together. Later, he made some sculptures but focused mostly on painting.

In 1922, Ernst moved to Paris, where he became involved in the growing Surrealist Movement, which was an offshoot of Dadaism. His 1923 painting *Of This Men Shall Know Nothing* is often considered among the finest Surrealist works ever created. In the 1930s, he fled Europe for America, where he spent most of the remainder of his life. His work would go on to influence many artists, including Jackson Pollock, one of the most famous abstract artists of the twentieth century.

*disillusioned: disenchanted or unsatisfied with one's current situation
*collage: a type of art in which various materials are pasted or attached to a single surface

---

1 In paragraph 1, the author's description of Max Ernst mentions which of the following?

Ⓐ The injuries he suffered fighting in World War I

Ⓑ The year when he started to attend his university

Ⓒ The name of the university which he attended

Ⓓ The influence that World War I had on his work

2 According to paragraph 2, which of the following is true about Max Ernst?

Ⓐ The first type of art which he worked on was paintings.

Ⓑ He utilized paper cut from catalogs to create collages.

Ⓒ His sculptures were more advanced than his collages or paintings.

Ⓓ He is considered one of the original founders of the Dada Movement.

Vocabulary

- _____ = to disturb; to stop something from happening
- _____ = battle; fighting
- _____ = not logical
- _____ = having pictures

B | The Andromeda Galaxy

The closest large galaxy to the Milky Way is the Andromeda Galaxy, which has been designated the M31 galaxy by astronomers. It is spiral shaped and is approximately 2.54 million light years away from Earth. At its broadest point, the Andromeda Galaxy is 220,000 light years wide, and it contains roughly one trillion stars, more than twice the number the Milky Way has. Due to its relatively close **proximity** to Earth as well as its brightness and size, the Andromeda Galaxy is the object farthest from Earth that can be seen with the naked eye. In the Northern Hemisphere, it is most easily seen in autumn in the eastern sky near the constellation Cassiopeia.

At the center of the Andromeda Galaxy is a dense cluster of stars. Astronomers also believe that a gigantic black hole lies in that part of it. The galaxy has two large spiral arms that appear **distorted** in shape due to the effects of the gravity fields of two nearby smaller galaxies, M32 and M110. It also contains a large ring of dust, which may be the result of a collision with galaxy M32 millions of years ago.

Astronomers are certain that a similar collision will occur between the Milky Way and the Andromeda Galaxy in the future. The two galaxies are currently approaching each other at a rate between 100 and 140 kilometers per second. It is estimated that the collision will take place sometime around four billion years from now.

*proximity: closeness; nearness
*distorted: twisted; irregular in shape

1　According to paragraph 1, the Andromeda Galaxy can be seen with the naked eye from Earth because

   Ⓐ it is only 220,000 light years away from Earth

   Ⓑ the stars in Cassiopeia help increase its brightness

   Ⓒ there are so many stars found in the galaxy

   Ⓓ it is a large, bright galaxy relatively close to Earth

2　Select the TWO answer choices from paragraph 2 that identify features of the Andromeda Galaxy. *To receive credit, you must select TWO answers.*

   Ⓐ It contains dust that might be from an impact with another galaxy.

   Ⓑ The effects of its gravity keep two smaller galaxies close to it.

   Ⓒ There are numerous stars and a large black hole in the middle of it.

   Ⓓ Its spiral arms are regular in shape despite the effects of gravity on them.

Vocabulary

- _____ = 1,000,000,000,000
- _____ = the eye without anything such as glasses, binoculars, or a telescope
- _____ = a group of stars that create a pattern in the sky
- _____ = a group formed by many things close to one another

C | The African Veldt

There is a vast region in southern Africa that mostly consists of dry grasslands. Known as the veldt, it is located in eastern South Africa and in sections of Swaziland, Botswana, Namibia, and Zimbabwe. The terrain is mostly flat, rolling **plains**, but it has a variety of elevations. This results in there being three distinct kinds of veldt: the low veldt, the middle veldt, and the high veldt.

The low veldt's elevation ranges from about 100 to 600 meters above sea level. The middle veldt stands 600 to 1,200 meters high while the high veldt is 1,200 to 1,800 meters above sea level. The high veldt is primarily part of a large interior **plateau** in South Africa. The middle and low veldts are on the borders of this plateau and are found both inside South Africa and its border nations. While the vegetation in all three areas varies to some extent, grasses and low shrubs dominate these regions.

The climate varies somewhat in each type of veldt. Mild winters last from May to September whereas extremely hot summers run from November to March. The high veldt is colder in winter and cooler in summer than the middle and low veldts, with the coldest temperatures in the high veldt not dropping much lower than ten degrees Celsius. The amount of rainfall varies as the high veldt gets more precipitation—between 400 and 800 millimeters annually—than the lower regions, but droughts are known to occur in all three regions.

*plain: a flat area of land that is not much higher than the surrounding area
*plateau: a relatively flat area of land which is higher than the land around it and which often has canyons

1 According to paragraph 1, why are there three different types of veldt?

   Ⓐ The climate in all three areas are vastly different.

   Ⓑ The elevations in the veldt differ to a great extent.

   Ⓒ The three regions have various types of vegetation.

   Ⓓ The animals living in the veldt tend to be different.

2 According to paragraph 3, which of the following is true about the high veldt?

   Ⓐ It suffers from droughts more than the middle and low veldts do.

   Ⓑ Its winters start in November while its summers begin in May.

   Ⓒ It has hot summers and winters with temperatures as low as ten degrees Celsius.

   Ⓓ Its rainfall can be double the amount that falls in the low veldt.

Vocabulary

- _____ = land
- _____ = the height above or below sea level something is
- _____ = moderate; not severe
- _____ = water in liquid or solid form that falls from the sky

◪ Mapping

The following chart shows the structure of the passage. Fill in the blanks with the appropriate words.

The African Veldt

Is found in southern ❶ _____
- are low veldt, middle veldt, and high veldt

Low Veldt
- 100-600 meters above sea level
- borders ❷ _____ in South Africa
- gets ❸ _____ precipitation than other regions

Middle Veldt
- 600-1,200 meters above sea level
- borders plateau in South Africa
- has ❹ _____ and low ❺ _____ like other regions

High Veldt
- 1,200-1,800 meters above sea level
- Has ❻ _____ winters and ❼ _____ summers than other areas
- Gets more ❽ _____ than other areas

◪ Summary

The following is a summary of the passage. Fill in the blanks with the appropriate words.

The veldt is a dry ❶ _____ found in eastern South Africa and some other countries. It has different ❷ _____, so it is divided into the low, middle, and high veldt. The low veldt is 100 to 600 meters above sea level, The middle veldt goes from 600 to ❸ _____ meters above sea level while the high veldt rises up to ❹ _____ meters above sea level. The ❺ _____ in each type of veldt differs somewhat. The ❻ _____ veldt gets colder weather and more rainfall than the other two areas.

Practice with Long Passages

A | The Library of Pergamum

🎧 CH03_3A

Located in the city of Pergamum in what is present-day Turkey, the Library of Pergamum was considered second in quality only to the Library of Alexandria in the ancient world. Most scholars agree that King Eumenes II built the library sometime during his reign between 197 B.C. and 159 B.C. An inscription found on a stone in the library's ruins reads that one donor was Flavia Melitene, the wife of a local politician. Through her efforts and those of others, the library came to be generously stocked with **scrolls**. Supposedly, more than 200,000 of them, a collection only exceeded in number by the Library of Alexandria, were stored in the library.

The Library of Pergamum was part of a building complex that was a temple to the Greek goddess Athena. The builders placed a large statue of Athena inside the library's largest room, the main reading room. Another statue, one of the Roman Emperor Hadrian, was installed inside it when the city came under Roman domination. The library also contained niches where the builders set smaller **busts** of famed scholars such as Herodotus and Homer. The entire temple-library complex was located at the northern end of a large hill, the Acropolis of Pergamum.

The library's main section consisted of four rooms attached to the temple complex. The largest of these was the central reading room, which was about sixteen meters by fourteen meters in dimension. It contained shelves that could hold nearly 17,000 scrolls along three of its walls. The reading room also had benches for scholars to sit at while they read. Some believe that scholars may have used this room for debates and meetings. The three smaller rooms were narrower and contained shelves of scrolls but had no places to read.

Each shelf was about two meters high, which permitted many scrolls to be stacked together. The upper portions of the walls contained windows to allow air and light into the library. The shelves throughout the library were spaced apart from the exterior walls, and this enabled air to circulate more freely. This was a precaution taken to prevent the scrolls, which were mostly made of papyrus, from getting moist and thereby being damaged.

Eventually, the library's collection of scrolls was lost, and the building itself fell into ruin. The reason that the scrolls were lost is unknown. Some believe that the Roman Mark Antony carted them away to Alexandria in an attempt to please the Egyptian ruler Cleopatra. Others say that Muslim invaders centuries later looted the library. How the library came to ruin is also uncertain, but earthquakes struck the city at times, and invaders sacked Pergamum on occasion as well.

*scroll: a roll of parchment, paper, or another substance that often has writing on it
*bust: a work of art such as a sculpture that shows the upper body and head of a person

---

Vocabulary

- _____ = a person who studies a topic in depth
- _____ = a person who gives money or other gifts away
- _____ = an area with several buildings used for similar purposes
- _____ = to take the valuables in a place such as a city after capturing it

1 The word "it" in the passage refers to

    (A) a temple to the Greek goddess Athena

    (B) a large statue of Athena

    (C) the main reading room

    (D) another statue

Factual Information Question

2 According to paragraph 3, which of the following is true about the Library of Pergamum's main section?

    (A) One of its main rooms contained places where people could read.

    (B) The four rooms that made it up were of roughly equal size.

    (C) It could hold no more than 17,000 scrolls at a single time.

    (D) Only a few scholars at a time were permitted to do research there.

Inference Question

3 In paragraph 5, the author implies that the Library of Pergamum

    (A) is known to have been looted by Muslim invaders

    (B) was burned by the Egyptian Cleopatra in a war against Rome

    (C) sent its scrolls to Alexandria when foreign invaders arrived

    (D) might have been destroyed because of a natural disaster

Prose Summary Question

4 An introductory sentence for a brief summary of the passage is provided below. Complete the summary by selecting the THREE answer choices that express the most important ideas of the passage. Some sentences do not belong because they express ideas that are not presented in the passage or are minor ideas in the passage.

The Library of Pergamum was one of the ancient world's great libraries and had numerous scrolls for scholars to look at.

ANSWER CHOICES

1. The library, with more than 200,000 scrolls, was the second largest one in the ancient world after the Library of Alexandria.

2. The library is believed to have been founded during the second century B.C. by King Eumenes II.

3. It is not known exactly what happened to the library, but the Romans or Muslims may have taken its scrolls.

4. There were not only thousands of scrolls in the library, but there were also a wide variety of statues.

5. The main section of the library contained large numbers of scrolls, and people were allowed to read and do work in this area.

6. The library had a large number of windows, which enabled air to circulate so that the scrolls could be preserved.

Opera Seria

In the eighteenth century, Italian opera was divided into two major types: opera buffa and opera seria. Opera buffa was comedic in nature while opera seria was serious and more akin to tragedies and modern melodramas. The term opera seria was not used at the time it first appeared and did not come about until studies on the history of opera were conducted in the early twentieth century. While opera seria was created in Italy, over time, it spread all throughout Europe and was popular almost everywhere except France.

Opera seria first developed in Venice and Naples, two Italian cities, around 1720. It was a product of the Enlightenment of the seventeenth century. It was intended to follow the clear thinking of the Enlightenment and to be rational in its ideas. This would result in a universal appeal that would give pleasure to its audience. Opera seria composers wished to emulate ancient Greek tragedies in operatic form. They strove for simple characters and simplified plots. Their goals were a **marked** contrast to the late seventeenth century's Baroque opera, which featured grand characterizations and complex plotting.

Two famed Italian opera composers, Pietro Metastasio and Apostolo Zeno, set the tone for the form of opera seria. It was performed in three acts and featured conflict centered on human emotions. Actual figures and historical occurrences based on Greek and Roman history were often its subjects. There were typically two pairs of lovers and a tyrant, who may or may not have been evil, of some kind. The plot usually concluded with a heroic deed or with one pair of lovers breaking up.

Arias and duets between the lead singers dominated the singing parts. Arias mostly came at the end of a scene. That gave the audience the opportunity to applaud as the singer exited the stage. **Recitatives** were interspersed with arias and duets. They were used to convey the plot and the characters' motives to the audience. The recitatives in opera seria had a common form as they tended to be unrhymed lines with seven to eleven syllables. This recitative form was called *versi sciolti*.

Lead male roles were sung by *castrati*, young singers with unnaturally high vocal ranges. The lead female role, the *prima donna*, was a soprano. She often carried the performance through the force of her talent at singing arias. As a consequence, opera seria came to be dominated by female singers. Many became such stars that entire operas were composed for them and their particular vocal talents.

*marked: obvious; clear; noticeable
*recitative: a style of music that is between singing and speaking

---

Vocabulary

- _____ = similar to
- _____ = logical
- _____ = the main story in a dramatic work
- _____ = an unelected leader who often rules harshly

1 Which of the sentences below best expresses the essential information in the highlighted sentence in the passage? Incorrect answer choices change the meaning in important ways or leave out essential information.

The term opera seria was not used at the time it first appeared and did not come about until studies on the history of opera were conducted in the early twentieth century.

Ⓐ In the twentieth century, the term opera seria was discovered by historians who were studying opera.

Ⓑ It was not until people began studying the history of opera in the 1900s that the term opera seria was used.

Ⓒ When people began to study the history of opera in the twentieth century, they created the term opera seria.

Ⓓ The term opera seria was created in the past and then gained widespread acceptance in the 1900s.

Vocabulary Question

2 The word "emulate" in the passage is closest in meaning to

Ⓐ influence

Ⓑ continue

Ⓒ imitate

Ⓓ expose

Factual Information Question

3 According to paragraph 4, the end of a scene usually had an aria because

Ⓐ it gave the members of the audience a chance to clap for the singer

Ⓑ it was easier to explain the plot with an aria than with a recitative

Ⓒ it was tradition to use an aria so that only one singer would be on stage

Ⓓ it enabled the other performers to get the opportunity to rest longer

Prose Summary Question

4 An introductory sentence for a brief summary of the passage is provided below. Complete the summary by selecting the THREE answer choices that express the most important ideas of the passage. Some sentences do not belong because they express ideas that are not presented in the passage or are minor ideas in the passage.

Opera seria was developed in Italy in the seventeenth century and had a number of characteristics that distinguished it from other types of performances.

ANSWER CHOICES

1 Pietro Metastasio and Apostolo Zeno were two of the first men ever to compose works of opera seria.

2 The genre was serious in nature and was intended to please the audience with its simple plots and characters.

3 Even though opera seria was popular in many European countries, the French never developed an appreciation for it.

4 Some soprano performers of opera seria became so famous that operas were specifically written for them to perform.

5 Arias, duets, and recitatives were used both to show off the voices of the performers and to explain the events in the story.

6 An opera seria had three acts and was typically about a story that came from ancient Greece or Rome.

CH03_4A

Portuguese Colonialism in Asia

In 1488 during the Age of Exploration, Portuguese sailors rounded the Cape of Good Hope in Africa and entered the Indian Ocean. Later expeditions reached India by 1499. In 1510, the Portuguese captured Goa in India and established a trading post and colony there. In 1511, they sailed to Malacca in Malaysia and quickly conquered it as well. Further efforts took them to Sri Lanka, Indonesia, the coast of China, and Japan. For nearly five centuries, their Asian empire endured. The Portuguese colony of Macau in China was the last to be lost in 1999.

The driving force between the exploration and colonization conducted by the Portuguese was trade. At the end of the fifteenth century, Venice and Genoa dominated the trade from Asia to the west that went through the Mediterranean Sea. Much of this trade was in spices that came from the east and made their merchants extremely wealthy. But in 1453, the Ottoman Turks conquered the Byzantine Empire, and that shut the door on trade in the eastern Mediterranean. Thereafter, the economic center of Europe shifted to western nations such as England, France, Spain, and Portugal. The Portuguese were the greatest navigators of that time, so they took advantage of the changing economic tide to use their ships to find new lands and to become wealthy.

In Asia, the Portuguese did not seek to establish large colonies like the English, French, Spanish, and even their fellow countrymen did in the Americas. Instead, they set up small, profitable trading posts. In that way, they could concentrate their efforts on occupying and fortifying small areas. By negotiating with local leaders from positions of strength, they secured trading rights. Large oceangoing vessels transported ruthless leaders and their followers to Asia, where they wrested away land from the natives and then carried trade goods back to Portugal. Most of the items they returned with were spices and luxury goods, but the Portuguese also engaged in the slave trade.

The major Portuguese trading posts in Asia were Goa, Malacca, the Moluccas Islands in Indonesia, Macau in China, and Nagasaki in Japan.

The Portuguese, however, were not alone in Asia. Spain and the Netherlands sent explorers into the region, and they began encroaching upon Portugal's trade, at times violently. Two treaties with Spain divided the world into domains for both of them, with the Spanish getting most of the New World and the Portuguese most of Asia. In 1580, Portugal became a part of the Hapsburg Spanish Empire after Spain invaded and defeated Portugal in a short war. This complicated matters in Asia to some extent.

However, Portugal managed to regain its independence from Spain in 1668. This marked the beginning of the decline of Portugal's Asian empire though. Portugal soon came into conflict with both England and the Netherlands, and both of them began assaulting Portugal's overseas empire. The powerful Dutch navy attacked and took over most of Portugal's important spice trading outposts. Nagasaki in Japan also became a Dutch outpost after the Portuguese there were defeated. The English started making inroads in India, and, before long, most of the subcontinent was under English rule. Soon, Portugal's Asian empire consisted only of Goa, Macau, and a small outpost in east Timor. By the twentieth century, only Goa and Macau were left.

*Glossary

navigator: a person who guides a ship to its destination

New World: North and South America; the lands discovered by European explorers beginning with Christopher Columbus

1 In paragraph 1, all of the following questions are answered EXCEPT:

Ⓐ In which lands did the Portuguese establish colonies after they founded one in Malaysia?

Ⓑ What caused Portugal to lose all of its colonies, including the one at Macau?

Ⓒ During which period of history did the Portuguese start founding Asian colonies?

Ⓓ Where did the Portuguese start their first colony after entering the Indian Ocean?

2 In paragraph 2, why does the author mention "the Ottoman Turks"?

Ⓐ To describe the manner in which they defeated the Byzantine Empire

Ⓑ To point out which lands in Asia they controlled in the fifteenth century

Ⓒ To discuss the relationship that they had with Venice and Genoa

Ⓓ To note the effect that they had on the economic history of Europe

3 The word "shifted" in the passage is closest in meaning to

Ⓐ resumed

Ⓑ moved

Ⓒ divided

Ⓓ appealed

4 The phrase "wrested away" in the passage is closest in meaning to

Ⓐ purchased

Ⓑ traded for

Ⓒ battled for

Ⓓ seized

5 Select the TWO answer choices from paragraph 3 that identify the strategy Portugal used in Asia. *To receive credit, you must select TWO answers.*

   Ⓐ It focused on dealing with the natives of Asian lands as equals.

   Ⓑ It emphasized dominating small areas rather than having large colonies.

   Ⓒ It gained the rights to trade with natives through its power.

   Ⓓ It brought goods from Portugal to give to the natives as gifts.

6 According to paragraph 4, which of the following is true about Portugal?

   Ⓐ It tried to establish some large colonies in the New World like Spain did.

   Ⓑ It came to an agreement with Spain regarding the locations of their colonies.

   Ⓒ It made war on the Spanish colonies that were located in Asia.

   Ⓓ It lost several of its Asian colonies due to the events of 1580.

7 Which of the sentences below best expresses the essential information in the highlighted sentence in the passage? Incorrect answer choices change the meaning in important ways or leave out essential information.

Portugal soon came into conflict with both England and the Netherlands, and both of them began assaulting Portugal's overseas empire.

   Ⓐ Portugal's colonies were attacked by both England and the Netherlands.

   Ⓑ England and the Netherlands joined forces to make war on Portugal.

   Ⓒ Portugal was defeated in several battles in Asia by England and the Netherlands.

   Ⓓ England and the Netherlands envied the Asian colonies owned by Portugal.

8 According to paragraph 5, what happened to Portugal's colony in Japan?

   Ⓐ It was peacefully returned to the Japanese.

   Ⓑ The Netherlands managed to take it away.

   Ⓒ The English captured it thanks to their navy.

   Ⓓ It remained in Portuguese control until the 1900s.

9   **Directions:** An introductory sentence for a brief summary of the passage is provided below. Complete the summary by selecting the THREE answer choices that express the most important ideas of the passage. Some sentences do not belong because they express ideas that are not presented in the passage or are minor ideas in the passage. **This question is worth 2 points.**

Drag your answer choices to the spaces where they belong. To remove an answer choice, click on it. To review the passage, click on VIEW TEXT.

Portugal established a number of colonies in Asia during the Age of Exploration, but the colonies were slowly lost over time.

-
-
-

ANSWER CHOICES

1   Portugal returned Macau, one of its Asian colonies, to China at the end of the twentieth century.

2   The Portuguese were Europe's best sailors, so they sailed around the western coast of Africa and past the Cape of Good Hope.

3   Many countries, such as the Netherlands and England, managed to take colonies away from Portugal by force.

4   Once the Portuguese entered the Indian Ocean by ship, they founded colonies in India, Malaysia, Japan, and other places.

5   Many of the colonies founded by Portugal, including Goa in India, were intentionally kept small, which let them focus on specific places.

6   The Spanish defeated Portugal and made it a part of their empire, so Portugal remained under Spanish control for almost a century.

How Birds Survive Storms

Storms are capable of causing severe amounts of damage to both human and animal habitats and are particularly dangerous to small animals, including birds. They may destroy bird nests, disrupt food supplies, damage living places such as trees and bushes, and injure or kill birds. Rain, snow, hail, sleet, strong winds, floods, lightning, and fires caused by lightning strikes are just some of the natural phenomena that are caused by storms and that can produce these negative effects. Despite these dangers, most birds survive storms because they have developed various methods enabling them to do so.

Birds have an innate ability to sense when storms are coming. For example, they can perceive changes in temperature, barometric pressure, and wind speed and direction in addition to the humidity in the air. These can indicate that inclement weather is approaching. When a bird realizes that a storm is coming, it responds by bulking up. It consumes more food, thereby endowing itself with extra fat to keep it warm and also to provide it with enough energy to survive the storm and a possible lack of food following it. Some birds even possess the ability to lower their metabolism so that they can consume stored energy at slower rates. Birds can additionally avoid storms they know are coming by flying away if the incoming weather system is not too large. However, when birds consume too much food, their airspeed velocity gets reduced, so they may be unable to fly away from a storm. Being slower in the air can also make birds more vulnerable to predators after a storm passes.

Another way birds can survive storms is by seeking shelter. Many tiny birds can fit comfortably inside cavities in trees to weather storms. Birds also hide behind trees, under brush, and in any other shelter they can find, usually on the lee sides of hills, mountains, or other large obstacles. Birds that cannot obtain shelter may survive by ducking their heads under their wings and by clinging onto anything they can grasp with their feet, such as tree branches or power lines. Birds' legs and talons are strong, so they can easily grip objects and hold onto them even during high winds.

In addition, birds' bodies help them survive storms. **1** Their feathers can trap air, increasing their ability to keep birds warm. **2** Besides providing birds with insulation, many feathers are waterproof. **3** Birds have a gland called the preen gland, which is near the tail and secretes an oil. **4** Birds use their beaks to collect this oil, rub it onto their feathers, and thereby increase their waterproofing. This ability to deflect rain enables birds to stay warm by keeping their feathers dry.

Yet another bird defense against storms is their ability to keep their internal organs warm. During cold weather, people lose heat because their skin emits heat into the surrounding air. This action chills the body's blood, and as the blood circulates through the body, it takes in even more coldness, and a damaging cycle develops. Birds, however, avoid this because the arteries and the veins in their feet and legs are close together. As warm blood flows down in the arteries, cold blood flows up through their veins. When the blood in each place passes, the warm blood in the arteries heats up the cold blood in the veins. This keeps birds' bodies warm but has the negative effect of not giving their feet much heat.

*Glossary

barometric pressure: the pressure produced by the Earth's atmosphere and measured by a barometer

lee side: a part that is sheltered or turned away from the direction the wind is blowing

10 In paragraph 1, all of the following questions are answered EXCEPT:

   (A) Why are the majority of birds able to survive when storms hit?

   (B) What kinds of injuries do small animals such as birds suffer during storms?

   (C) Which phenomena produced by storms can harm birds in various ways?

   (D) In what ways is it possible for birds to be negatively affected by storms?

11 According to paragraph 2, why do many birds consume food before storms?

   (A) They want to eat their food before too much of it gets blown away by storms.

   (B) The food that they eat helps them stay warm during stormy weather.

   (C) Eating provides them with enough energy to fly away from coming storms.

   (D) They are decreasing their food supply since animals may steal their food following storms.

12 According to paragraph 2, which of the following is true about birds?

   (A) Their metabolism increases during storms and makes them expend lots of energy.

   (B) They are not able to detect changes in the atmosphere indicating that a storm is coming.

   (C) It is easy for predators to catch them when they are flying in the middle of storms.

   (D) Those that eat too much before storms may not be able to fly away from bad weather.

13 The word "cavities" in the passage is closest in meaning to

   (A) passageways

   (B) holes

   (C) entrances

   (D) branches

14 Which of the sentences below best expresses the essential information in the highlighted sentence in the passage? Incorrect answer choices change the meaning in important ways or leave out essential information.

Birds that cannot obtain shelter may survive by ducking their heads under their wings and by clinging onto anything they can grasp with their feet, such as tree branches or power lines.

(A) Some birds grasp things with their feet and put their heads beneath their wings if they cannot find a safe place.

(B) One preferred method that birds use to keep themselves safe during storms is to grab branches or power lines.

(C) Many birds simply cover their heads with their wings whenever stormy weather begins.

(D) It is not possible for some birds to fly away during storms, so they may look for other ways to keep themselves safe.

15 The author discusses "the preen gland" in paragraph 4 in order to

(A) explain the way that birds use it to make their feathers waterproof

(B) point out that only certain types of birds actually have it in their bodies

(C) describe how it assists birds in keeping warm during cold weather

(D) mention that it helps birds trap air between their feathers to stay warm

16 According to paragraph 5, birds' bodies avoid losing heat during storms because

(A) the small sizes of their bodies enable them to conserve body heat well

(B) both their arteries and their veins transport warm blood through their bodies

(C) blood in their arteries heats up cold blood flowing through their veins

(D) their feathers prevent them from losing any body heat through the skin

17 Look at the four squares [■] that indicate where the following sentence could be added to the passage.

This feature of their feathers is especially useful for wading birds such as herons and egrets, which spend large amounts of time in ponds and lakes.

Where would the sentence best fit?

Click on a square [■] to add the sentence to the passage.

18 **Directions**: An introductory sentence for a brief summary of the passage is provided below. Complete the summary by selecting the THREE answer choices that express the most important ideas of the passage. Some sentences do not belong because they express ideas that are not presented in the passage or are minor ideas in the passage. **This question is worth 2 points.**

There are several reasons why birds are able to survive storms.

-

-

-

ANSWER CHOICES

1 Birds often find places that provide shelter where they are able to get away from storms when they come.

2 Some storms can cause a great amount of damage by harming both birds and the places where they live.

3 It is possible for birds to detect when bad weather is coming, so they typically eat plenty of food before that happens.

4 Birds' feathers are able to keep them warm while the blood in their bodies can also help keep them from getting too cold.

5 Some birds are capable of flying high enough in the air that they can get above rainclouds and avoid storms.

6 All of the feathers on birds are waterproof, so they are capable of staying dry when rain is falling.

Vocabulary Review

A Complete each sentence with the appropriate word from the box.

interrupt	elevation	internal	insulation	cluster

1 This mountain has the highest _____ of any place in the country.

2 It is considered rude to _____ a person in the middle of a conversation.

3 Ted has an _____ bleeding problem as a result of a car accident.

4 By using _____, you can make sure that your house keeps heat in it during winter.

5 It is possible to see the _____ of stars by using a telescope.

B Complete each sentence with the correct answer.

1 A **tyrant** is a person who rules a country with _____.

   a. kindness   b. no mercy

2 When a galaxy has **trillions** of stars, it has _____ of them.

   a. a small number   b. very many

3 An **irrational** person is not able to act in a _____ manner.

   a. logical   b. creative

4 When writing the **plot** of a novel, it is important to make sure the _____ is interesting.

   a. background   b. story

5 An individual who works in an office **complex** likely works in a large _____.

   a. building   b. city

6 People on an **expedition** to the jungle are _____ there.

   a. living   b. on a trip

7 When there is rough **terrain**, the _____ is often hard to drive or walk on.

   a. land   b. road

8 Because Jason is a **scholar**, he prefers to be in _____ environment.

   a. a business   b. an academic

9 During times of **inclement** weather, there are normally _____ skies.

   a. dark and cloudy   b. clear and sunny

10 When one animal **encroaches** in another's territory, it _____ that animal's space.

   a. departs   b. invades

Chapter **04**

Negative Factual
Information

Question Type | Negative Factual Information

◪ About the Question

Negative Factual Information questions focus on information that is not included in the passage. You are asked to answer a question asking about facts or information that is NOT covered in the passage. Three of the four answer choices contain accurate information appearing in the passage while the correct answer choice has either incorrect information or information that does not appear in the passage. The information asked about in these questions is always included in a small section of the passage. There are 0-2 Negative Factual Information questions for each passage.

Recognizing Negative Factual Information questions:

• According to paragraph 1, which of the following is NOT true about X?

• The author's description of X mentions all of the following EXCEPT:

• In paragraph 2, all of the following questions are answered EXCEPT:

Helpful hints for answering the questions correctly:

• The question identifies one or two paragraphs where the correct answer can be found. Focus only on that part of the passage when looking for the correct answer.

• The correct answer may contain information that is factually correct but does not appear in the passage.

• The answer choices often restate the information mentioned in the passage but use different words and phrases. Be careful of slight deviations that can make these restatements become the correct answer.

The Moons of Pluto

➡ Pluto is no longer considered a major planet but is classified as a dwarf planet. Unlike two of the major planets though, Pluto has satellites orbiting it. There are five moons known to be in orbit around Pluto: Charon, Nix, Hydra, Styx, and Kerberos. The largest of the moons is Charon, which is tidally locked with Pluto. As a result, much like Earth and its moon, only one side of Charon can be seen from Pluto's surface as it orbits the dwarf planet. Charon was also the first of Pluto's moons to be discovered, which happened in 1978. The other four moons were discovered by the Hubble Space Telescope between the years 2005 and 2012. They are all relatively small, having diameters ranging between seven and fifty-five kilometers. Because of their size, distance from the sun, and fairly recent discovery, very little is known about the four smallest of these satellites.

According to paragraph 3, which of the following is NOT true about the moons of Pluto?

Ⓐ All of them are tidally locked with Pluto as they orbit it.

Ⓑ Not much is known about four of the moons yet.

Ⓒ The four smallest moons have diameters no larger than fifty-five kilometers.

Ⓓ Most of them were discovered within a decade of one another.

Paragraph 3 is marked with an arrow (➡).

| **Answer Explanation** |

Choice Ⓐ is the correct answer. The information in answer choices Ⓑ, Ⓒ, and Ⓓ is correct. However, it is not true that all of the moons of Pluto are tidally locked with it. That is only true of Charon.

A | Tree Rings

🎧 CH04_2A

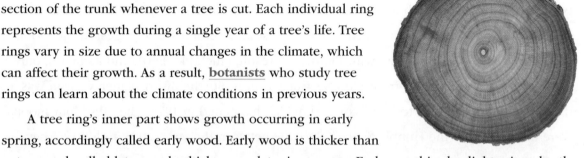

As a tree becomes bigger, a ring of new growth forms around it. Individual tree rings can be seen in a horizontal cross section of the trunk whenever a tree is cut. Each individual ring represents the growth during a single year of a tree's life. Tree rings vary in size due to annual changes in the climate, which can affect their growth. As a result, <u>botanists</u> who study tree rings can learn about the climate conditions in previous years.

A tree ring's inner part shows growth occurring in early spring, accordingly called early wood. Early wood is thicker than outer wood, called late wood, which grows later in summer. Early wood is also lighter in color than late wood. Because <u>temperate zones</u> have distinct variations between seasons, the trees growing in them have pronounced differences in their individual rings.

To examine tree rings, botanists take core samples of trees, typically by extracting samples from a large number of trees in a given region. If they find a pattern in a substantial number of tree ring samples, they can make assessments about past climate conditions. For example, wide early wood suggests heavy spring rains whereas thin early wood implies the late arrival of spring rains. A series of extremely thin tree rings for several years is normally indicative of a prolonged drought. At present, botanists are able to utilize the tree rings of living and dead trees to research climate conditions from up to 10,000 years ago.

*botanist: a scientist who studies plants
*temperate zone: an area that gets hot summers, cold winters, and moderate springs and falls

---

1 According to paragraphs 1 and 2, which of the following is NOT true about tree rings?

Ⓐ They only appear in trees that grow in temperate zones.

Ⓑ They are formed from combinations of early wood and late wood.

Ⓒ They grow in trees over the course of an entire year.

Ⓓ They are different each year depending upon the weather.

2 In paragraph 3, all of the following questions are answered EXCEPT:

Ⓐ What does it mean when many tree rings in a row are very thin?

Ⓑ What are botanists able to determine by studying tree rings?

Ⓒ What do tree rings look like when there is a lot of precipitation in spring?

Ⓓ How do botanists use tree rings millions of years old to study climate?

Vocabulary

• _____ = level; flat; parallel to the ground   • _____ = to remove; to take out

• _____ = clearly shown; obvious   • _____ = an evaluation; an analysis

B | Manatees

Manatees are among nature's more unusual animals. They are mammals, but they dwell in the sea and are sometimes called sea cows due to their bulky size. They are native to the Atlantic Ocean and live in coastal waters from Florida to Brazil on the ocean's western side and along parts of West Africa's coast and in some of its river systems in the eastern Atlantic. One species also inhabits the Amazon River in South America. Manatees have a life expectancy of forty years, grow to four meters in length, and can weigh approximately 600 kilograms.

While manatees live in water, they breathe air. Swimming manatees surface to breathe every few minutes whereas resting ones can remain **submerged** for up to fifteen minutes. They utilize two short fins on their sides and a large, flat tail to swim. When born, their mother helps them swim to the surface, but within an hour, they can swim on their own. As babies, manatees drink their mother's milk, but mature animals are **herbivores** that consume water grasses, weeds, and algae. They frequently devour their entire body weight in plant matter in a single day.

While the manatee population was once large, they are an endangered species today. The primary reason concerns the fact that they live in shallow coastal and river waters. This makes them easy to hunt, which people do for their hides, oil, and bones. Additionally, recreational boaters sometimes hit surfacing manatees and kill them because of the impact of the collision.

*submerge: to go beneath the surface of the water
*herbivore: an animal that only eats plant matter

1 According to paragraph 1, which of the following is NOT true about the manatee?

Ⓐ It can be found living on both sides of the Atlantic Ocean.

Ⓑ The largest of the species resides in the Amazon River.

Ⓒ It has been known to live for around four decades.

Ⓓ Its large size results in some people calling it a sea cow.

2 In paragraph 2, the author's description of the manatee mentions all of the following EXCEPT:

Ⓐ how much food it is capable of eating in one day

Ⓑ the type of food that it consumes after being born

Ⓒ the lengths of both of its short fins and tail

Ⓓ the amount of time that it can stay under the water

Vocabulary

- _____ = how long someone or something usually lives
- _____ = to go to the surface of the water from underneath it
- _____ = adult
- _____ = to eat, often in great amounts

The Economic Effects of the Erie Canal

The first major manmade inland transportation route in the United States was the Erie Canal. Built between 1817 and 1825, it had thirty-six locks and ran for 580 kilometers between Albany and Buffalo in upstate New York. The canal opened in an era prior to the invention of the railway and when small boats and horses were the primary means of inland transportation. It revolutionized the trade system of the United States and had a tremendous economic impact on the young country.

The new canal made it possible for small ships to navigate from the Atlantic Ocean to the Great Lakes. Starting at New York City, ships sailed up the Hudson River to Albany, <u>traversed</u> the canal, and then entered Lake Erie. This let bulk goods move quickly and cheaply to various parts of the nation. It also enabled crops to move from western states and territories to the east just as efficiently. This caused an explosion of trade between the eastern and western parts of the country and also helped increase the grain trade between the United States and Europe.

The canal further impacted the region it passed through. Upstate New York became a tourist attraction, and many visitors were <u>induced</u> to settle there. Masses of people used the canal as they moved westward to settle in uninhabited lands as well. And the Erie Canal served as an example of an efficient construction project. This encouraged the building of more canals, which benefitted the nation's economy.

*traverse: to navigate; to travel through
*induce: to persuade; to convince

1 In paragraph 1, the author's description of the Erie Canal mentions all of the following EXCEPT:

Ⓐ the manner in which the canal influenced the United States

Ⓑ the types of transportation prevalent when the canal was built

Ⓒ the amount of time that was required to construct the canal

Ⓓ the organization that was responsible for building the canal

2 According to paragraphs 2 and 3, which is NOT true about the effects of the Erie Canal?

Ⓐ The eastern United States lost population as more people moved west.

Ⓑ People became able to sail to the Great Lakes from the Atlantic Ocean.

Ⓒ The land around the canal turned into a popular place for tourists to visit.

Ⓓ There was an increase in trade between the United States and Europe.

Vocabulary

· _____ = away from the coast

· _____ = an enclosed part of a canal that can raise or lower ships by adding or releasing water

· _____ = to have an effect on

· _____ = having no people living in a place

Mapping

The following chart shows the structure of the passage. Fill in the blanks with the appropriate words.

The Economic Effects of the Erie Canal

First major ❶ _____ transportation route in U.S.

– was between Albany and Buffalo in New York

– Had tremendous ❷ _____ on country

Let small ships sail from Atlantic Ocean to ❸ _____

– bulk goods move cheaply and quickly through country

– ❹ _____ moved from west to east quickly

– increased ❺ _____ between states and also with Europe

Affected ❻ _____ New York

– area became ❼ _____

– people used canal when traveled to settle in west

– was efficient ❽ _____ project

– encouraged building of more canals

Summary

The following is a summary of the passage. Fill in the blanks with the appropriate words.

The Erie Canal was the first major ❶ _____ inland transportation route in the United States. It went from Albany to ❷ _____ in New York. It let small ships travel from the ❸ _____ Ocean to the Great Lakes. Thanks to it, bulk ❹ _____ could move cheaply and quickly to parts of the country. And crops from western states could be moved easily to the ❺ _____. The canal increased the grain trade between the United States and ❻ _____. It made ❼ _____ New York a tourist attraction and let people move to settle uninhabited lands in the ❽ _____ more easily.

A | Ironmaking in the Industrial Revolution

🎧 CH04_3A

Metallurgists have been aware of the process of how to make iron ever since ancient times. Yet by the time the Industrial Revolution got underway in the eighteenth century, ironmaking had still not been perfected. During the Industrial Revolution, iron makers used trial and error to produce iron of better quality, and their efforts ultimately culminated with the mass production of steel in the late-nineteenth century.

Iron ore that is **smelted** draws in carbon impurities, which give iron its strength, from charcoal fires. Iron with a carbon level of 0.02 to 0.08 percent is called wrought iron. If the amount of impurities ranges from 0.2 to 1.5 percent, then it is steel. Finally, cast iron has a carbon content of 3 to 4.5 percent. Wrought iron is more malleable than steel but not as strong whereas cast iron is more brittle and less flexible than the other two.

Before the Middle Ages, ironworkers mostly dealt with wrought iron that was smelted from small amounts of ore in small charcoal fires. Then, the blast furnace was developed during the thirteenth century and enabled ironworkers to make cast iron in greater quantities. They poured molten cast iron into molds to make a wide variety of items, among them being pots and pans, stoves, cannons, cannonballs, and bells.

In 1784, Englishman Henry Cort invented a process for transforming cast iron into wrought iron by oxidizing the carbon impurities out of cast iron. In this manner, ironworkers could produce large masses of more malleable wrought iron, which were then made into various products. Despite this advance, it was still an inefficient method that produced smaller amounts of wrought iron than was necessary to satisfy the ongoing demand. Steel was always the preferred choice because it was stronger than wrought iron and more malleable than cast iron. Unfortunately, it was difficult to make. Steel was typically created from wrought iron after a slow process which infused more carbon into it.

Then, in 1856, Englishman Henry Bessemer developed a way to mass-produce steel. His Bessemer process injected cold air into large containers of molten cast iron. This procedure reduced the carbon level of the cast iron to the amount needed to make steel. There were some drawbacks, particularly that it did not remove any phosphorus—a yellow, poisonous, solid element—and made the steel too brittle. Thus only phosphorous-free ores could be used. Finally, in 1876, Welshman Sidney Thomas discovered that adding limestone to molten cast iron made the phosphorous float to the top of the molten steel, whereupon workers could draw it off as **slag**. With cheap mass-produced steel readily available, ironmaking had reached its peak.

*smelt: to melt ore in order to separate the metal in it
*slag: waste; the leftover material after metal has been removed from ore

Vocabulary

• _____ = easily breakable; fragile   • _____ = to combine with oxygen
• _____ = melted; liquefied   • _____ = a disadvantage

1 Which of the sentences below best expresses the essential information in the highlighted sentence in the passage? Incorrect answer choices change the meaning in important ways or leave out essential information.

During the Industrial Revolution, iron makers used trial and error to produce iron of better quality, and their efforts ultimately culminated with the mass production of steel in the late-nineteenth century.

Ⓐ Iron workers tried hard to develop processes that could make iron and steel of exceptional quality.

Ⓑ The Industrial Revolution was a time when people made many inquiries into the process of making various metals.

Ⓒ It was not until the Industrial Revolution occurred that people learned the secrets of making iron and steel.

Ⓓ Ironworkers managed to produce high-quality iron during the Industrial Revolution, and that let them later make steel in large amounts.

Rhetorical Purpose Question

2 The author discusses "carbon impurities" in paragraph 2 in order to

Ⓐ explain how they affect iron ore when it is smelted

Ⓑ describe how they can be removed from iron ore

Ⓒ point out that they are desired in the making of steel

Ⓓ compare the amount of them in various types of iron ore

Negative Factual Information Question

3 In paragraph 5, all of the following questions are answered EXCEPT:

Ⓐ What can be added to iron in its melted form to separate phosphorus from it?

Ⓑ Where were phosphorus-free ores commonly found in the Industrial Revolution?

Ⓒ What were some of the disadvantages to using the method Henry Bessemer devised?

Ⓓ How did the process that was invented by Henry Bessemer produce steel?

Prose Summary Question

4 An introductory sentence for a brief summary of the passage is provided below. Complete the summary by selecting the THREE answer choices that express the most important ideas of the passage. Some sentences do not belong because they express ideas that are not presented in the passage or are minor ideas in the passage.

There were a number of innovations in the Industrial Revolution that led to improvements in both the development of iron and steel.

ANSWER CHOICES

☐ 1 Henry Cort developed a method to make wrought iron from cast iron, which people found useful for making many products.

☐ 2 Depending on the percentage of carbon impurities in iron, cast iron, wrought iron, and steel can all be made.

☐ 3 People first learned to make iron thousands of years ago, but their methods were mostly inefficient.

☐ 4 The Bessemer method permitted people to mass-produce steel despite its various drawbacks.

☐ 5 The blast furnace let medieval iron makers produce iron that could be utilized to make weapons and other objects.

☐ 6 Once Sidney Welsh made his discovery, it became easy for ironworkers to remove phosphorus from steel in its molten form.

Grecian Pottery Art

Pottery is durable and is therefore one of the most common items to have survived from ancient times. This is especially true in Greece, where a vast number of examples of pottery have been unearthed and examined. The ancient Greeks were renowned for their exquisite pottery and the art they painted on it. In fact, pottery art is often utilized by historians and archaeologists to understand ancient Greek society.

The style of Greek pottery painting changed over time. In the early years, the most common form of painting was a white base coat with more elaborate designs added on top in red paint. During the ninth and eighth centuries B.C., geometric shapes were commonly painted on pottery. Among these shapes were triangles, ovals, and meandering lines, all of which usually encircled the pottery. Groups of shapes were separated by horizontal lines, and soon afterward, animals and human figures began appearing on the pottery. **1** This period has become known as the Geometric Period. **2** As the Greeks started trading with people in lands in the eastern Mediterranean region, their pottery art came to be influenced by that area. **3** New designs included palm trees, lotus plants, lions, and more curved lines, which were commonly featured on eastern pottery. **4**

At the end of the seventh century B.C., a new style—called black-figure pottery art—originated in Corinth and soon spread elsewhere throughout the Greek world. Painters used an undercoat of orange-red with black figures painted on top. This pottery is noted for its highly stylized human figures. Pottery artists typically painted historical figures from Greek myths, with warriors in battle poses being a common motif.

Red-figure pottery art began replacing black-figure pottery art after around 150 years. It was the opposite of black-figure pottery art as it had a black undercoat and red painted figures on top. Red-figure pottery art is noted for its more refined details of figures, especially of the human body, faces, and clothing. Pottery artists also made more of an effort to use depth and overlapping figures to represent reality, and they often painted common people engaging in everyday activities.

Around the fourth century B.C., pottery art went into decline in Greece. After the Macedonian conquest and the beginning of the Hellenistic Period, artists turned their attention more to clay figurines and metalwork. Yet the large number of extant Grecian pottery art indicates a great deal about Greek society. Greek clothing styles and hairstyles, tools, weapons, and other minute details can be understood in part thanks to it. The pottery art additionally provides insights into their beliefs and daily lives that would otherwise be unknown.

*exquisite: attractive; beautiful; ornate
*undercoat: a first layer; a primer

Vocabulary

- _____ = to dig up from out of the ground
- _____ = a person who studies civilizations from the past
- _____ = wandering
- _____ = existing; surviving

1   In paragraph 2, the author's description of the Geometric Period mentions all of the following EXCEPT:

   Ⓐ the types of figures that were painted on pottery during it

   Ⓑ the reason that certain figures were so popular

   Ⓒ the period of time during which it happened

   Ⓓ the colors in which most pottery was painted

2   According to paragraph 5, why did pottery art become less popular after the fourth century B.C.?

   Ⓐ The Macedonians disliked art being made on pottery.

   Ⓑ Art became less important due to the wars during that time.

   Ⓒ Greek artists began working in other mediums.

   Ⓓ The process of making pottery was lost to the Greeks.

3   Look at the four squares [▪] that indicate where the following sentence could be added to the passage.

   The one which immediately followed it is known to art historians as the Orientalizing Period.

4   Select the appropriate statements from the answer choices and match them to the period of pottery art to which they relate. TWO of the answer choices will NOT be used.

Geometric Period (Select 3)	Black-Figure Pottery Art (Select 2)	Red-Figure Pottery Art (Select 2)
•		
•	•	•
•	•	•
•		

STATEMENTS

1 Showed scenes that were based upon regular life

2 Was inspired by artists from the eastern Mediterranean area

3 Had black figures that were painted on a red surface

4 Was the pottery art practiced in the ninth and eighth centuries B.C.

5 Often featured pictures of lotuses, lions, and curved lines

6 Featured pictures of warriors that were usually stylized

7 Depicted shapes such as triangles and squares on it

8 Had horizontal lines that separated the shapes on the pottery

9 Contained details of people such as their faces

🎧 CH04_4A

Ecological Zones in the Rocky Mountains

There are mountains located on each of the world's continents. Depending upon the height of a mountain, it may possess up to four distinct ecological zones, making the conditions at the bottom much different from those at its peak. The four zones, moving from the lowest level to the highest, are known as the foothills, the montane zone, the subalpine zone, and the alpine zone. Where each zone begins and ends depends upon a variety of factors, including the region's latitude, its distance from the ocean, the prevailing weather patterns, and the nature of the terrain in the region. Consequently, the ecological zones in the Andes Mountains of South America and the Rocky Mountains in North America are slightly different from those of the Alps in Europe and the Himalayas in Asia.

The foothills of the eastern slopes of the Rocky Mountains generally rise between 1,500 and 2,600 meters above sea level. They tend to be forested areas containing a combination of deciduous trees and coniferous trees. This is normal since the Rockies are in a temperate zone. In tropical and subtropical zones, however, foothills commonly have rainforests. The foothills in the eastern Rockies have sandstone ridges and shale valleys and show strong evidence of glacial activity from prior ice ages. All kinds of wildlife—as well as humans—can be found dwelling in the foothills of these mountains.

The region immediately above the foothills is the montane zone. In some places, it can begin as low as 1,500 meters above sea level and rise to a maximum of around 3,300 meters above sea level. In the eastern part of the Rockies, the montane zone covers the area from 2,400 to 3,000 meters above sea level. The terrain varies as there are steep slopes in some places and broad valleys in others. Some regions are cold and receive substantial amounts of snowfall whereas others are warmer due to the winds blowing down certain valleys. As the altitude gets higher, there are fewer and fewer deciduous trees in this zone. Most of the vegetation consists of coniferous trees, low shrubs, and wild grasses, and much less animal life is found there than in the foothills.

Once the montane zone ends, the subalpine zone begins. There, the trees, many of which are pines and spruces, become fewer, shorter, and more twisted and gnarled, especially as the elevation rises. In the eastern Rockies, this zone extends from roughly 3,000 to 3,600 meters above sea level. The land there is rugged, shows evidence of glacial scouring, and features steep slopes and plenty of snowfall. Only hardy animals, such as bighorn sheep, lynxes, mountain goats, and red-tailed hawks, reside in this unforgiving region.

The uppermost zone of the eastern Rocky Mountains is the alpine zone. This region begins where the treeline is found. ■ As a general rule, it is 3,600 meters above sea level and extends all the way to the peaks of the mountains, no matter how high they may reach. ■ The alpine zone is barren land often covered with snow and ice for the majority of the year. ■ Some places that are high enough have snow and ice on their peaks year round. ■ Resultantly, only mosses, heather, and some sturdy wildflowers manage to grow there, and there are just a few animals that make their homes this high up the mountains.

*Glossary

deciduous tree: a type of tree with broad leaves which fall off during the fall or winter
coniferous tree: a type of tree with leaves that are needlelike in appearance and which keeps its leaves year round

1. In paragraph 1, why does the author mention "the Himalayas in Asia"?

   Ⓐ To emphasize how high they are in comparison to other mountains

   Ⓑ To state that their ecological zones differ from those of other mountains

   Ⓒ To describe some of the features that make them distinct from other mountains

   Ⓓ To mention that their alpine regions are the biggest of their ecological zones

2. In paragraph 1, all of the following questions are answered EXCEPT:

   Ⓐ Which features can help determine the starting and ending points of ecological zones on mountains?

   Ⓑ How do the conditions in the different ecological zones on mountains vary from one another?

   Ⓒ What are the names of some of the mountain chains that are found around the world?

   Ⓓ What is the order in which the ecological zones on mountains occur?

3. According to paragraph 2, which of the following can be inferred about foothills?

   Ⓐ Humans prefer to make their homes in these areas because of their rivers and valleys.

   Ⓑ The land can have trees growing on it but may also be desert, prairie, or plains.

   Ⓒ The types of forests they have are determined by which temperature zone they are in.

   Ⓓ They rise to be no more than 1,500 meters above sea level in most places.

4. The word "substantial" in the passage is closest in meaning to

   Ⓐ apparent

   Ⓑ significant

   Ⓒ various

   Ⓓ accumulated

5   Which of the following can be inferred from paragraphs 2 and 3 about the montane zone?

(A) The steep slopes make it an ideal place for mountain climbing.

(B) The temperature in it can stay below zero all year round.

(C) Almost no humans make their homes in this mountain zone.

(D) There are fewer forests in it than there are in the foothills.

6   In paragraph 4, the author's description of the subalpine zone mentions all of the following EXCEPT:

(A) It covers an area of around 600 meters in altitude in many places.

(B) It is a difficult place to live in for the majority of animals.

(C) The higher the altitude, the fewer large plants that grow in this region.

(D) The smaller amount of oxygen in the air makes breathing there difficult.

7   According to paragraph 5, few plants grow in the alpine zone because

(A) the land is constantly eroded by the high winds and icy weather

(B) much of it has snow or ice cover for the majority of the year

(C) high winds tend to prevent many plants from growing in it

(D) the soil is poor in nutrients, so most plants cannot grow there

8   Look at the four squares [■] that indicate where the following sentence could be added to the passage.

This is the place beyond which no trees are capable of growing due to the wind, temperature, and poor soil conditions.

Where would the sentence best fit?

Click on a square [■] to add the sentence to the passage.

9 **Directions:** Select the appropriate statements from the answer choices and match them to the mountain ecological zone to which they relate. TWO of the answer choices will NOT be used. **This question is worth 4 points.**

Drag your answer choices to the spaces where they belong. To remove an answer choice, click on it. To review the passage, click on VIEW TEXT.

STATEMENTS

1   Is the mountain ecological zone where trees no longer grow

2   Has some deciduous trees but many more coniferous ones

3   Often features land that was affected by the movement of glaciers

4   Is the home of large animals such as lynxes and bighorn sheep

5   May vary in height from 1,500 meters above sea level to more than 3,000

6   Is only limited in height by how far up above sea level a mountain rises

7   Has varying weather that may include warm winds and heavy snowfall

8   Is the second highest of the ecological zones found on most mountains

9   Has rainforests in some regions as well as other types of forests

MOUNTAIN ECOLOGICAL ZONE

Foothills (Select 2)

-
-

Montane Zone (Select 3)

-
-
-

Alpine Zone (Select 2)

-
-

The Economic Effects of Subsistence Farming

© Therina Groenewald

One of the most vital basic necessities for life is food. During the past ten thousand years, humans have obtained the majority of their food through agriculture. However, for most of history, farming has been at the subsistence level, so most people only grew enough to supply their family's needs and had little or no surplus food. This has had wide-ranging economic effects up to the present time. Even today, despite modern farming technology and enormous farms, in large parts of Asia, Africa, and Latin America, subsistence farming remains a part of life.

Growing food requires land, which is one of the first bottlenecks to large-scale farming. Yet arable land is not always available in great amounts. In regions with little arable land and large populations, subsistence farming was the only alternative for millennia. Another bottleneck is a lack of labor for large farms. A single family is only capable of working so much land at one time. In the past, when everyone was growing their own food, there was no extra labor to expand a farm even if land had been available. As a result, throughout history, most farms were small, so their yields were similarly small. This affected local economies negatively. When most people were working the land merely to feed themselves, there was no labor available for other economic endeavors.

Gradually, people in many places, through innovative farming techniques and the invention of various tools and machinery, achieved the ability to grow more than a single family needed. Therefore, economic activity in other areas grew. A prime example of this was Britain in the eighteenth and nineteenth centuries. There, creative farming methods and tools resulted in larger farms needing fewer people to work on them. That allowed farmers to grow more food than they needed, and the labor no longer required on farms was absorbed by the factories in Britain's growing industrial base. This did not happen everywhere though. For the most part, by the mid-twentieth century, subsistence farming had mainly disappeared in North America and Western Europe but remained a fact of life in most of the rest of the world. This led to a widening economic gap between various regions.

Today, subsistence farming still exists in places in sub-Saharan Africa, Southeast Asia, and India as well as in some mountainous regions of Latin America. Many subsistence farmers in those regions also practice a trade to supplement their incomes. ◼ Some insist their way of life has benefits. ◼ For instance, the food they grow is consumed at the source, so time and money are not wasted on transporting food from rural areas to urban centers. ◼ Farmers can also stay in their home villages, where housing and the cost of living are generally affordable. ◼

Yet not all of the news is positive. In theory, subsistence farmers do not need to depend on other people, but that is not always the case. Nature has a way of interfering with such a utopian dream. Droughts, which result from a lack of rain, can cause widespread crop failures and famines in places where subsistence farming dominates. In addition, pests such as locusts can destroy crops quickly and therefore adversely affect the lives of subsistence farmers. Subsistence farming is also a dead-end job for most people. They have no opportunity for upward economic mobility, leaving generation after generation to depend on a highly fragile method of survival. This, in turn, causes the stagnation of the economies of nations where this farming method remains a way of life for many.

*Glossary
Latin America: South America, Central America, and some islands in the Caribbean Sea
bottleneck: a place or stage in a process where progress is stopped or slowed down

10 The word "surplus" in the passage is closest in meaning to

Ⓐ nutritious

Ⓑ leftover

Ⓒ abundant

Ⓓ salable

11 In paragraph 2, all of the following questions are answered EXCEPT:

Ⓐ What is the result when the majority of people have to grow food only to support themselves?

Ⓑ Why did some people in the past have no choice but to turn to subsistence farming?

Ⓒ What are some obstacles people must deal with when it comes to large-scale farming?

Ⓓ How much land was a single family capable of working on at one time in the past?

12 Which of the sentences below best expresses the essential information in the highlighted sentence in the passage? Incorrect answer choices change the meaning in important ways or leave out essential information.

Gradually, people in many places, through innovative farming techniques and the invention of various tools and machinery, achieved the ability to grow more than a single family needed.

Ⓐ Over time, improvements in farming methods and the development of technology let people grow more food than they needed.

Ⓑ It is only when people farm creatively and use various inventions that they can successfully grow crops in their fields.

Ⓒ The main reason that people were able to grow more than enough food for themselves was the utilization of technology.

Ⓓ Advanced equipment has been shown to be better for improving crop yields than innovative farming techniques are.

13 In paragraph 3, the author uses "North America and Western Europe" as examples of

- (A) areas with large populations which require huge farms to produce a lot of food
- (B) regions in the world that made good use of advanced farming techniques
- (C) parts of the world where subsistence farming was practiced for several centuries
- (D) places where farming had gone beyond the subsistence level by the mid-1900s

14 According to paragraph 4, which of the following is true about subsistence farmers?

- (A) The ones in places in Africa, Asia, and Latin America are improving their farming methods.
- (B) Many are uninterested in working other jobs and enjoy the farming that they do.
- (C) Lots of them in various places have second jobs that allow them to earn more money.
- (D) The majority of them today can be found in certain countries in Latin America.

15 The word "stagnation" in the passage is closest in meaning to

- (A) idling
- (B) destruction
- (C) development
- (D) altering

16 According to paragraph 5, which of the following is NOT true about subsistence farming?

- (A) It is often practiced by several generations of families in certain areas.
- (B) The majority of problems that are faced by its practitioners are manmade ones.
- (C) The people who practice it are often unable to improve their lives at all.
- (D) Natural disasters such as droughts can cause great damage in places where it is practiced.

17 Look at the four squares [■] that indicate where the following sentence could be added to the passage.

Finally, little harm is done to the environment since farmers are not working in factories that pollute the air.

Where would the sentence best fit?

Click on a square [■] to add the sentence to the passage.

18 **Directions:** An introductory sentence for a brief summary of the passage is provided below. Complete the summary by selecting the THREE answer choices that express the most important ideas of the passage. Some sentences do not belong because they express ideas that are not presented in the passage or are minor ideas in the passage. **This question is worth 2 points.**

Subsistence farming has been practiced for thousands of years and is still a fact of life in many places around the world.

-
-
-

ANSWER CHOICES

1. When farming methods and equipment improved in places, people were able to abandon the subsistence farming lifestyle.

2. People in certain places around the world still practice subsistence farming, and they benefit by living in affordable places and by saving money.

3. Humans first began farming the land several thousand years ago when they learned how to engage in agriculture.

4. Britain was affected by the Industrial Revolution, and many laborers departed farms and went to work in factories.

5. People who practice subsistence farming cannot improve their lives, and they may also be harmed by natural causes.

6. Places in Europe and North America no longer have subsistence farmers because of their good economies.

◢ Vocabulary Review

A Complete each sentence with the appropriate word from the box.

interfere with	archaeologist	extract	mature	endeavors

1 One of the adventurer's most famous _____ was traveling around the world.

2 It is possible to _____ gold found in ore by melting it.

3 Janet became a(n) _____ in order to study ancient cultures.

4 George requested that nobody _____ him while he was working.

5 _____ fruit tastes better than unripe fruit since it is juicier and sweeter.

B Complete each sentence with the correct answer.

1 The **altitude** of a place is how _____ the ground it is.

   a. high above   b. low under

2 Something that is **brittle** is highly likely to _____.

   a. break apart   b. be valuable

3 People who **unearth** ancient artifacts _____.

   a. sell them   b. dig them up

4 A **horizontal** line is one that goes _____.

   a. from left to right   b. up and down

5 When lions **devour** their prey, they _____ it.

   a. kill   b. eat

6 Most farmers prefer to _____ on **arable** land.

   a. grow crops   b. raise animals

7 An asteroid will _____ the Earth if it is going to **impact** the planet.

   a. hit   b. avoid

8 A recipe that requires a **combination** of ingredients has _____ of them.

   a. few   b. many

9 When a hurricane travels **inland**, it _____.

   a. moves onto land   b. stays offshore

10 If a deal has some **drawbacks**, then it has a few _____.

   a. advantages   b. disadvantages

Chapter **05**

Sentence Simplification

Question Type | Sentence Simplification

About the Question

Sentence Simplification questions focus on a single sentence. You are asked to choose a sentence that best restates the information in the sentence that is highlighted in the passage. You need to note the primary information that is found in the sentence and make sure that it is included in the answer choice that you select. The words, phrases, and grammar in the answer choices vary from those in the highlighted sentence. There are 0-1 Sentence Simplification questions for each passage.

Recognizing Sentence Simplification questions:

- Which of the sentences below best expresses the essential information in the highlighted sentence in the passage? Incorrect answer choices change the meaning in important ways or leave out essential information.

  [You will see a sentence in bold.]

Helpful hints for answering the questions correctly:

- The highlighted sentence typically contains at least two separate clauses. Make sure that you know what the main point or idea of each clause is.

- The answer choice you select must contain all of the important information that is in the highlighted sentence.

- Do not select answer choices that contain incorrect information or that omit important information.

- The answer choices for these questions are approximately half the length of the sentences being asked about. Therefore, you should consider how to summarize information in long sentences.

Lanternfish

The sun's light cannot penetrate deep beneath the surface of the world's oceans. Nevertheless, there is still light down below because many marine creatures dwelling in the deep sea utilize something called bioluminescence. Through a variety of ways, these creatures create their own light, which allows them to see hundreds or thousands of meters beneath the surface. One such animal that creates its own light is the lanternfish. There are more than 200 species of lanternfish, which can be anywhere from one to twelve centimeters in length. It has small organs, called photophores, which emit light. They are located on the head, underside, and tail of the fish. The light not only allows the lanternfish to see but also attracts other smaller fish, which the lanternfish feeds upon. On the other hand, the light created by the lanternfish makes it an attractive target for creatures larger than it.

Which of the sentences below best expresses the essential information in the highlighted sentence in the passage? Incorrect answer choices change the meaning in important ways or leave out essential information.

Through a variety of ways, these creatures create their own light, which allows them to see hundreds or thousands of meters beneath the surface.

Ⓐ Any animals that can produce their own light thousands of meters beneath the surface are unique.

Ⓑ The animals are able to see deep underneath the surface thanks to various methods that they use.

Ⓒ It requires a combination of ways for animals to be able to see when they are far beneath the ocean's surface.

Ⓓ There are only a few types of animals that are capable of creating their own light.

❘ **Answer Explanation** ❘

Choice Ⓑ is the correct answer. The sentence points out that creatures use various methods to enable themselves to see when they are very far beneath the surface of the ocean. This thought is best expressed by the sentence in answer choice Ⓑ.

A | The Battle of Manzikert

🎧 CH05_2A

The Battle of Manzikert took place in Anatolia on August 26, 1071, and was fought between the Byzantine Empire and the Seljuk Turks. The battle was among the most significant ones in the entire history of the Byzantine Empire. During the fighting, the Turks used archers and cavalry to harass the Byzantines and hence avoided getting involved in a **pitched battle**. When night fell, the Byzantines initiated an orderly retreat, but confusion caused some troops to panic.

The Turks promptly attacked, causing the Byzantines to flee the field of battle. During the ensuing events, the Turks managed to capture the Byzantine emperor, Romanus IV.

The defeat had serious long-term repercussions for the Byzantines despite the fact that they suffered a fairly small number of casualties. The psychological effects were enormous. The Turks had long feared the Byzantine army, but they gained confidence from their victory. In contrast, the defeat and capture of the emperor humiliated the Byzantines. The Turks released Romanus once he promised to make peace and to pay a large ransom. But after returning to Constantinople, he was overthrown in a <u>coup</u>. Exiled, Romanus died soon afterward.

The coup caused internal turmoil in the empire. This further weakened the Byzantines and let the Turks continue advancing and win victories over the next few decades. They eventually conquered much of Anatolia, which left the Byzantines with only the land near Constantinople. The Byzantines never recovered and were finally conquered in 1453.

*pitched battle: a fight in which the forces on both sides are arranged in position before the clash begins
*coup: a sudden change in the government, often through the use of violence

---

Which of the sentences below best expresses the essential information in the highlighted sentence in the passage? Incorrect answer choices change the meaning in important ways or leave out essential information.

The defeat had serious long-term repercussions for the Byzantines despite the fact that they suffered a fairly small number of casualties.

Ⓐ Because they suffered so many casualties, the Byzantines were hurt by the battle for a long time afterward.

Ⓑ There were long-term effects of the battle for the Byzantines, especially due to the loss of their soldiers.

Ⓒ While only a few Byzantine soldiers were killed or injured, the loss affected them for many years.

Ⓓ The Byzantine army was never the same again after its defeat in spite of only losing a small number of soldiers.

Vocabulary

- _____ = soldiers who fight while on horseback
- _____ = the act of moving back away from a battle
- _____ = an effect; a result of some action
- _____ = a state of great confusion or disturbance

B | Crow Intelligence

Of the approximately forty species of crows, many show high levels of intelligence. This is particularly true of crows residing on the Pacific island of New Caledonia. They have shown themselves to be remarkably clever and capable of employing tools. Two studies performed in **controlled demonstrations** showed their ability to solve complex problems.

For the first test, small pieces of food were **inserted** into three clear tubes of water. One tube was narrow, another contained a minimal level of water, and the other was wide with a high water level. The crow attempted to reach the food but could not. A few objects, some solid and heavy and others hollow and light, were arranged nearby. The crow grabbed the heavy objects and deposited them in the wide tube with the most water, thereby causing the water level to rise so that it could obtain the food.

The second test involved a box with food inside and a short stick. Additionally, there were a longer stick in another clear plastic box with a small opening and three open boxes containing small stones. Showing its puzzle-solving ability, the crow took the short stick and dragged the stones out, and then it picked up the stones and placed them inside the small opening in the first box. The weight of the stones opened a compartment, which provided access to the longer stick. The crow then used the longer stick to obtain the food in the first box.

*controlled demonstration: a test in which the conditions are measured or prevented from being random
*insert: to place something inside another thing

Which of the sentences below best expresses the essential information in the highlighted sentence in the passage? Incorrect answer choices change the meaning in important ways or leave out essential information.

The crow grabbed the heavy objects and deposited them in the wide tube with the most water, thereby causing the water level to rise so that it could obtain the food.

Ⓐ The crow was able to get the food when it made the water level go up in one tube by putting some heavy objects in it.

Ⓑ The crow put some of the heavier objects in the tube and made the water level increase, but it could not get any food.

Ⓒ By making the water level rise in the tube that was wide and had lots of water, the crow was able to get the food it contained.

Ⓓ When it used all of the objects to make the water level rise, the crow got access to the food and then consumed it.

Vocabulary

- _____ = highly; amazingly
- _____ = very small; slight; minor
- _____ = having nothing in one's center
- _____ = to pull something on the ground

C Desertification

The process of turning fertile land into desert is known as desertification. It typically takes place in regions called drylands, which have limited amounts of water that are barely enough to sustain agriculture and human usage. Examples of drylands are the Great Plains of North America, the steppes of Russia, the lands to the south of the Sahara Desert, and some parts of Australia. Changes in climate and human actions are the major causes of desertification.

A sudden variation in the climate can result in a region receiving less rainfall. Should this persist for a long time, vegetation will begin dying due to a lack of water. When that happens, the soil will become less **cohesive** since there is little or no vegetation anchoring the soil to the ground. Soon, the wind starts blowing away the topsoil. If these conditions continue, the land will transform into desert. On the southern edges of the Sahara Desert, this process results in land lost to desertification each year.

Human overuse of land and water can similarly result in desertification. When humans clear trees and other vegetation to plant crops, soil erosion may result. Likewise, if too many animals such as cattle or sheep graze on drylands, the vegetation may be destroyed, and the soil may be eroded. Finally, poor management of water resources plays a role by **depleting** both surface water and groundwater. All three of these factors can result in desertification.

*cohesive: unified
*deplete: to use entirely or almost entirely

Which of the sentences below best expresses the essential information in the highlighted sentence in the passage? Incorrect answer choices change the meaning in important ways or leave out essential information.

Likewise, if too many animals such as cattle or sheep graze on drylands, the vegetation may be destroyed, and the soil may be eroded.

Ⓐ There are many examples of animals like sheep and cows grazing on drylands.

Ⓑ Some animals that graze on drylands eat all the vegetation they can find.

Ⓒ Animals grazing on land can eat all the vegetation and thus erode the soil.

Ⓓ The destruction of vegetation in a region can lead to the erosion of the land.

Vocabulary

- _____ = to do or happen for a long period of time
- _____ = to keep something from moving
- _____ = to change
- _____ = to eat grass or other vegetation in a field

◼ Mapping

The following chart shows the structure of the passage. Fill in the blanks with the appropriate words.

Desertification

Process of turning ❶ _____ land into desert

– often takes place in ❷ _____ that get little water

– major ❸ _____ are changes in climate and human actions

❹ _____ in climate can happen

– area gets less rainfall

– vegetation dries up, and soil loses ❺ _____

– wind blows away ❻ _____

– if continually happens, can turn land into desert

– is happening at southern edges of ❼ _____ Desert

Humans ❽ _____ land and water

– clear trees and other vegetation to ❾ _____ land

– soil ❿ _____ happens

– too many ⓫ _____ grazing on land can erode soil

– poor water management can reduce surface water and ⓬ _____

– all three can lead to desertification

◼ Summary

The following is a summary of the passage. Fill in the blanks with the appropriate words.

When fertile land becomes desert, ❶ _____ occurs. This typically happens in ❷ _____, such as the Great Plains, Russian steppes, and lands south of the Sahara Desert, which get ❸ _____ amounts of water. When a region receives less rainfall than normal for a long time, ❹ _____ starts dying. The soil becomes less ❺ _____, and then the wind blows away the topsoil. This can cause the land to become a desert. ❻ _____ can cause desertification, too. When they clear land for ❼ _____, soil erosion may happen. And poor water ❽ _____ can remove surface and groundwater, resulting in desertification.

A | *Paranthropus Robustus*

CH05_3A

In 1938, Robert Broom discovered the remains of a hominid in a cave in South Africa. Around a decade later, anthropologists heard about people unearthing the skeletal remains of humans in the caves at the nearby Swartkrans Cave Complex. This caused them to begin digging for bones there as well. Since then, the remains of more than 400 hominids have been unearthed in Swartkrans. While some of them were the bones of **Homo erectus**, most of them were the remains of *Paranthropus robustus*, a different type of hominid.

The *Paranthropus robustus* remains that have been found are estimated to be between one and two million years old. This makes *Paranthropus robustus* much older than *Homo erectus*. As such, the two species clearly lived in the cave complex at different times. Nevertheless, anthropologists must take care when exhuming remains to be sure that those from one time period are not mixed with those of another. Fortunately, the remains are often found in different sedimentary layers, making it easy to determine the time period to which they belong.

When Broom first discovered the remains of *Paranthropus robustus*, he realized he was looking at a new species of hominid. He gave *Paranthropus robustus* its name because he observed that the teeth and jaws were bigger and more robust than those of other early hominids. The remains found in the first cave and later in Swartkrans have given anthropologists a very clear picture of what *Paranthropus robustus* was like. The skeletal structures indicate that it could walk upright. Males grew to around 120 centimeters in height and weighed more than fifty kilograms. Females grew to about 100 centimeters in height and weighed around forty kilograms.

Paranthropus robustus had a large, wide jaw like that of a gorilla. It had heavy **molars**, which were much bigger than human molars, at the back of its jaw. This suggests that it ground its food by using its teeth. Its bone structure also indicates a muscular system allowing the jaw to grind hard, chewy food. Based on these discoveries, anthropologists believe that the diet of *Paranthropus robustus* consisted of foods such as hard fruits, nuts, and plant roots.

In addition, research on the hand bone and muscle structure of *Paranthropus robustus* shows that it had the ability to grasp and use tools. Thus it is clear that some of the bone and stone tools found by a few skeletons at the Swartkrans Cave Complex were used by *Paranthropus robustus*. One theory is that *Paranthropus robustus* utilized tools to dig up termite mounds in order to consume termites. Others also believe the tools were used to dig for plant roots and to cut thick skin off various hard fruits.

*Homo erectus: an extinct ancestor of man that walked upright
*molar: a large tooth with a broad surface that is used to grind food

Vocabulary

- _____ = a living or extinct primate capable of walking on two legs
- _____ = the makeup of something
- _____ = to reduce to small pieces by crushing
- _____ = to grab with one's hands

1 The word "them" in the passage refers to

  Ⓐ anthropologists

  Ⓑ people

  Ⓒ the skeletal remains of humans

  Ⓓ the caves

Inference Question

2 Which of the following can be inferred from paragraph 3 about skeletons of *Paranthropus robustus*?

  Ⓐ They have been examined by people using advanced technology.

  Ⓑ Those belonging to both males and females have been discovered.

  Ⓒ The majority of the ones exhumed have been complete skeletons.

  Ⓓ Some of them have been found in places other than South Africa.

Sentence Simplification Question

3 Which of the sentences below best expresses the essential information in the highlighted sentence in the passage? Incorrect answer choices change the meaning in important ways or leave out essential information.

Based on these discoveries, anthropologists believe that the diet of *Paranthropus robustus* consisted of foods such as hard fruits, nuts, and plant roots.

  Ⓐ The evidence shows that *Paranthropus robustus* consumed a variety of hard foods.

  Ⓑ *Paranthropus robustus* was a skilled hunter that ate a diet of meat and fruits.

  Ⓒ Anthropologists have learned a great amount of information about *Paranthropus robustus*.

  Ⓓ The diets of *Paranthropus robustus* have been guessed at by anthropologists.

Prose Summary Question

4 An introductory sentence for a brief summary of the passage is provided below. Complete the summary by selecting the THREE answer choices that express the most important ideas of the passage. Some sentences do not belong because they express ideas that are not presented in the passage or are minor ideas in the passage.

Thanks to the discoveries of many remains of *Paranthropus robustus*, anthropologists have learned a lot about this distant ancestor of humans.

ANSWER CHOICES

☐ 1 Remains from hundreds of different examples of *Paranthropus robustus* have been found, letting anthropologists study them closely.

☐ 2 The bones and muscles in *Paranthropus robustus* show that it was able to use tools, some of which have been unearthed alongside their remains.

☐ 3 *Paranthropus robustus* had large teeth and jaws and likely used them to grind the food that it consumed.

☐ 4 Robert Broom was the first anthropologist to do serious work on *Paranthropus robustus*, and he also named the species.

☐ 5 Regarding the sizes and weights of *Paranthropus robustus*, males were taller and weighed more than females.

☐ 6 The only place that remains of *Paranthropus robustus* have been found is in a single cave in South Africa.

B Scholasticism

In Europe, the prevailing method of university education from the twelfth to the seventeenth century was scholasticism. Essentially, students and teachers read works in a chosen field and then discussed their contents. They would attempt to reach conclusions, especially when there were contradictions. The main point of most of their studies was to try to reconcile Christian theology with the classical writings of ancient philosophers, most notably Aristotle.

The primary focus of the scholastic method was <u>dialectical</u> reasoning. In class discussions, one person would argue for a certain viewpoint, known as the thesis. **1** Others would argue against that viewpoint. **2** During their discussion, the students and teacher would attempt to reach a conclusion, which they named the synthesis. **3** At times, even though students might have disagreed with an argument, they were obligated to argue in favor of it. **4** Therefore, they learned how to use <u>rhetoric</u> to argue for a side in a dispute in which they did not believe. While most of their discussions were related to theology and ancient philosophers, in later times, new topics were studied by using the scholastic method. These included economics, psychology, and the philosophy of nature and science.

Class discussions always began either with a question being raised or a reading being selected. A student or the teacher could suggest a question for debate. As for the reading method, the teacher selected the work to be read as well as any secondary documents related to the work and its author. The teacher often read the material aloud. Then, there was a period of reflection allowing students to contemplate the reading for the purpose of discussing it later.

For both methods, the next step was an open discussion. The students argued the points that appeared to contradict one another. Some argued for one side while others argued for the opposite one. When readings were examined, the discussion included a study of the exact wording to eliminate any perceived ambiguities in the meaning of the text. As they argued, one student took notes to use when summarizing the argument. Sometimes there seemed to be no way to resolve the contradictions. In other instances, students discovered that there were no contradictions and that any perceived ones were the result of their own subjective points of view.

The scholastic method taught students to think critically. Students learned to use language to present formal arguments and to be able to rebut any points that were raised in refutation of their own arguments. Eventually, however, people began to regard scholasticism as too rigid and formalistic. As a result, it began to fall out of favor with the rise of humanism in later centuries.

*dialectical: relating to logical arguments
*rhetoric: the art of using oratory or persuasive language

Vocabulary

- _____ = a statement that goes against itself or another one
- _____ = to settle a problem
- _____ = unclearness in meaning
- _____ = a disagreement

1 Which of the sentences below best expresses the essential information in the highlighted sentence in the passage? Incorrect answer choices change the meaning in important ways or leave out essential information.

As for the reading method, the teacher selected the work to be read as well as any secondary documents related to the work and its author.

(A) Students were obligated to be familiar with both the author's original work and other writings that were about it.

(B) The professor often read works by a specific author and then assigned secondary writings for the students to read.

(C) The authors that were studied had written both primary and secondary works about their topics.

(D) When the reading method was used, the instructor chose everything that the students looked at.

2 The word "rebut" in the passage is closest in meaning to

(A) define

(B) counter

(C) support

(D) acknowledge

3 Look at the four squares [■] that indicate where the following sentence could be added to the passage.

Their counterargument was called the antithesis.

4 An introductory sentence for a brief summary of the passage is provided below. Complete the summary by selecting the THREE answer choices that express the most important ideas of the passage. Some sentences do not belong because they express ideas that are not presented in the passage or are minor ideas in the passage.

Scholasticism was the dominant method of study in Europe for hundreds of years and involved the art of making arguments.

ANSWER CHOICES

[1] Scholasticism began to go into decline when the humanists of the Renaissance gained more prominence.

[2] When using this method, students often read works by a specific writer and then used dialectic to discuss them.

[3] Most of the teachers who lived during the time that scholasticism was dominant focused on the writings of Plato and Aristotle.

[4] Students were taught to argue for and against various viewpoints, which enabled them to develop their critical thinking skills.

[5] Teachers that used this method of education allowed their students to participate in discussions to find and resolve contradictions in texts.

[6] Nearly all of the most famous educators and philosophers in the Middle Ages were taught using the scholastic method.

CH05_4A

The Art of Albrecht Dürer

Melencolia I (1514)

Albrecht Dürer (1471-1528) was an artist who lived during the German Renaissance and is noted for his woodcut prints, engravings, portraits, self-portraits, and watercolors. He is particularly renowned for his introduction of classical motifs into Northern European works of art. Born in Nuremburg to a large family whose head was a goldsmith, Dürer apprenticed with his father as a youth but exhibited a talent for drawing. He then began studying with a local artist who specialized in making woodcut illustrations for books. With him, Dürer learned many of the basic skills that would transform him into a great woodcut artist. In time, he helped make woodcut illustration an independent form of art.

Some of Dürer's earliest works were self-portraits, which he created throughout his entire life. One that has survived of him shows him as a child in 1484. It was done in silverpoint, a form of drawing which is difficult to correct if the artist using it makes mistakes. The self-portraits that Dürer made during his lifetime were in several different mediums and show the increasing skill and maturity of the artist. In the early 1490s, he spent some time traveling, including making a trip to Italy. While there, he came under the influence of some artists of the Italian Renaissance. He promptly began showing skill at drawing well-proportioned human forms and added depth and perspective to his works. At that time, Dürer also began to interweave Northern European styles with the classical forms that he had learned in Italy.

Dürer turned to religious themes for his most famous series of woodcut illustrations. These were

The Apocalypse, done between 1496 and 1498, the *Large Passion* cycle, which was worked on from 1497 to 1511, and *The Life of the Virgin*, which he created between 1500 and 1511. *The Apocalypse* was a series of fifteen woodcut prints depicting the Biblical story of the end of the world. The death and resurrection of Jesus was told in the *Large Passion* series of eleven woodcut illustrations. *The Life of the Virgin* told the story of Jesus's mother, Mary, and was completed in nineteen woodcut illustrations. These three series of woodcuts brought fame to Dürer. They were often sold as books, and Dürer engraved elaborate title pages for them.

In 1505, Dürer returned to Italy for two years and spent a great deal of time in Venice to learn more from the Italian school of art. He further developed his ability accurately to paint human forms during these two years, and he additionally became interested in painting nudes. At that time, he created one of his more enduring works, the nude *Adam and Eve* (1507). Further fame came with a series of engravings in 1513 and 1514. These included *Knight, Death, and the Devil, St. Jerome in His Study,* and *Melencolia I.* The last has intrigued artists ever since its creation, and there has been a significant amount of debate over its meaning.

In his final years, Dürer continued to be prolific, producing many paintings and engravings. He also passed on his knowledge through two series of books. The first series, *Four Books on Measurement*, was intended to impart his knowledge of geometry as it applied to many disciplines, including art, architecture, and engineering. The next one, *Four Books on Human Proportion*, was meant for artists. The books deal with the human body, how it is measured and drawn, and how it moves.

---

*Glossary

motif: a theme; a style
woodcut: a carved block of wood that is used to make prints with

1. In paragraph 1, all of the following questions are answered EXCEPT:

   (A) What did Albrecht Dürer do with the classical styles of art that he learned?

   (B) How did Albrecht Dürer influence other artists during the German Renaissance?

   (C) Where did Albrecht Dürer learn the skills that enabled him to make woodcuts?

   (D) Which types of art is Albrecht Dürer known for making during his life?

2. In paragraph 2, why does the author mention "silverpoint"?

   (A) To show how skilled at a difficult type of art Dürer was

   (B) To claim that Dürer did most of his self-portraits in that style

   (C) To describe the manner in which it was used by Dürer

   (D) To claim that Dürer learned how to do it on a trip to Italy

3. The word "interweave" in the passage is closest in meaning to

   (A) study

   (B) practice

   (C) abandon

   (D) unite

4. In paragraph 2, which of the following can be inferred about Albrecht Dürer?

   (A) He had little interest in creating self-portraits until after he visited Italy.

   (B) He learned how to use perspective in artwork while he was in Italy.

   (C) He decided to become a professional artist after living in Italy for a while.

   (D) He was one of the few German artists influenced by the Italian Renaissance.

5   In paragraph 3, the author uses "*The Apocalypse*" as an example of

   Ⓐ a woodcut made by Dürer that was influenced by religion

   Ⓑ the type of work that Dürer is mostly remembered for today

   Ⓒ a work of art that earned Dürer a large amount of money

   Ⓓ one of the few series of works that Dürer made during his life

6   According to paragraph 4, what happened to Albrecht Dürer while he was in Italy?

   Ⓐ He began to make woodcuts of nudes for the first time.

   Ⓑ He learned the skills he needed to paint *St. Jerome in His Study.*

   Ⓒ He met several famous artists involved in the Italian Renaissance.

   Ⓓ He improved his ability to depict the human body accurately.

7   Which of the sentences below best expresses the essential information in the highlighted sentence in the passage? Incorrect answer choices change the meaning in important ways or leave out essential information.

The first series, *Four Books on Measurement*, was intended to impart his knowledge of geometry as it applied to many disciplines, including art, architecture, and engineering.

   Ⓐ *Four Books on Measurement* was a mathematical study on the field of geometry.

   Ⓑ Dürer wrote about art, architecture, and engineering in one series of books he published.

   Ⓒ The series of books on measurement focused on geometry as it applied to various fields.

   Ⓓ The first series of books that Dürer wrote discussed the importance of geometry to people.

8   According to paragraph 5, which of the following is true about Albrecht Dürer?

   Ⓐ He produced not only artwork but also written works in the final years of his life.

   Ⓑ He abandoned creating art in order to write several nonfiction books.

   Ⓒ The first set of books that he wrote was meant to teach artists the finer points of art.

   Ⓓ The books that he wrote included notes about his in-depth studies of the human body.

9   **Directions:** An introductory sentence for a brief summary of the passage is provided below. Complete the summary by selecting the THREE answer choices that express the most important ideas of the passage. Some sentences do not belong because they express ideas that are not presented in the passage or are minor ideas in the passage. **This question is worth 2 points**

> Drag your answer choices to the spaces where they belong. To remove an answer choice, click on it. To review the passage, click on VIEW TEXT.

Albrecht Dürer was a German Renaissance artist who created a wide variety of works during the course of his life.

-
-
-

ANSWER CHOICES

1. When Dürer spent time in Italy, he learned some skills that helped him improve the quality of the art he created.

2. Dürer apprenticed with a goldsmith when he was a child, but he was more interested in creating art than jewelry.

3. It was the written works that Dürer published near the end of his life that influenced people more than his art.

4. Dürer excelled at creating woodcuts, and some of the ones he created with religious themes made him a noted artist.

5. Dürer made self-portraits all throughout his life, and he also created a number of nudes later in his life.

6. Some of the paintings that Dürer made have confused art historians as to what messages he was trying to impart.

Balamku Cave

The ancient Mayan city of Chichen Itza is located in Mexico's Yucatan Peninsula. Under it lie a series of cave chambers that may conceal secrets explaining the collapse of Mayan civilization. One of the caverns there is known as Balamku Cave or the Cave of the Jaguar God. Inside it, archaeologists have discovered artifacts which they believe may offer insights into the ancient Mayan way of life.

Balamku Cave was discovered in 2018. Some archaeologists were searching for an underground water system beneath Chichen Itza. To their surprise, they stumbled upon a series of narrow tunnels. They followed the tunnels and eventually came upon Balamku Cave. So far, the team excavating the region has discovered seven large chambers. One of the first things they unearthed was a treasure trove of artifacts. The initial discovery of more than 150 objects included incense burners, decorated plates, vases, pots, and vessels for carrying water. Many were adorned with the faces of ancient Mayan gods and other religious symbols. Archaeologists believe the objects were placed in the cave more than 1,000 years ago.

The archaeological team soon learned that they had not been the first individuals to discover Balamku Cave. In 1966, another archaeologist, Victor Segovia Pinto, found a different entrance to the underground system. He wrote a report on his findings and then had the cave entrance sealed by local farmers. Nobody today knows exactly what happened next or what Segovia's intentions were at that time. Some believe he had planned to return to the site to conduct an extensive excavation, but that never occurred. ▮1 Few others knew about his find, and his report was lost. ▮2 More delays in the rediscovery of the cave resulted due to the nature of Mayan archaeology in the past few decades. ▮3 A great amount of effort was directed toward aboveground ruins, such as the remains of Mayan cities. ▮4 But it has only been in recent years that cave archaeology has taken a prominent role in revealing the secrets of Mayan civilization. This resulted in widespread knowledge of the existence of the cave not occurring until 2018.

Knowledge of Mayan culture is necessary to understand why they left so many artifacts in the cave. For Mayans, caves were a window into the underworld and were therefore some of the most sacred places for the Mayan people. One theory as to why they placed artifacts in the cave has to do with the decline of Mayan culture. The main theory is that Mayan lands endured a severe drought around a millennium ago. As a result, there were crop failures, and a famine devastated the Mayan people. This ultimately led the survivors to abandon the Yucatan Peninsula. The discovery of artifacts dedicated to the gods alongside vessels for carrying water suggests that the Mayans went deep into the cave to pray to their gods for rain to end the drought. Unfortunately for them, their prayers went unanswered.

By studying the cave and the artifacts found inside it, archaeologists hope to obtain some insight into the demise of the Mayans. The incense burners, for example, have residue of organic matter that was burned in them. It may be useful for dating the exact time when the cave was used as a place of supplication by the Mayans. This, in turn, could provide more information on the collapse of Mayan civilization, including approximately when it began.

---

*Glossary

underworld: the place beneath the world where the souls of the dead are believed to go

residue: something that remains, especially after an item is burned or used in some other way

10 The word "conceal" in the passage is closest in meaning to

Ⓐ hide

Ⓑ report

Ⓒ explain

Ⓓ approach

11 In paragraph 2, which of the following can be inferred about Balamku Cave?

Ⓐ It contains a number of chambers that descend seven levels beneath the ground.

Ⓑ Its existence was well known to locals despite archaeologists not knowing about it.

Ⓒ The discovery of it by a team of archaeologists in 2018 was entirely accidental.

Ⓓ Doing research inside it has been temporarily banned by the Mexican government.

12 According to paragraph 2, what did archaeologists find in Balamku Cave?

Ⓐ A large cave system that had been enlarged by humans long ago

Ⓑ Seven chambers, all of which contained artifacts left by the Mayans

Ⓒ Artifacts around a millennium old that are thought to be of Mayan origin

Ⓓ A temple that was dedicated to some old Mayan gods and goddesses

13 What is the author's purpose in paragraph 3 of the passage?

Ⓐ To argue that Balamku Cave was not actually discovered in 2018

Ⓑ To point out why the natives did not want Balamku Cave rediscovered

Ⓒ To describe the research done on Balamku Cave by Victor Segovia Pinto

Ⓓ To explain why almost nobody knew about Balamku Cave until 2018

14 According to paragraph 3, which of the following is true about Victor Segovia Pinto?

Ⓐ He failed to go back to Balamku Cave to excavate it after he discovered it.

Ⓑ He did a great amount of research on the Mayans and Chichen Itza in particular.

Ⓒ He conducted an extensive excavation on Balamku Cave and found artifacts there.

Ⓓ He published a report detailing information about his discovery of Balamku Cave.

15 Which of the sentences below best expresses the essential information in the highlighted sentence in the passage? Incorrect answer choices change the meaning in important ways or leave out essential information.

The discovery of artifacts dedicated to the gods alongside vessels for carrying water suggests that the Mayans went deep into the cave to pray to their gods for rain to end the drought.

Ⓐ Archaeologists have determined that the Mayans went into the cave to pray for the drought to be over and also left all of the artifacts in it.

Ⓑ Some believe that anytime there was a time of drought, the Mayans entered the cave with various offerings to the gods and then prayed to them.

Ⓒ It is thought that since the Mayans left items for their gods as well as water containers, they entered the cave to pray for an end to the drought.

Ⓓ Because the Mayans went deep into the cave to pray to the gods, they brought various items, including water vessels, along with them.

16 The word "supplication" in the passage is closest in meaning to

Ⓐ donation

Ⓑ prayer

Ⓒ discovery

Ⓓ safety

17 Look at the four squares [■] that indicate where the following sentence could be added to the passage.

As time passed, those individuals who were aware of the existence of the cave became smaller in number.

Where would the sentence best fit?

Click on a square [■] to add the sentence to the passage.

120

18 Directions: An introductory sentence for a brief summary of the passage is provided below. Complete the summary by selecting the THREE answer choices that express the most important ideas of the passage. Some sentences do not belong because they express ideas that are not presented in the passage or are minor ideas in the passage. **This question is worth 2 points.**

The discovery of Balamku Cave in Chichen Itza should help archaeologists learn more about ancient Mayan society.

-

-

-

ANSWER CHOICES

1 Archaeologists are still trying to determine what happened to the Mayans and why they disappeared centuries ago.

2 Chichen Itza, which is located in the Yucatan Peninsula, is one of the most important of all ancient Mayan sites.

3 Archaeologists hope that some of the artifacts found in the cave will help them learn about the reason Mayan civilization collapsed.

4 The cave was initially discovered by Victor Segovia Pinto, but he failed to excavate it, so knowledge of it was lost.

5 Archaeologists believe the Mayans may have left items in the cave because they were asking their gods to end a drought.

6 There are seven chambers that have been discovered in Balamku Cave, which is also called the Cave of the Jaguar God.

◢ Vocabulary Review

A Complete each sentence with the appropriate word from the box.

decline	turmoil	contradiction	accurately	ambiguity

1 By _____ predicting the stock market, Jeff became a wealthy man.

2 Nobody believed him since his second statement was a _____ of his first one.

3 The _____ in sales of the item happened due to there being less demand for it.

4 Some people speak with a lot of _____ to avoid taking sides in arguments.

5 There was a lot of _____ as soon as the building caught on fire.

B Complete each sentence with the correct answer.

1 Items that **adorn** the walls in a room help _____ it.

   a. decorate   b. camouflage

2 Work that is **accurately** done is done _____.

   a. properly   b. quickly

3 People who **grind** pepper _____.

   a. add it to food   b. break it into small pieces

4 If some food is **remarkably** good, it tastes _____ good.

   a. very   b. a little

5 Jeremy **persisted** and _____ during the race.

   a. kept running   b. gave up

6 The **entrance** to the building is the place where people _____.

   a. do their work   b. go inside

7 The **retreat** of the army happened when the general ordered the soldiers to _____.

   a. move forward   b. move backward

8 A person **grasping** at something is trying to _____ it.

   a. purchase   b. grab

9 When someone does a **minimal** amount of work, that person _____.

   a. barely works at all   b. works very hard

10 When cows **graze** in a field, they _____.

   a. eat grass   b. get some rest

Chapter **06**

Inference

Question Type | Inference

◢ About the Question

Inference questions focus on the implications that are made in the passage. You are asked to analyze the information presented in the passage and then to come to logical conclusions about it. The answers to these questions are never explicitly written in the passage. Instead, you need to infer what the author of the passage means. These questions often require you to understand cause and effect and also to compare and contrast various events, people, or ideas. There are 0-2 Inference questions for each passage. Most passages have at least 1 Inference question though.

Recognizing Inference questions:

• Which of the following can be inferred about X?

• The author of the passage implies that X . . .

• Which of the following can be inferred from paragraph 1 about X?

Helpful hints for answering the questions correctly:

• Inference questions often focus on various cause and effect relationships. Think about the possible unstated effects of various events, ideas, or phenomena that are presented in the passage.

• You need to be able to read between the lines to answer these questions properly. Focus not only on what the author is overtly writing but also on what the author is hinting at in the text.

• Avoid selecting answer choices because they contain words that are found in the passage. These are frequently misleading.

• The correct answer will never contradict the main point of the passage. Avoid answer choices that go against the main point or theme of the passage.

• Some Inference questions use words such as *suggest* rather than *imply* or *infer*.

• The difficulty level of these questions has increased. In some cases, test takers must be able to understand an entire paragraph rather than only a part of it.

Taiga

➡ The largest land biome is called the taiga. It is one of the three primary forest biomes, with the other two being the tropical rainforest and the temperate forest. The taiga is distinguished from these other two ecosystems in several ways. First, the climate in the taiga is much colder and drier than the other two as winter in some regions can last for half the year, and summer is typically extremely short. This results in a short growing season in the region. Additionally, the majority of trees in the taiga are evergreen trees such as pines and cedars. Since these trees do not lose their leaves in fall like deciduous ones do, there is only a thin layer of fertile soil in the land. Most taiga are found in the Northern Hemisphere, particularly in Siberia, Canada, and Alaska in the United States.

In paragraph 3, which of the following can be inferred about the taiga?

Ⓐ Most crops are unable to grow well there.

Ⓑ It covers more land in Canada than anywhere else.

Ⓒ There are many species of animals that live in it.

Ⓓ It can have warmer weather than some temperate forests.

Paragraph 3 is marked with an arrow (➡).

| Answer Explanation |

Choice Ⓐ is the correct answer. The passage reads, "The climate in the taiga is much colder and drier than the other two as winter in some regions can last for half the year, and summer is typically extremely short. This results in a short growing season in the region." In pointing out how cold the weather is and how short the growing season it, it can be inferred that most crops are unable to grow well in the taiga.

A | **How Sound Waves Move**

🎧 CH06_2A

When something releases energy through vibrations, it produces sound. These vibrations pass through the air and hit a person's eardrum, which vibrates. The brain recognizes this vibrating energy as a particular sound. Sound vibrations move through the air or other mediums, such as water, in the form of waves. Sound cannot move through a **vacuum** though, a principle English scientist Robert Boyle discovered in the seventeenth century.

Sound waves resemble the waves produced when someone throws a rock into a pond. They originate at a source and move in circles away from it. As sound waves travel through the air, they do not move in regular patterns but instead push together and pull apart, creating some areas where air is squashed together and other areas where it is pulled apart. Scientists call the former sound waves compressions and the latter ones rarefactions.

Sound waves do not move at constant rates as the medium they travel through affects their velocity. For example, they move four times faster in water than in air. As sound waves travel, they lose energy and eventually completely **dissipate**. That is why sounds from close sources are louder than those created far away. Obstacles also influence how sound waves travel as they can bounce off some objects and produce echoes or bend around obstacles. The ability of sound to bend is called diffraction. It lets people hear sounds despite obstacles standing between the source and the listener.

*vacuum: an area that has no gas or air in it
*dissipate: to disperse; to break apart

---

1 Which of the following can be inferred from paragraph 2 about sound waves?

Ⓐ They vibrate in ways that scientists are able to predict.

Ⓑ They move quickly in some directions but slowly in other ones.

Ⓒ They use compressions to increase the speed at which they travel.

Ⓓ They travel in all directions away from where they were made.

2 In paragraph 3, the author implies that sounds waves

Ⓐ travel faster through the ground than they do in air

Ⓑ create echoes when they cannot move through an object

Ⓒ are capable only of traveling a limited distance

Ⓓ use the process of diffraction to move through water

Vocabulary

- _____ = to move back and forth
- _____ = to compress; to make something very small by crushing it
- _____ = an object that is blocking someone or something
- _____ = a repeated sound produced when a sound wave reflects off a surface

B | Bumblebees

Bumblebees are stout, hairy black and yellow insects that gather nectar from flowers. Similar in appearance to honeybees, they are larger and hairier though. There are more than 200 species of bumblebees, most of which are native to the Northern Hemisphere, but some species reside in South America. Due to their role as pollinators, they are vital to the ecosystems in which they live.

Living in nests which they build underground or in vegetation near the ground, bumblebees prefer their homes to be in cool, dry, shaded places. A bumblebee nest has fewer than 400 members, including a queen, many female worker bees, and a few male reproductive bees called drones. There are also some specialized female bees that will become queens in the future. Once they are fertilized, they leave the nest, become **dormant** until the next spring, and then establish a new nest. Until the new queen's eggs hatch, she is entirely alone.

Bumblebees use their long tongue to **lap up** nectar from flowers. As they feed, they gather flower pollen on the rear sections of their bodies. Female bumblebees have a special basketlike structure that helps them collect pollen. As they move from flower to flower, this pollen falls off their bodies and pollinates the flowers. This is the most important role of bumblebees. Without them pollinating various plants, numerous flowers, crops, and other types of vegetation would be in grave danger of being unable to reproduce and would therefore eventually go extinct.

*dormant: inactive
*lap up: to lick up; to consume

1 In paragraph 2, which of the following can be inferred about queen bees?
   (A) They are territorial and will fight other bumblebees that are nearby.
   (B) They take no males or females with them when they build new nests.
   (C) They are capable of fertilizing themselves if they are alone.
   (D) They create honey that their larvae consume after they are born.

2 In paragraph 3, the author implies that bumblebees
   (A) pollinate the flowers that they visit by accident
   (B) have caused some flowers to go extinct in the past
   (C) use the pollen they gather to create honey
   (D) need to gather pollen to create energy for themselves

Vocabulary

- _____ = a sweet substance produced by a plant that attracts insects or birds
- _____ = an animal or thing that fertilizes a plant
- _____ = to come out from an egg to be born
- _____ = serious; great

C | Ribonucleic Acid

Ribonucleic acid, otherwise known as RNA, is one of the essential components of the human body. It is a molecule created from DNA. Each RNA molecule is comprised of one or more **nucleotides**, which individually contain a base such as adenine, cytosine, guanine, or uracil, a ribose sugar, and a phosphate. RNA has several functions, including assisting the body in accelerating chemical reactions and playing roles in cell division, cell aging, and cell death. Finally, its primary purpose is to control how proteins in the body are made.

Every cell in the body contains DNA. This DNA carries the entire genetic code for the body, among them being the genes that are needed to create and activate important proteins. However, the DNA needs to be protected, so it cannot leave the nucleus of the cell. It therefore utilizes RNA to carry messages to create proteins in a procedure known as transcription.

This form of messenger RNA is known as mRNA. It carries instructions for creating and activating proteins from DNA to structures that are called **ribosomes**. Each ribosome consists of proteins and another form of RNA. It is called ribosomal RNA, or rRNA for short. When the mRNA enters the ribosome, it tells the ribosome to form a protein. The body then uses the proteins that are created to carry out a wide range of functions.

*nucleotide: a group of molecules that form the building blocks of RNA or DNA when they are linked to one another
*ribosome: a specialized part of a cell in which proteins are manufactured

---

1   Which of the following can be inferred from paragraph 1 about RNA?

(A) Each molecule of it is responsible for a single task in the body.

(B) The body requires it in order to create various types of proteins.

(C) It can mutate so that it causes some cells to age at a rapid rate.

(D) One of its roles is to create sugar that the body uses for energy.

2   In paragraphs 2 and 3, which of the following can be inferred about mRNA?

(A) It can move to places in the body that DNA cannot go to.

(B) It is capable of forming rRNA with the help of ribosomes.

(C) It helps DNA create the genetic code of the entire body.

(D) It can be responsible for some cell problems that bodies develop.

Vocabulary

•   _____ = important; necessary

•   _____ = to increase the rate of

•   _____ = total; complete

•   _____ = the center or core of something

▌ Mapping

The following chart shows the structure of the passage. Fill in the blanks with the appropriate words.

Ribonucleic Acid

Is essential ❶ _____ in human body

– Comprised of nucleotide, ribose sugar, and phosphate

– Has many ❷ _____ , including controlling how proteins are made

---

DNA in all cells in body

– carries ❸ _____ code

– has genes needed to make and control ❹ _____

– DNA can't leave ❺ _____ of cell

– uses ❻ _____ to send messages to cells to make protein

– process is called ❼ _____

---

mRNA = messenger RNA

– has instructions for creating and ❽ _____ proteins

– takes to ribosomes

– mRNA enters ❾ _____ and tells it to form protein

▌ Summary

The following is a summary of the passage. Fill in the blanks with the appropriate words.

Ribonucleic acid, or RNA, is an essential component of the human body. RNA molecules contain at least one ❶ _____ . RNA has many functions, but its main purpose is ❷ _____ how proteins in the body are made. ❸ _____ has the entire genetic code for the body but cannot leave the nucleus of the cell. So it uses RNA to carry ❹ _____ to create proteins. ❺ _____ is messenger RNA. It takes ❻ _____ for creating and activating proteins to ribosomes. There, rRNA, or ribosomal RNA, tells the ribosomes to form a ❼ _____ .

A | Tropical Seagrasses

🎧 CH06_3A

Some aquatic plants live in warm, shallow salt water in tropical zones. Known as tropical seagrasses, they evolved from land plants to live beneath the sea. Like plants on land, they have roots, flowers, seeds, and leaves. However, they lack strong supporting structures such as stems and trunks. Seagrasses produce food through **photosynthesis**, so they cannot live in deep water or in places where the water is too murky for sunlight to penetrate.

There are more than fifty species of seagrasses, around fifteen of which grow in tropical zones. All of them share some features. For instance, they usually have long, thin leaves that are around ten to thirty centimeters long, but one species has leaves up to 150 centimeters in length while a few have shorter, more rounded leaves. Tropical seagrasses also anchor themselves to sandbanks and mud banks. They grow in beds that may cover many **hectares**. These beds typically contain a single species of seagrass, but mixed groups are not unknown.

Tropical seagrasses are of great importance to numerous marine life forms. First, they serve as food for many animals, including manatees, dugongs, turtles, crabs, sea urchins, and various species of fish. Even when they die, they provide nutrients for creatures as they decay. Second, many tropical marine life forms hide from predators in the dense beds of seagrass and also find their own food in them. Third, many tiny forms of life, including bacteria and algae, which other creatures feed upon, gather in seagrass beds in vast numbers.

Another benefit tropical seagrasses provide is that they slow down moving water, which allows silt in the water to drop and gather in seagrass beds. The silt increases the density of the seabed, thereby giving plants better homes. The roots of the seagrasses in these beds of sediment help prevent erosion. They additionally serve as filters by absorbing nutrients from the water. In this way, they can deter algae blooms that are caused when too many nutrients enter the water due to coastal farm runoff. On top of all that, seagrasses consume large amounts of carbon dioxide in the oceans. According to one estimate, all of the seagrasses worldwide absorb ten percent of the oceans' carbon dioxide.

Unfortunately, tropical seagrass habitats are in danger, which, in turn, is endangering many seagrasses. The main problem concerns the overuse of fertilizers on farms that produce so much runoff polluted by nutrients that seagrasses cannot filter all of it. This runoff clouds the water, which blocks sunlight, so the seagrasses die. As they die, they decay, which provides more nutrients for algae to grow and causes even more seagrasses to die.

*photosynthesis: the process through which plants use sunlight to create food for themselves
*hectare: a unit of land measuring around two and a half acres

Vocabulary

- _____ = to go into
- _____ = to connect one thing to another
- _____ = to eat
- _____ = silt; dirt; soil

1 The word "murky" in the passage is closest in meaning to

(A) unexplored

(B) rapid

(C) salty

(D) cloudy

2 Select the TWO answer choices from paragraphs 2 and 3 that identify characteristics of seagrasses. *To receive credit, you must select TWO answers.*

(A) Enable large predators to hide from smaller creatures they are hunting

(B) Live only in places with seagrasses of the same species

(C) Grow from the bottom of the sea in either sand or mud

(D) Provide sustenance for animals in a variety of ways

3 In paragraph 4, the author implies that seagrasses

(A) can eliminate the conditions that allow algae to thrive

(B) are planted by people to attempt to prevent erosion

(C) play a major role in keeping the oceans unpolluted

(D) are found only in areas of the ocean with lots of silt

4 An introductory sentence for a brief summary of the passage is provided below. Complete the summary by selecting the THREE answer choices that express the most important ideas of the passage. Some sentences do not belong because they express ideas that are not presented in the passage or are minor ideas in the passage.

The various species of tropical seagrasses share several characteristics and also provide a number of benefits to the areas in which they grow.

ANSWER CHOICES

1 Many animals feed upon seagrasses, and the seagrasses additionally help creatures after dying by decomposing.

2 The actions of some humans are causing pollution, which is a source of danger for some species of seagrasses.

3 The leaves of most seagrasses are nearly identical in appearance, and they tend to grow in similar areas.

4 Seagrasses are effective at helping silt accumulate at the bottom of the ocean and can prevent soil from eroding.

5 Of the more than fifty types of seagrasses in the world, nearly all of them can be found in tropical climates.

6 Algae blooms have killed many seagrasses around the world and may cause them to go extinct in the future.

B The Chinese Song Dynasty

The Song Dynasty of China lasted from 960 to 1279 and encompassed much of what is eastern China today. This period is notable for its high level of social, economic, artistic, and technological innovations, which made it the most advanced land in the world. However, the dynasty was doomed by constant warfare and was eventually overthrown by a Mongol invasion.

The Song Dynasty can be divided into two distinct times: the Northern Song (960-1126) and the Southern Song (1127-1279) periods. The Northern Song Dynasty got its start when a general in the Zhou Dynasty named Zhao Kuangyin overthrew the emperor in a coup. He named himself Emperor Taizu and established his capital in the city of Kaifeng in northern China. Emperor Taizu and his descendants are commonly recognized for their reforms, which established China as the leading nation in the world in many areas.

One of these reforms was the creation of a highly sophisticated administrative arm staffed by educated men who had passed a rigorous examination. The Song additionally established many social welfare programs to aid the poor. They built numerous internal canals, which helped trade flourish as well. Song land reforms improved crop outputs, which led to an increase in the population. During that time, the Chinese were the world's leaders in science, engineering, and technology. They developed gunpowder weapons, invented the compass, created wood block printing, and issued the world's first paper currency.

However, the Song Dynasty was not always prosperous. Nor was it peaceful as along its borders were many warring states, which resulted in costly, endemic warfare. The greatest threat to the Song was the northern Liao Empire. The Song allied with the Jurchen people, who were enemies of the Liao. They had rebelled against their Liao overlords and founded a state of their own, called the Jin Empire. Together, they defeated the Liao by 1125. Yet the alliance did not last. The Jin recognized that the Song military was not as strong as theirs, so they attacked the Song. By 1127, the Jin had defeated the Song, prompting the Song emperor and his court to flee south of the Yangtze River.

The Song government established itself in what is today the city of Hangzhou. This marked the beginning of the Southern Song Dynasty. Clashes with the Jin continued, especially along the coast and the Yangtze River. But the Mongols began raiding Jin lands. In 1211, an enormous Mongol army invaded northern China and, over time, conquered the Jin. In the last 1260s, Mongol leader Kublai Khan launched an invasion of the Southern Song lands across the Yangtze River. After more than a decade of warfare, the Song were defeated in 1279.

*staff: to man; to run; to operate
*endemic: constant; widespread

Vocabulary

- _____ = advanced
- _____ = difficult
- _____ = a device that always points to the north
- _____ = to cause something to happen

1 Which of the sentences below best expresses the essential information in the highlighted sentence in the passage? Incorrect answer choices change the meaning in important ways or leave out essential information.

Emperor Taizu and his descendants are commonly recognized for their reforms, which established China as the leading nation in the world in many areas.

(A) The emperor and his children focused on ways to make China one of the leading countries in the entire world.

(B) In order to become one of the top countries in the world, China had to institute a large number of reforms.

(C) Thanks to the reforms made by the emperor and his descendants, China became one of the world's greatest nations.

(D) There were some reforms made in China, but the emperor and his descendants could not change the country to a great extent.

2 In paragraph 3, which of the following can be inferred about the Song Dynasty?

(A) Its rulers desired to improve the conditions of the people they ruled.

(B) Many of the reforms that it made were imitated by people in other lands.

(C) The first documented usage of money happened during the Song Dynasty.

(D) The canals that were built during it took many years to construct.

3 According to paragraph 4, which of the following is NOT true about the Jin Empire?

(A) It was comprised of a group that was known as the Jurchen people.

(B) Its army managed to defeat the Song and to drive the Song away from their lands.

(C) Its people had migrated to China from lands that were somewhere in the west.

(D) It worked together with the Song to defeat an enemy they had in common.

4 An introductory sentence for a brief summary of the passage is provided below. Complete the summary by selecting the THREE answer choices that express the most important ideas of the passage. Some sentences do not belong because they express ideas that are not presented in the passage or are minor ideas in the passage.

The Song Dynasty was a period in which many reforms took place in China, but it was also a time of warfare, which eventually caused the dynasty to end.

ANSWER CHOICES

1 China was an advanced country during this time and made many advances in the fields of science, engineering, and technology.

2 There were no wars during the Northern Song Period, but there were many fought during the Southern Song Period.

3 The Southern Song Period was marked by wars that were fought both against the Jin Empire and the Mongols.

4 The Liao Empire was one of the enemies of the Song, who had to fight it along its northern lands.

5 The reforms of Emperor Taizu and others improved the internal conditions of the land, both economically and socially.

6 The Song Dynasty originated when its founder defeated the emperor in a coup and began to rule the land.

CH06_4A

The Development of Birds in Eggs

A female bird produces eggs inside her body after a male bird fertilizes her ovum. She then commonly lays her eggs in some type of nest. Within each egg is an embryo that subsequently grows into a chick. While the embryo is developing, the female—and occasionally the male—sits atop the egg, thereby keeping it warm. Once the embryo has fully developed into a baby bird, the chick cracks the egg and emerges.

In the majority of cases, birds inside eggs develop in a similar manner. The common chicken is a typical example of how an embryo develops to become a bird. The chick begins its life as an oocyte—the yolk of an egg—which is produced by the hen's ovary organ. The yolk travels into a tube called an oviduct, whereupon it comes into contact with male sperm. The sperm fertilizes the small, circular white part on the yolk called the blastodisc. ■ After being fertilized, it becomes a blastoderm, which marks the beginning of a new chicken. ■ The yolk then continues traveling down the oviduct and acquires structural fibers called chalazae and two membrane layers called albumin. ■ It creates a thick inner layer near the yolk in addition to a thinner outer layer. ■

As the growing egg moves down the oviduct, it turns, which twists each chalaza to make something resembling a rope. There are two chalazae—one at each end of the egg. Their function is to anchor the egg yolk inside the albumin. Next, the eggshell grows around the yolk and the albumin as it forms from the new two-layer membrane that grows around the egg white. The shell itself comes from calcite, a form of calcium carbonate which is found in the membrane. While the egg spins in the lower part of the oviduct, the calcite crystallizes and gradually builds up to form a complete eggshell.

The entire journey takes about one day, after which the egg is laid. Afterward, the mother hen sits on the eggs in her nest to incubate them. While this is happening, the blastoderm divides several times and transforms into an embryo. Once it forms, it takes approximately twenty-one days for an embryo to become a chick. Developing chicks get the required nutrients from the egg yolk. Waste eliminated from the growing chick is collected in a special sac known as the allantois, and the chick receives oxygen from another sac located within the egg. After the egg is laid, it is quite warm but immediately begins losing heat. While cooling, it shrinks slightly, and the two membrane layers underneath the eggshell pull apart, creating a small air sac. The chick breathes oxygen from this sac and expels carbon dioxide into it. Numerous microscopic holes in the eggshell permit oxygen to enter and depart the membrane air sac.

The embryo gradually starts resembling a chicken. After developing for eight days, it weighs about a gram, and upon hatching, it weighs somewhere around thirty grams. Once the chick becomes too big for the egg, it hatches. Most baby birds have a special growth on their beak called an egg tooth, which they utilize to break out of the shell. Most chicks do this slowly, spending their remaining time in the shell consuming whatever is left of the yolk before emerging completely. After the chicks hatch, mother hens feed them and keep them warm for several more weeks.

*Glossary

ovary: the female reproductive gland

chalazas: a twisted cord that attaches the yolk to the shell membrane

1   According to paragraph 1, which of the following is true about bird eggs?

   Ⓐ They are primarily taken care of in nests by male birds.

   Ⓑ They have to be protected from predators that try eating them.

   Ⓒ They are heated while the embryos are developing in them.

   Ⓓ They are cracked by female birds when the chicks are ready to hatch.

2   The word "it" in the passage refers to

   Ⓐ an oviduct

   Ⓑ the sperm

   Ⓒ the yolk

   Ⓓ the blastodisc

3   In paragraph 3, why does the author mention "calcite"?

   Ⓐ To discuss its role in helping the membrane develop

   Ⓑ To note that it is the material the eggshell is formed from

   Ⓒ To describe how it forms inside the eggshell

   Ⓓ To explain what its chemical structure is

4   In paragraph 3, the author implies that the chalazae

   Ⓐ are responsible for preventing the yolk from getting out of the albumin

   Ⓑ provide the calcite which is necessary for the eggshell to develop

   Ⓒ twist and become ropelike due to the action of the egg yolk

   Ⓓ enable the eggshell to develop and grow around the albumin

5   The word "incubate" in the passage is closest in meaning to

   Ⓐ protect

   Ⓑ observe

   Ⓒ warm

   Ⓓ hide

6   Which of the following can be inferred from paragraph 4 about chicks developing in eggs?

   Ⓐ They need oxygen in order to develop properly.

   Ⓑ More heat can enable them to hatch in two weeks.

   Ⓒ They get access to water from the holes in the eggs.

   Ⓓ Excessive carbon dioxide can kill them.

7   Select the TWO answer choices from paragraph 5 that identify what happens when a chick hatches. *To receive credit, you must select TWO answers.*

   Ⓐ They eat the remainder of the yolk before hatching.

   Ⓑ They are assisted by their mothers when they hatch.

   Ⓒ They try to get out of the egg as quickly as possible.

   Ⓓ They make use of the egg tooth to crack the eggshell.

8   Look at the four squares [■] that indicate where the following sentence could be added to the passage.

These layers are also known as the egg white.

Where would the sentence best fit?

Click on a square [■] to add the sentence to the passage.

9 **Directions:** An introductory sentence for a brief summary of the passage is provided below. Complete the summary by selecting the THREE answer choices that express the most important ideas of the passage. Some sentences do not belong because they express ideas that are not presented in the passage or are minor ideas in the passage. **This question is worth 2 points.**

Drag your answer choices to the spaces where they belong. To remove an answer choice, click on it. To review the passage, click on VIEW TEXT.

The development of a bird inside an eggshell is a complicated process that takes around three weeks to complete.

-
-
-

ANSWER CHOICES

1 Birds usually sit on their eggs after they are laid so that they can keep the eggs warm.

2 Only a few chicks rely upon an egg tooth to help them break out of the eggshell as soon as they are ready to hatch.

3 When a yolk gets fertilized by male sperm, it can then become a chicken, so it becomes a blastoderm and starts developing.

4 The eggshell itself is made of calcite, and it covers the entire egg yolk and albumin as it develops.

5 Developing embryos get their nutrients from the egg yolk and can also breathe oxygen through holes in the eggshell.

6 Inside the eggshell, the embryo slowly develops to become a chick and eventually hatches once it becomes big enough.

CH06_4B

The Decline of Sensory Perception with Age

As people age, their bodies begin to wear out. One of the primary effects of this is a decline in sensory perception. Humans have five senses: hearing, sight, touch, taste, and smell. The deterioration of each sense produces both physical and mental effects on the body. While some can be altered or slowed, in most cases, the decline in sensory perception is total and permanent.

Hearing loss is one of the leading problems people, especially those seventy-five or older, face as they age. The loss of hearing is based on a person's inability to hear sounds at different decibel levels. A mild case of hearing loss can result in a person being unable to hear sounds quieter than twenty decibels. ■ In comparison, a person who cannot hear anything lower than ninety decibels, which is comparable to the sound made by a lawnmower, is considered deaf. ② Hearing loss is normally dealt with through the utilization of hearing aids or by surgically implanted devices that repair physical problems inside the ear. ③ A loss of hearing can result in an increase in depression as a person can no longer communicate as freely as in the past. This may produce feelings of isolation. ④

The decline of sight is another major result of age. The human eye changes shape as people age, which can lead to progressively worsening eyesight requiring the use of more powerful glasses as well as reading glasses. Another common problem is the formation of cataracts, which cause the clouding of the eye lens. It is estimated that thirty percent of all adults over the age of sixty-five will develop cataracts at some time in their lives. Fortunately, cataracts can be dealt with by replacing them with artificial lenses in a simple surgical procedure. Other vision problems are not so easily solved. Glaucoma, the increase of pressure inside the eyeball, often damages the optic nerve and may cause total blindness. The loss of sight can negatively impact a person's quality of life by restricting the individual's ability to work, read, drive, watch television, and live independently.

People's senses of taste and smell also worsen as they age. Approximately seventy-five percent of people eighty or older report declines in their olfactory functions. While some diseases may cause this, research indicates that the main reason is the slowing of cell replacement in the olfactory fibers in the nose. As people become older, they may lose their sense of taste, typically due to oral and respiratory diseases. Both the loss of smell and taste are associated with heavy smoking. Negative results of this include a decline in a person's desire for food and the loss of enjoyment of pleasant smells such as flowers.

A decline in nerve functions produces a loss in the sensation of feel regarding things that a person touches. This is part of the process of aging but may also be a secondary effect of certain diseases. A common side effect of diabetes, for instance, is damage to the nerve endings, which can make a person lose feeling in the extremities. This can result in unnoticed injuries, especially in the feet, which can lead to serious infections and even amputation. A stroke can cause the loss of sensation, but this usually happens only on one side of the body. The loss of feeling can hamper people by causing them to suffer injuries without feeling pain.

*Glossary

decibel: a unit that is used to means the intensity of sound waves
olfactory: relating to the sense of smell

10 Which of the following can be inferred from paragraph 1 about the five senses?

Ⓐ They tend to decline an equal amount in people as they become older.

Ⓑ Hearing and sight are the two senses that decline the most in older people.

Ⓒ Some people have managed to improve their senses during their elderly years.

Ⓓ It is possible to prevent some of them from worsening as a person ages.

11 The author discusses "the sound made by a lawnmower" in paragraph 2 in order to

Ⓐ make a comparison between that sound and the sound of someone whispering

Ⓑ point out that exposure to noise that loud can harm people's sense of hearing

Ⓒ describe a common noise that the majority of people are familiar with

Ⓓ state that people unable to hear that sound are regarded as being deaf

12 Which of the sentences below best expresses the essential information in the highlighted sentence in the passage? Incorrect answer choices change the meaning in important ways or leave out essential information.

The human eye changes shape as people age, which can lead to progressively worsening eyesight requiring the use of more powerful glasses as well as reading glasses.

Ⓐ If an elderly person's eyes change shape, that individual may need to wear reading glasses or get stronger glasses.

Ⓑ As people get older, their eyes change shape, so they may require vision aids since their eyesight declines in quality.

Ⓒ By wearing stronger glasses or even reading glasses, it is possible for the elderly to overcome their decline in eyesight.

Ⓓ People whose eyesight gets worse as they become older may need to get powerful glasses or at least reading glasses.

13 According to paragraph 3, glaucoma can affect the eye by

(A) clouding the eye lens and making it harder for a person to see

(B) causing harm to a nerve that may then make a person go blind

(C) changing the shape of the eye and making a person's eyesight worse

(D) darkening a person's vision and causing a decline in that person's eyesight

14 In paragraph 4, the author implies that smoking may

(A) make people no longer able to taste or smell things very well

(B) make people more interested in eating because of their lack of taste

(C) cause people to suffer from a variety of respiratory diseases

(D) cause some cells in parts of people's bodies to be replaced more slowly

15 The word "hamper" in the passage is closest in meaning to

(A) inform

(B) hinder

(C) annoy

(D) trick

16 In paragraph 5, the author's description of the sense of feel mentions all of the following EXCEPT:

(A) the reason a loss of feeling can cause additional damage to some people

(B) the parts of the body that are particularly vulnerable to a loss of feeling

(C) some ways that people can prevent their sense of feeling from declining

(D) a reason some people can lose their sense of feeling on one side of their bodies

17 Look at the four squares [■] that indicate where the following sentence could be added to the passage.

However, these treatments are not always effective or may have results that are less than expected.

Where would the sentence best fit?

Click on a square [■] to add the sentence to the passage.

142

18 **Directions**: An introductory sentence for a brief summary of the passage is provided below. Complete the summary by selecting the THREE answer choices that express the most important ideas of the passage. Some sentences do not belong because they express ideas that are not presented in the passage or are minor ideas in the passage. **This question is worth 2 points.**

When people become older, all five of their senses start to become worse in quality.

-
-
-

ANSWER CHOICES

1. Doctors are developing medical solutions, such as hearing aids, that can prevent a decline in a sense from harming people too much.

2. All five senses are important, so the deterioration of one of them can lead to a decline in a person's quality of life.

3. People who are in their seventies and eighties often report a decline in the quality of their sense of hearing.

4. Some older people report the loss of their senses of taste and smell, and human actions may account for these declines.

5. In some cases, it is possible for a person to slow down or even prevent the decline of one of the five senses.

6. Older people's eyesight can start to decline, and they might also suffer problems such as cataracts and glaucoma.

■ Vocabulary Review

A Complete each sentence with the appropriate word from the box.

worsen	nucleus	sophisticated	sediment	progressively

1 _____ that is washed downstream by rivers can be stopped by dams.

2 The patient's health got _____ better thanks to the medicine.

3 This is a _____ piece of machinery that is difficult to use.

4 The scientist is looking at the _____ of the cell with a microscope.

5 Mark's condition began to _____, so he hurried to the hospital to see a doctor.

B Complete each sentence with the correct answer.

1 If a knife cannot **penetrate** an object, it is unable to _____ it.

   a. cut   b. sharpen

2 It is possible to **eliminate** problems and to make them all _____.

   a. disappear   b. become worse

3 A machine that is **vibrating** is _____.

   a. not working   b. shaking

4 If you **prompt** a person to act in a certain way, you _____ that person do something.

   a. make   b. request

5 As soon as a bird egg **hatches**, a baby _____.

   a. flies away   b. comes out

6 David **accelerated** the car, so the vehicle began to _____.

   a. slow down   b. move faster

7 If a machine suffers from **deterioration**, then it begins to _____.

   a. break down   b. be upgraded

8 When there are **obstacles** in a road, there are some things _____ the road.

   a. destroying   b. blocking

9 Mr. Anderson **restricted** Amy's access to the room by telling her she could _____.

   a. not enter it   b. work in there anytime

10 A person who is in **grave** danger is in a _____ situation.

   a. bad   b. safe

Chapter **07**

Rhetorical Purpose

▋ About the Question

Rhetorical Purpose questions focus on the reasons that certain information is included in the passage. You are asked to answer a question about why the author decided to write about something in the passage. The function of the material rather than its meaning is important for these kinds of questions. The information asked about in these questions is always included in a small section of the passage. There are 1-2 Rhetorical Purpose questions for each passage.

Recognizing Rhetorical Purpose questions:

- The author discusses "X" in paragraph 2 in order to . . .

- Why does the author mention "X"?

- The author uses "X" as an example of . . .

Other Rhetorical Purpose questions ask about the function or purpose of an entire paragraph. The questions are phrased like this:

- Paragraph 4 supports which of the following ideas about . . . ?

- Paragraphs 2 and 3 support which of the following ideas about . . . ?

- What is the author's purpose in paragraph 4 of the passage?

Helpful hints for answering the questions correctly:

- Read only the paragraph that is mentioned in the question itself. Then, think about how the topic mentioned in the question relates to that paragraph or the entire passage.

- The words that are used in the answer choices, particularly the verbs, are very important when you try to find the answer. Look for words such as *define, illustrate, explain, argue, compare, contrast, criticize, refute, note, example,* and *function.*

- There is a special emphasis on these questions. Some questions ask about entire sentences, not just words or phrases.

Roman Aqueducts

　　The Romans were among the most advanced of all the ancient civilizations. Their towns and cities, for example, frequently had running water, indoor plumbing, and sewage systems. Even in places far from abundant sources of fresh water, the Romans managed to provide water. They did this primarily through their aqueduct system. The city of Rome had up to eleven aqueducts providing its people with their daily water needs. There were hundreds of other aqueducts located all throughout the empire. Some ran above ground while others were located beneath it. While most aqueducts were a few kilometers long, several, such as the Aqua Augusta in Italy, were more than fifty kilometers in length. The quality of engineering was such that after the Roman Empire fell in the fifth century, some aqueducts remained in use for centuries afterward. Even today, the remains of some of them can be seen dotting the countryside in Europe.

Why does the author mention "the Aqua Augusta"?

Ⓐ　To note that its remains can be seen today

Ⓑ　To claim that it provided Rome with water

Ⓒ　To give an example of an underground aqueduct

Ⓓ　To point out that it was a very long aqueduct

❘ Answer Explanation ❘

Choice Ⓓ is the correct answer. The passage reads, "While most aqueducts were a few kilometers long, several, such as the Aqua Augusta in Italy, were more than fifty kilometers in length." The author therefore mentions that Aqua Augusta for the purpose of pointing out how long it was.

A | The Dewey Decimal System

🎧 CH07_2A

In the second half of the nineteenth century, libraries began springing up around the Western world. While most of them carried similar books, each had their own way of cataloging the material they housed. Some individuals began devising ways to unify the ordering methods of libraries. One such classification method was created by American librarian Melvil Dewey. In 1876, he published a pamphlet explaining his system, which became known as the Dewey Decimal System.

His method was a success. By the mid-1800s, libraries across the United States were using it. Today, it is used by more than 200,000 libraries in around 130 countries. The system is numerical and utilizes groupings of ten to **categorize** all types of information. Dewey came up with ten major classes, each of which received a number from zero to nine. The categories in the major classes included religion, science, and literature. For every class, Dewey created ten divisions, and each had ten sections.

The result was that every book had at least three numbers as its **call number**. For example, Dewey used the number 941 to represent the history of the British Isles. Nine represented the major class of history, four was the division of Europe, and one was for the British Isles. He then added a decimal point and one, two, or three more numbers to narrow down the subject fields even more. This resulted in a logical and easily used system that remains popular to this day.

*categorize: to classify; to organize by putting into various groupings
*call number: a number on a library book that is used to identify and locate it

---

1 In paragraph 1, why does the author mention "American librarian Melvil Dewey"?

   Ⓐ To explain his role in creating a categorization method

   Ⓑ To point out that he worked in a library for many years

   Ⓒ To credit him as the author of a pamphlet on libraries

   Ⓓ To claim he made the only classification method of books

2 In paragraph 2, the author uses "religion, science, and literature" as examples of

   Ⓐ topics which Melvil Dewey was particularly interested in

   Ⓑ subjects that were major categories in the Dewey Decimal System

   Ⓒ minor divisions according to the Dewey Decimal System

   Ⓓ fields of study that received the number 9 in Dewey's system

---

Vocabulary

- _____ = to make a list or record of something
- _____ = to create; to make
- _____ = a booklet
- _____ = to make small in size; to focus on

The Neolithic Period

The Neolithic Period happened at the conclusion of the Stone Age and lasted from roughly 10,000 B.C. to 3000 B.C., when humans took the first steps toward establishing modern civilization. During this period, humans made copious advances, such as creating more sophisticated stone tools and weapons and learning the arts of agriculture and <u>animal husbandry</u>. Furthermore, pottery and weaving became commonplace while people started dwelling in small villages and towns.

For approximately 2.5 million years, humans had utilized stone tools and weapons that were simple implements created by chipping flakes off stones. However, by 10,000 B.C., people in several locations worldwide had mastered the art of stone grinding. This permitted them to employ hard stones to grind and polish softer ones into more efficient tools and weapons. These improved implements were used until around 3000 B.C., when how to make bronze was discovered.

Another feature of the Neolithic Period was farming, which was initially learned in the Middle East around 10,000 B.C. Early farmed crops included wheat and millet, which were bred from wild plants, and people domesticated animals such as sheep, goats, cattle, and horses. The development of pottery and weaving provided vessels and baskets for carrying and storing food supplies. These improvements tied people to the land, making them depend upon it for food, and resulted in them abandoning their <u>hunter-gatherer lifestyles</u> and establishing permanent settlements, the first of which were in Mesopotamia, Egypt, China, and the Indus Valley.

*animal husbandry: the taming, raising, and breeding of animals, especially those living on farms
*hunter-gatherer lifestyle: a way of living in which a person hunts for food and gathers fruits, grains, vegetables, and other vegetation to eat

---

1   The author discusses "stone grinding" in paragraph 2 in order to

Ⓐ explain how it created better tools and weapons than bronze

Ⓑ show the way that early humans made swords and farming implements

Ⓒ mention that it and farming were learned at around the same time

Ⓓ describe its usefulness to people living in the Neolithic Period

2   In paragraph 3, the author uses "Mesopotamia, Egypt, China, and the Indus Valley" as examples of

Ⓐ some places where humans first began to establish early civilizations

Ⓑ the locations of early Neolithic communities discovered by archaeologists

Ⓒ settlements in which improvements in farming and animal husbandry were made

Ⓓ areas in which many hunter-gatherers lived for thousands of years

Vocabulary

- _____ = numerous
- _____ = a tool
- _____ = to tame an animal
- _____ = to give up; to stop doing something

C | The Orbits of the Inner Planets

The solar system's inner planets are Mercury, Venus, Earth, and Mars. They are the four planets closest to the sun and have numerous differences from Jupiter, Saturn, Uranus, and Neptune, which are the outer planets. The inner planets are rocky in nature, which is unlike the gaseous outer planets. They are also fairly small and lack the rings which the outer planets have. Finally, the orbits of the inner planets are tighter and much shorter in duration than those of the outer planets.

Mercury is the closest planet to the sun so has the shortest orbit, taking only eighty-eight Earth days to complete its year. Mercury's orbit is highly **eccentric**, with its distance from the sun varying from anywhere between forty-six and seventy million kilometers. Interestingly, the planet **rotates** on its axis so slowly that a day on Mercury lasts fifty-nine Earth days. The duration of a single orbit of the next closest planet, Venus, is 225 Earth days. Like Mercury, it rotates slowly. In fact, a day on Venus lasts longer than a year as a single rotation of the planet takes 243 Earth days to complete.

Earth's orbit is longer, requiring 365 days to accomplish, while its daily rotation takes only twenty-four hours to complete. Mars has the longest orbit of all four inner planets at 687 days, and it has a daily rotation of almost twenty-five hours. Like Mercury, it has an eccentric orbit, so its distance from the sun varies a great amount during its orbit.

*eccentric: not consistent; erratic
*rotate: to spin around in a circle

---

1 The author discusses "the outer planets" in paragraph 1 in order to

Ⓐ provide their names as well as details on their rotations

Ⓑ contrast their characteristics with those of the inner planets

Ⓒ describe the manner in which they orbit the sun

Ⓓ argue that they have less eccentric orbits than the inner planets

2 In paragraph 2, why does the author mention "a day on Venus"?

Ⓐ To describe the temperature changes during that time

Ⓑ To compare a day on Venus with a day on Mars

Ⓒ To state that it is longer than an orbit around the sun

Ⓓ To point out that it takes less time than a day on Mercury

Vocabulary

- _____ = the sun and all the objects, including the planets and the moons, that orbit it
- _____ = a length of time
- _____ = the line on which a rotating object turns
- _____ = to finish; to do

■ Mapping

The following chart shows the structure of the passage. Fill in the blanks with the appropriate words.

The Orbits of the Inner Planets

Inner planets are Mercury, ❶ _____ , Earth, and Mars

- are rocky, small, and lack ❷ _____ like outer planets have

- have tighter and shorter ❸ _____ than outer planets

Mercury and Venus are ❹ _____ planets

- Mercury ❺ _____ one year in eighty-eight Earth days

- has highly ❻ _____ orbit

- day on Mercury lasts fifty-nine Earth days

- Venus orbits sun in ❼ _____ days

- day on Venus lasts ❽ _____ Earth days

Earth and Mars have ❾ _____ orbits

- Earth takes 365 days to complete orbit

- one day is twenty-four hours

- Mars orbits sun in ❿ _____ days

- day on Mars lasts ⓫ _____ hours

■ Summary

The following is a summary of the passage. Fill in the blanks with the appropriate words.

The ❶ _____ planets are Mercury, Venus, Earth, and Mars. They are small, rocky planets that lack rings and have tight, short ❷ _____ .

❸ _____ is the closest to the sun and takes eighty-six days to complete its orbit. It has an eccentric orbit and ❹ _____ slowly, so one day there lasts fifty-nine Earth days. ❺ _____ orbits the sun in 225 days and takes 243 Earth days to complete one rotation. ❻ _____ completes its orbit in 365 days. It rotates once every twenty-four hours. ❼ _____ requires 687 days to orbit the sun. A ❽ _____ on Mars lasts twenty-five hours.

A | Kurt Lewin and Behavior

🎧 CH07_3A

Kurt Lewin was a German psychologist famous for his work in the field of social psychology. Born to a middle-class family in 1890, he served in the German army in World War I. After being wounded in battle, he returned home and later received a PhD in psychology from the University of Berlin. In 1933, he and his family departed Germany for the United States. He spent the remainder of his life there working at various universities until his death in 1947.

Today, Lewin is primarily known for his work on human behavior. He was a student of the Gestalt school of thinking, in which he believed that behavior was a result of the entirety of a person's experience. In particular, he thought that human behavior was the product of both a person's personality and the environment in which the person lived. This environment included social **parameters** such as laws and the accepted modes of social interaction. Lewin created an equation to express this: $B = f(P, E)$. According to it, behavior (B) is a function (f) of personality (P) and environment (E).

The main theme of his notion was field theory. It stated that human behavior was influenced by fields of forces. These fields exist around a person in a space which Lewin called the person's life space. He felt that human behavior is purposeful and motivated by needs and desires. As a person moves to achieve them, surrounding the person are different fields of forces that are dynamically interacting with that individual. Some are attracting the person while others are repelling the person. The blending of these forces creates a tension in which the person either approaches or avoids a particular situation. How the person reacts to each field determines that individual's behavior. Lewin further believed that changes in the fields can force a person to learn and adapt to them.

Lewin not only theorized on human behavior but also devised experiments to study it. In his experiments, he created situations and then manipulated the variables to see if there would be different outcomes. Action research was the name that he gave this way of experimenting. In addition, Lewin used diagrams and geometric figures to demonstrate the patterns of relationships between the fields which influenced human behavior.

Today, Lewin's work is applied to a wide range of fields inside and outside of psychology. His theories on behavior have also influenced thinking on how groups behave. He even **coined** the term group dynamics to describe intergroup relations. Lewin's theories have been of particular importance in the field of education, especially to study and understand child development, motivation, and social behavior.

*parameter: a guideline; a limit
*coin: to create something new, especially a word or expression

Vocabulary

- _____ = how a person acts
- _____ = a manner or method
- _____ = to push away
- _____ = to create; to come up with

1 In paragraph 2, the author's description of Kurt Lewin's work mentions which of the following?

   (A) The mathematical equation he borrowed to explain his work

   (B) His thoughts on what caused humans to behave the way they do

   (C) The manner in which human laws altered the behavior of people

   (D) How much the Gestalt school of thinking affected him

Negative Factual Information Question

2 According to paragraph 3, which of the following is NOT true about field theory?

   (A) There are fields that attract people and none that repel them.

   (B) The life space is the place where various fields can be found.

   (C) There are fields around people that affect their behavior.

   (D) The fields determine how people respond in certain situations.

Rhetorical Purpose Question

3 The author discusses "Action research" in paragraph 4 in order to

   (A) give a name to the geometric research that Lewin did at times

   (B) describe the type of experiments that Lewin conducted on behavior

   (C) point out that Lewin's research contained mathematical formulas

   (D) argue that Lewin's method of research had a number of flaws in it

Prose Summary Question

4 An introductory sentence for a brief summary of the passage is provided below. Complete the summary by selecting the THREE answer choices that express the most important ideas of the passage. Some sentences do not belong because they express ideas that are not presented in the passage or are minor ideas in the passage.

Kurt Lewin conducted research in the field of social psychology and is mostly known for the work he did on human behavior.

ANSWER CHOICES

1 By using action research, Lewin was able to develop his theories on behavior by conducting experiments on people.

2 Lewin's work had a great amount of influence on the behaviorists of his day and is still important for individuals in child development.

3 The fields that Lewin believed existed around people could either attract or repel them depending on the situation.

4 Lewin spent the majority of his life doing his research while living in either Germany or the United States.

5 Lewin developed the idea of field theory, which attempted to explain why humans behave in certain manners.

6 It was Lewin's belief that a person's behavior was determined by both the environment and the individual's personality.

Coal

Millions of years ago, various plants and animals died, fell to the ground, and formed layers in sedimentary rock. Over time, intense heat and pressure transformed this biological matter into seams of fossilized carbon, which is better known as coal. There are four main types of coal: lignite, subbituminous, bituminous, and anthracite. Each kind formed on account of several factors, including the degrees of heat and pressure that acted upon them, the length of time they were buried, and the amount of time they took to become coal.

The four types of coal are classified as low-rank coal or high-rank coal. Lignite and subbituminous are low ranked whereas bituminous and anthracite are high ranked. Lignite has the lowest rank due to its brownish color, relative softness in comparison to the other types of coal, and poor burning qualities. **1** It is the youngest coal and has not been subjected to long periods of high heat and pressure. **2** Today, lignite is mostly used to generate electricity at power plants and to make fertilizer. **3** It comprises roughly seventeen percent of the world's known coal reserves. **4**

After much more time passes and more heat and pressure are applied, seams of lignite become subbituminous coal. It is darker and harder than lignite and contains between forty and fifty percent carbon. Subbituminous coal has little sulfur content compared to other types of coal, so it burns more cleanly than they do. It is mostly used in power generators, and roughly thirty percent of the world's coal reserves consist of it.

The next higher-ranked coal is bituminous coal. It has a carbon content of between sixty and eighty percent and is the most useful coal with the most applications. There are two separate types of bituminous coal: thermal and metallurgical. Thermal bituminous coal burns very well, so it is often used for the purpose of creating electricity at power plants as well as in certain industrial processes. Metallurgical bituminous coal, on the other hand, has ideal qualities for making coke, which can then be used to create iron and steel. Approximately fifty-two percent of the world's coal reserves are bituminous in nature.

As for anthracite, it is the hardest, blackest, and rarest of the types of coal and comprises only around one percent of the entire world's known coal reserves. It is the oldest kind of coal, having spent more time under pressure than the other types. Its high carbon content generates great heat and virtually no smoke when it is burned, making it ideal for domestic heating and various industrial uses.

*seam: a fairly thin level or line
*coke: the solid product that results when coal is distilled in an oven and which is made mostly of carbon

---

Vocabulary

- _____ = to create; to make
- _____ = a layer
- _____ = a use
- _____ = to make up

1   In paragraph 3, which of the following can be inferred about coal?

   Ⓐ A lot of pollution is produced when coal with sulfur is burned.

   Ⓑ Subbituminous coal is the most common type of coal in the world.

   Ⓒ Most coal is found in seams that are close to the surface.

   Ⓓ It is the most common type of fuel used by power generators.

Rhetorical Purpose Question

2   In paragraph 4, the author uses "Metallurgical bituminous coal" as an example of

   Ⓐ the kind of coal that is favored by power plants

   Ⓑ the more common type of bituminous coal

   Ⓒ the type of coal that has the most applications

   Ⓓ a kind of coal which is useful to the steel industry

Insert Text Question

3   Look at the four squares [■] that indicate where the following sentence could be added to the passage.

   It is, however, not as soft as peat, which is a type of sedimentary rock sometimes called brown coal.

Fill in a Table Question

4   Select the appropriate statements from the answer choices and match them to the type of coal to which they relate. TWO of the answer choices will NOT be used.

Lignite (Select 3)	Bituminous (Select 2)	Anthracite (Select 2)
•		
•	•	•
•	•	•
•		

STATEMENTS

☐1 Comprises around one third of the world's coal reserves

☐2 Is considered a low-rank type of coal

☐3 Has more uses than any other type of coal

☐4 Creates almost no smoke when it is burned

☐5 Does not burn as well as other types of coal

☐6 Has a darker color than any other kind of coal

☐7 Does not contain large amounts of sulfur

☐8 Has uses in the fertilizer industry

☐9 Is the most common type of coal in the world

The Environmental Impact of Farming

Ever since humans first learned how to farm the land more than 10,000 years ago, the crops they have harvested have ensured that mankind has not only survived but flourished. Yet despite the obvious benefits to people, farming has had mostly negative effects on the environment anywhere that it is practiced. Among the problems associated with the art of agriculture are the loss of animal habitats, soil erosion, and the overconsumption of water. Other issues include the polluting of both the land and the oceans with chemicals and the injecting of various types of noxious gases, including methane, into the atmosphere.

Before an area can be planted with crops, the land must be cleared of vegetation, which can be in the form of tall trees or small shrubs and bushes. However, there are numerous animals that make their homes in these places, so cutting down trees and digging up other plants deprives them of their natural habitats. Today, an enormous amount of land all around the world has been cleared for farming. In some places, this has resulted in extensive habitat loss for some animals. For instance, in Indonesia, large swaths of jungle have been cleared for palm oil plantations, which has resulted in the endangerment of many species, including elephants, rhinoceroses, and tigers. In Brazil, countless rainforest dwellers have lost their homes since Brazilian farmers started clearing the land for soybean farms and cattle ranches.

Once land has been cleared, soil erosion becomes an issue. Vegetation typically anchors soil due to its roots, but when the land is cleared to make it suitable for farming, the soil loses much of its cohesion. As new crops grow, the wind and rain may degrade the soil and carry away a sizable amount of topsoil. It is estimated that Brazil alone loses up to fifty-five million tons of topsoil each year. Worldwide, perhaps ten million hectares of arable land are degraded through erosion annually.

As soil erodes, it often moves into rivers, lakes, and oceans, where it blocks waterways and harms marine life. In extreme situations, the loss of soil can lead to the desertification of the land.

According to some experts, human water consumption for farming accounts for around seventy percent of all the fresh water people use. Much of this water is wasted when it leaks from substandard irrigation systems or is mishandled when applied to crops. Waste such as this has led to the lowering of water tables and the drying up of land and river systems. One consequence of irrigating land too much is that there is a large amount of water runoff into rivers, lakes, and oceans. This water often carries both eroded soil and chemicals such as pesticides and fertilizers. While pesticides are beneficial in that they kill harmful creatures which can damage or eat crops, they can also harm animals in addition to the pests that they are aimed at. As for fertilizers, they contain large quantities of nitrogen. When they enter the water system, they may have ruinous effects by causing algae blooms. These deplete the water of oxygen and cause other life forms to die.

Another problem is that farming can often release various gases into the atmosphere. One of these is methane, which can be harmful. Methane is actually produced in large amounts by the digestive systems of many animals kept as livestock. In addition, when farmers burn the land on which they farm, other harmful particles can be released into the environment. These can contaminate the air and cause harm to humans and other animals.

*Glossary

noxious: poisonous

swath: a strip

1 According to paragraph 1, farming harms the environment because

(A) it provides new types of habitats for animals to live in

(B) it can cause the land, air, and water to become unclean

(C) it removes nutrients from the soil and makes it infertile

(D) it causes harm to the land due to irrigation systems

2 In paragraph 2, why does the author mention "palm oil plantations"?

(A) To point out that they have more advantages than disadvantages

(B) To criticize the countries that allow them to become so large

(C) To compare the damage they cause with that of other farms in Asia

(D) To name some of the animals that they have directly harmed

3 The word "cohesion" in the passage is closest in meaning to

(A) attractiveness

(B) fertility

(C) solidity

(D) appearance

4 In paragraph 3, the author uses "the desertification of the land" as an example of

(A) something that often happens after a few years of farming

(B) a phenomenon that is primarily taking place in Brazil

(D) the most dangerous issue that is caused by farming

(D) a problem that can be caused by the erosion of the soil

5   According to paragraph 3, which of the following is NOT true about topsoil?

    (A) It can be washed away due to the action of water.

    (B) Most crops are not able to grow well without it.

    (C) It can be eroded and then swept into bodies of water.

    (D) The loss of it may reduce the quality of the soil.

6   Which of the sentences below best expresses the essential information in the highlighted sentence in the passage? Incorrect answer choices change the meaning in important ways or leave out essential information.

While pesticides are beneficial in that they kill harmful creatures which can damage or eat crops, they can also harm animals in addition to the pests that they are aimed at.

    (A) The best way to kill animals that harm or eat crops is to spray the crops with pesticides in order to kill the creatures.

    (B) Pesticides kill all types of animals, including both pests and other animals which they are not intended to harm.

    (C) Even though pesticides are used on many crops, they do not always stop creatures from damaging them.

    (D) Because so many pesticides are used these days, they kill large numbers of animals that are not considered pests.

7   Which of the following can be inferred from paragraph 4 about the water used for farming?

    (A) It is possible to prevent a great amount of it from being wasted.

    (B) The overuse of it is causing the levels of some seas to decline.

    (C) The cost of irrigating land is causing the prices of crops to rise.

    (D) It cannot be purified later because there are too many chemicals in it.

8   According to paragraph 5, which of the following is true about methane?

    (A) The smell that it gives off is easily recognizable.

    (B) It can be produced whenever farmers burn the land.

    (C) Large concentrations of it have been known to explode at times.

    (D) Animals are responsible for producing large amounts of it.

9 **Directions:** An introductory sentence for a brief summary of the passage is provided below. Complete the summary by selecting the THREE answer choices that express the most important ideas of the passage. Some sentences do not belong because they express ideas that are not presented in the passage or are minor ideas in the passage. **This question is worth 2 points.**

Drag your answer choices to the spaces where they belong. To remove an answer choice, click on it. To review the passage, click on VIEW TEXT.

Farming can have a large number of negative effects on the environment.

-
-
-

ANSWER CHOICES

☐1 Various irrigation methods have helped farmers grow crops but have also depleted groundwater levels in many places.

☐2 Many animals in places around the world are losing their homes due to the need for people to farm the land.

☐3 Because of farming, humans have survived in great numbers but have also caused damage to the land they live on.

☐4 Fertilizers cost large amounts of money and do not often succeed at making the soil become more fertile.

☐5 Clearing the land for farming can sometimes lead to the erosion of topsoil and cause the land to become desert at times.

☐6 Water usage for farming can deplete supplies in some places while runoff can add pollutants to waterways.

Sheep Wool Manufacturing

The sheep was among the first animals domesticated by humans thousands of years ago. This hardy animal has several characteristics that made it ideal for domestication. It was fairly docile, it fed on different types of plants, it could survive harsh weather conditions, it was a source of milk and meat, and its hide was useful. Over time, people began to regard the sheep not merely as a food source but also as a renewable source of wool for manufacturing clothing. Sheep wool has several advantages over other animal furs and hairs, among them being excellent thermal characteristics. Sheep wool fibers also cling together well, which allows for the easy spinning of wool into longer threads of yarn. Eventually, the mass-processing of wool for clothing became a major focus of the Industrial Revolution in the 1700s, and it continues to be an important part of the textile industry in modern times.

There are numerous breeds of sheep that have different types of wool, but all wool manufacturing starts with shearing. This takes place once a year—normally in spring—with each sheep producing between two and eight kilograms of wool. The wool is removed with clippers and is still done by hand with electric devices on many sheep ranches today. ■ Wool from different parts of the sheep has varying characteristics, so after shearing, it is graded and sorted into piles. ■ Once these steps have been taken, sheep ranchers sell the wool in lots to wool buyers, who are experts capable of distinguishing the quality of the material. ■ They look for high-quality wool with the characteristics needed to make fine clothing. ■ Coarser wool is used to manufacture carpets and heavy apparel such as jackets and sweaters.

Sheep wool is dirty, so it must be cleaned and scoured to remove impurities such as vegetation, dirt, and grease. The most common method for cleaning wool is to soak it in baths containing water, soap, and an alkali such as soda ash. The wool then passes through a series of rollers to squeeze out the water yet is not completely dry. Once the cleaning process is complete, lanolin, a waxy substance produced by sheep and used by the cosmetics industry, can be extracted from the wool and sold.

The next step in wool manufacturing is carding. Once done by hand, it is completed by machines nowadays. The wool passes through a series of metal teeth that remove any remaining residue and additionally straighten the wool fibers into slivers that can be more easily spun into yarn. To produce wool of higher quality, another carding step separates short and long wool fibers. After carding, the wool is spun into yarn as the wool fibers are drawn together on a spindle or cone. This process was once arduous and slow when done by hand, but gradually over time, efficient machines were invented to increase the speed and quality of production.

When the spinning is complete, the wool is sent to weavers, who utilize large looms to manufacture fabric from it. The various types of fabric are the results of different qualities of wool produced by sheep. For example, the merino sheep produces fine wool fibers used in high-quality clothing manufacturing. After the weaving is done, the fabric is soaked in water to make the fibers bond more closely together. The final step involves dying. Sheep wool easily absorbs dyes, allowing it to be transformed into an array of colors. Once dry, the wool is finally ready to be used to create various textiles.

*Glossary

alkali: a base that is capable of neutralizing an acid and turning it into salt
spindle: a rod on a spinning wheel on which thread is wound

10 In paragraph 1, the author implies that sheep wool

(A) can be used to create fabric that is more expensive than other types of cloth

(B) has various qualities which allow it to help keep people using it warm

(C) has only been used to create textiles since the Industrial Revolution

(D) can be difficult to weave but creates textiles that are strong and waterproof

11 According to paragraph 1, which of the following is true about sheep wool?

(A) It has been mass-produced to create textiles from the 1700s to the present day.

(B) It is collected by farmers on every continent on the planet where sheep are raised.

(C) It was not used to make textiles until the beginning of the Industrial Revolution.

(D) It will become cheaper in price in the future as it is produced on a larger scale.

12 The word "shearing" in the passage is closest in meaning to

(A) culling

(B) categorizing

(C) breeding

(D) shaving

13 Which of the following can be inferred from paragraph 2 about sheep wool?

(A) Some wool that is taken from certain parts of the sheep is of no use.

(B) Sheep that produce large amounts of wool typically have coarse wool.

(C) It has certain characteristics that can be identified by various individuals.

(D) Sheep wool that is high in quality is used to make clothing and carpets.

14 In paragraph 3, the author uses "soda ash" as an example of

- (A) a waxy substance found in sheep wool that has value to the cosmetics industry
- (B) a material that is useful for removing dirt from sheep wool and making it clean
- (C) an impurity that is commonly found in sheep wool and needs to be removed
- (D) an alkali that assists in the removal of lanolin from sheep wool

15 The word "arduous" in the passage is closest in meaning to

- (A) expensive
- (B) complicated
- (C) plausible
- (D) difficult

16 According to paragraph 5, sheep wool must be soaked in water because

- (A) it helps the dye that will be applied to the wool to be absorbed
- (B) more impurities need to be removed from the wool at that stage in the process
- (C) it helps the individual fibers in the wool connect more strongly with one another
- (D) doing so improves the overall quality and softness of the wool

17 Look at the four squares [■] that indicate where the following sentence could be added to the passage.

Wool of the finest quality comes from the sides and shoulders of the sheep.

Where would the sentence best fit?

Click on a square [■] to add the sentence to the passage.

18 **Directions**: An introductory sentence for a brief summary of the passage is provided below. Complete the summary by selecting the THREE answer choices that express the most important ideas of the passage. Some sentences do not belong because they express ideas that are not presented in the passage or are minor ideas in the passage. **This question is worth 2 points.**

There are several steps involved in preparing sheep wool to be used to make clothing and other textiles.

-
-
-

ANSWER CHOICES

[1] After sheep wool is graded and sorted, it must be cleaned in order to remove various impurities from it.

[2] Some sheep produce large quantities of wool whereas others only produce a couple of kilograms of it each year.

[3] Once sheep wool is turned into fabric, it can be dyed a variety of colors thanks to its absorbent qualities.

[4] Depending upon how high in quality it is, sheep wool can be used to make clothes, carpets, or sweaters.

[5] Carding straightens sheep wool, and then it is spun into yarn either by hand or by machines.

[6] The use of sheep wool for textiles has been going on ever since the Industrial Revolution began.

◼ Vocabulary Review

A Complete each sentence with the appropriate word from the box.

comprised	catalog	repel	generate	consequences

1 Actions have _____, so be sure to act in a proper manner.

2 Bug spray can _____ insects and prevent them from biting people.

3 The group is _____ of people who work in various industries.

4 Scientists are busy trying to _____ the new species they found in the rainforest.

5 The power plant is able to _____ enough electricity to supply the entire city.

B Complete each sentence with the correct answer.

1 Something that lasts for the **duration** of a show takes place until the show _____.

   a. starts   b. finishes

2 All of the **impurities** in the liquid caused it to be _____.

   a. pure   b. unclean

3 When you **remove** the garbage, please be sure to _____ somewhere.

   a. take it away   b. recycle it

4 The group wants to **devise** a plan by _____ an idea.

   a. rejecting   b. thinking of

5 When a man **accomplishes** a goal, he _____ his objective.

   a. achieves   b. considers

6 Factories that **manufacture** computers _____ them by using various parts.

   a. design   b. produce

7 If a woman has **copious** amounts of money, she is likely _____.

   a. rich   b. poor

8 Someone whose **behavior** is good _____ like a good person.

   a. thinks   b. acts

9 When people learned to **domesticate** animals, they _____ sheep, cows, and chickens.

   a. tamed   b. ate

10 Deanna **deprived** the workers of the employee lounge by _____ it for a couple of weeks.

   a. closing   b. repairing

Chapter **08**

Insert Text

■ About the Question

Insert Text questions focus on an additional sentence that could be included in the passage. You are asked to read a new sentence and then to determine where in the passage it could be added. These questions require you to consider several factors, including grammar, logic, flow, and connecting words, when you are trying to determine the correct answer. There are 0-1 Insert Text questions for each passage. There is a special emphasis on these questions. Almost every passage now has 1 Insert Text question.

Recognizing Insert Text questions:

- Look at the four squares [■] that indicate where the following sentence could be added to the passage.

  [You will see a sentence in bold.]

  Where would the sentence best fit?

Helpful hints for answering the questions correctly:

- The squares are always placed after four consecutive sentences.

- Try reading the passage to yourself by adding the sentence after each square. That can help you determine where it should be added.

- Many times, the sentence to be added contains a connecting word or phrase. Pay attention to words or phrases such as *in addition, for instance, for example, therefore, consequently, on the other hand, finally,* and *as a result*. These connecting words and phrases can affect the flow of the passage.

Pampas Grass

The Pampas is a low-lying region of land that is located in parts of both Argentina and Brazil. Most of the area has a temperate climate, but some parts have semiarid weather. A large amount of the region is susceptible to forest fires; therefore few forests grow there. Instead, much of the Pampas is covered with various species of grasses. Among the best known of these is pampas grass. ■ There are more than twenty species of pampas grass, many of which can grow to be more than three meters in height. ■ Pampas grass is considered an ornamental grass because of the enormous silver-colored plumes that emerge from it at the end of summer. ■ Appreciated for its beauty, pampas grass has been exported to countries around the world and is currently cultivated in places in North America, Europe, and Asia. ■

Look at the four squares [■] that indicate where the following sentence could be added to the passage.

The flowers of some species can be nearly half a meter long.

Where would the sentence best fit?

| Answer Explanation |

The third square is the correct answer. The sentence before the third square reads, "Pampas grass is considered an ornamental grass because of the enormous silver-colored plumes that emerge from it at the end of summer." First, note that the sentence in the passage describes plumes, which are the flowers of the pampas grass. It also points out the great size of the plumes by calling them "enormous." The sentence to be added mentions "flowers," which refers to the plumes. It also states that the flowers "can be nearly half a meter long," which is an enormous size for flowers. Therefore, the two sentences go well together.

A | The Stratosphere

🎧 CH08_2A

The Earth's atmosphere has four main layers, the second of which is the stratosphere. Beneath it is the troposphere while the mesosphere is located above it. The stratosphere extends from an average of ten kilometers above sea level up to fifty kilometers above the planet's surface. The height where the stratosphere begins differs. For instance, it starts twenty kilometers above the surface at the <u>equator</u> but only seven kilometers above the ground at the North and South poles.

Due to the dry air with little moisture, the stratosphere has few clouds. Interestingly, the higher the altitude in the stratosphere, the higher the temperature. This is unusual because the temperature usually decreases at higher altitudes in the other layers. **1** However, the stratosphere contains the <u>ozone</u> layer, which protects the Earth from the sun's ultraviolet radiation. **2** As the sun's rays hit the ozone layer, their heat gets absorbed, causing the temperature to rise. **3** The temperature at the top of the stratosphere is nearly zero degrees Celsius, which is much warmer than the temperature at its lower levels. **4**

Another feature of the stratosphere is that the air there is roughly one thousand times thinner than it is at sea level. **5** The air is also stable with little turbulence. **6** Due to these conditions, it is an ideal place for commercial jet aircraft to fly since the thin air reduces drag and increases fuel efficiency. **7** As a result, many jets fly at low levels of the stratosphere approximately nine to twelve kilometers above the ground. **8**

*equator: the imaginary line that runs around the center of the Earth from east to west
*ozone: a form of oxygen in which three molecules of it are joined to one another

---

1 Look at the four squares [**1** – **4**] that indicate where the following sentence could be added to the passage.

It can be more than fifty degrees below zero where the stratosphere meets the troposphere.

2 Look at the four squares [**5** – **8**] that indicate where the following sentence could be added to the passage.

This enables jets to fly faster than if they remain in the layer beneath the stratosphere.

Vocabulary

* _____ = to stretch out in a certain direction
* _____ = to soak up
* _____ = the irregular movement of the atmosphere
* _____ = resistance to movement through the air

Red-Tailed Hawk Migration

The red-tailed hawk ranks among the most common birds of prey in North America. It resides from Alaska in the north to Central America in the south and may even be found living on islands in the Caribbean Sea. Of the sixteen subspecies of hawks, those living in warm southern lands do not migrate, but those dwelling in cold northern lands annually fly south for winter. Therefore, southern lands see an increase in the number of hawks each year.

Red-tailed hawk chicks **fledge** at around six to seven weeks of age and quickly improve their flying skills. When colder weather arrives, these juveniles are the first to migrate south and are subsequently followed by the older mating pairs. **1** Juveniles generally fly farther south than more mature hawks. **2** The southern migration takes place from August to January. **3** The departure time depends upon how far north the hawks reside. **4** The return migration in spring happens from February to early June.

The hawks prefer to soar as they fly, so they use **updrafts** from the ground to carry them long distances. **5** There are several travel corridors which the hawks make use of when they migrate south. **6** Found along ridge lines, these flyways have good updrafts, making the process faster and easier. **7** However, not every hawk follows these migratory routes, especially since they are flying south from places virtually everywhere on the North American continent. **8**

*fledge: to be raised until one is capable of flight for the first time
*updraft: the upward movement of air

---

1 Look at the four squares [**1** – **4**] that indicate where the following sentence could be added to the passage.

They are less able to tolerate lower temperatures than older hawks, so young birds require warmer places.

2 Look at the four squares [**5** – **8**] that indicate where the following sentence could be added to the passage.

They tend to avoid migrating over open water due to the lack of air moving upward there.

Vocabulary

- _____ = a small group within a species
- _____ = a youth; an immature organism
- _____ = to fly high in the sky without any visible movement
- _____ = nearly; practically

C | African Mangrove Forests

Mangrove trees grow in tropical swamps and other watery areas and have roots that descend from their branches. The resulting mangrove forests, which are created where many of these trees grow, are densely **tangled** areas that create unique ecosystems. In Africa, around 3.2 million hectares of coastline contain mangrove forests. **1** The majority are found along the continent's western and southeastern coasts as well as on the island of Madagascar. **2** Mangrove forests straddle the boundary between freshwater and saltwater habitats. **3** They provide an abundance of riches for people and wildlife while also serving as shields against storms and large waves. **4**

More than fifteen species of mangrove trees grow in Africa and serve as homes for both land and sea animals. Monkeys live in their branches while manatees dwell in the water nearby the trees' roots. The mud beds the trees' roots systems lie in are home to a diverse group of shellfish and crustaceans. In addition, countless species of fish and waterfowl make their homes in mangrove forests. Humans also use mangrove forests for their wildlife, wood, and diverse plant life.

5 African mangrove forests protect coastal regions when there is **inclement** weather. **6** For instance, mangroves are capable of absorbing the destructive forces of rushing water caused by hurricanes, typhoons, and tsunamis. **7** Unfortunately, mangrove forests in Africa are in danger from pollution and human overuse as roughly thirty percent of the mangrove forests there have vanished in the last twenty-five years. **8**

*tangled: twisted; snarled
*inclement: extreme; rough

---

1 Look at the four squares [**1** – **4**] that indicate where the following sentence could be added to the passage.

One reason for this is their ability to grow well in brackish water that would kill most other types of vegetation.

2 Look at the four squares [**5** – **8**] that indicate where the following sentence could be added to the passage.

A study conducted in 2003 showed that a small stand of mangrove trees can reduce the destructive force of a large wave by ninety percent.

Vocabulary

- _____ = an area of wet, spongy land that often has trees growing in it
- _____ = to be located between two things
- _____ = birds that live in or around water
- _____ = a very large wave often produced by an earthquake or underwater volcanic eruption

Mapping

The following chart shows the structure of the passage. Fill in the blanks with the appropriate words.

African Mangrove Forests

Grow in swampy and ❶ _____ areas near coast

- most on ❷ _____ and southeastern coasts of Africa
- are on ❸ _____ between freshwater and saltwater habitats

15 species of mangroves in Africa

- homes for land and sea animals
- monkeys and ❹ _____ live there
- ❺ _____ and shellfish live in mud beds
- fish and ❻ _____ live in them
- humans use forests

Protect coastal regions from bad ❼ _____

- can ❽ _____ destructive forces of rushing water
- keep land safe from hurricanes, typhoons, and ❾ _____
- being polluted and overused by humans so have ❿ _____ in number

Summary

The following is a summary of the passage. Fill in the blanks with the appropriate words.

Mangrove trees grow near the ❶ _____ in both western and southeastern Africa and in Madagascar. They live on the boundary between ❷ _____ and saltwater habitats. There are more than ❸ _____ species of mangroves in Africa. Both land and sea animals live in mangrove ❹ _____. These include monkeys, manatees, shellfish, ❺ _____, fish, and waterfowl. Mangrove forests also ❻ _____ the land from inclement weather. Rushing water from hurricanes, typhoons, and tsunamis can be ❼ _____ by them. Unfortunately, they are being polluted and overused by humans, so mangrove forests are ❽ _____.

A | Ancient Irrigation Methods

🎧 CH08_3A

The process of bringing water to crops in areas that receive an insufficient amount of rainfall is irrigation. There is evidence that the ancient Mesopotamians, Egyptians, and Chinese all had extensive irrigation systems. These enabled the people in those societies to establish flourishing civilizations since they could grow large quantities of food.

Mesopotamia developed along the banks of two great rivers, the Tigris and the Euphrates. To create farmland, the people first drained swamps and built canals in dry land between and alongside the rivers. Next, they made dikes by the riverbanks. When the water levels were high, the Mesopotamians opened gaps in the dikes to allow water to pour into the canals and to spread across the land. **1** When the water levels were low, they hauled water from the rivers to the canals by using buckets on the ends of ropes that were attached to a counterweighted pivot boom, a device known as a **swape**. **2** The Mesopotamians had to carefully manage their water resources lest the land become too salty. **3** They therefore enacted many laws concerning water usage and spent countless man-hours of labor on their enormous irrigation system. **4**

The people of Egypt had methods similar to those of the Mesopotamians as they employed both canals and swapes to obtain water from the Nile River. However, at times, the yearly flooding of the Nile was too powerful, so it destroyed lowlands. The Egyptians thus tended to grow their crops on relatively high lands nearby the river. They also surrounded their fields with dikes. When the yearly flood arrived, they used **sluices** in the dikes that diverted water from the Nile through short canals into flat-bottomed basins. They let the water remain in the basins for forty to sixty days before draining it. The silt the water carried settled at the bottoms of the basins and provided nutrients that helped crops grow. The key to the Egyptian irrigation system was timing. They had to know when the floodwaters were coming so that they could open the sluice gates at the correct time.

In China and many other Asian lands, rice was the staple of their diet for thousands of years. Rice requires plenty of water to grow though. One method of irrigation that the Chinese discovered was terrace farming. This involved the carving out of flat areas of land on hillsides to make them resemble a series of steps. When it rained, water got trapped in the areas which were flat. By carefully managing the water levels, the Chinese were able to keep some of their fields wet and others dry during the various stages of the rice-growing season.

*swape: a long pole attached to a tall post that can raise and lower buckets for the purpose of moving water
*sluice: an artificial channel that is used to move water to prevent flooding

Vocabulary

- _____ = not enough
- _____ = a hole or a break in something solid
- _____ = land that is lower than other land around it
- _____ = a natural or manmade hollow area with water in it

1   The word "flourishing" in the passage is closest in meaning to

(A) expanding

(B) thriving

(C) advanced

(D) urban

2   According to paragraph 3, the crops the Egyptians grew were on elevated land because

(A) the land got higher each year due to the accumulation of silt

(B) doing so was easier for the Egyptians to irrigate the land

(C) Egyptian technology let them raise water to higher levels easily

(D) it kept them from being harmed when the Nile River flooded

3   Look at the four squares [■] that indicate where the following sentence could be added to the passage.

Thanks to the time invested in these projects, they managed to harvest enough crops each year to support large populations of people in their urban centers.

4   Select the appropriate statements from the answer choices and match them to the ancient civilization to which they relate. TWO of the answer choices will NOT be used.

Mesopotamia (Select 3)	Egypt (Select 2)	China (Select 2)
•	•	•
•	•	•
•		

STATEMENTS

1   Made use of sediment carried downriver by water

2   Developed a method of irrigating crops grown on hills

3   Made people carry buckets of water from rivers to fields

4   Had regulations governing how water could be used

5   Needed large amounts of water to grow rice

6   Got rid of swampland by removing water from it

7   Had the most advanced irrigation techniques in ancient times

8   Put dikes all around their fields to prevent flooding

9   Built canals that were between two large rivers

William Gilbert (1836-1911) and Arthur Sullivan (1842-1900) were the two most famous comic opera writers and composers of Victorian England. They are renowned for their stage works, which include *HMS Pinafore*, *The Pirates of Penzance*, and *The Mikado*. Their works have an absurdist quality which found humor in flouting the strict social norms of the time. Altogether, they penned fourteen comic operas between 1871 and 1896. Their compositions were performed around the globe and are still put on today.

Gilbert was the dramatist of the pair and wrote the scenarios for their comic operas while Sullivan composed the music. Prior to meeting in 1869, each of them had enjoyed somewhat successful careers in the theater world. They collaborated on their first comic opera, *Thespis*, in 1871. It was a minor success, but the duo did not have the opportunity to work together again for four years. The occasion for their reunion was the writing of the comic opera *Trial by Jury* in 1875. It was a smash hit, and the pair suddenly found themselves in high demand.

Their next work was the somewhat less successful *The Sorcerer* in 1877. But their greatest works, *HMS Pinafore* in 1878 and *The Pirates of Penzance* in 1879, quickly followed. Both operas were highly successful, which put the duo at the peak of the English theater world. Minor hits followed until they once again struck gold with *The Mikado* in 1885. Their last major success was *The Gondoliers* in 1889.

Gilbert and Sullivan lived in a society that was extremely strict, and their comic operas often injected ridiculous, **topsy-turvy** situations into that world. **1** *HMS Pinafore* laughed at the rigid Royal Navy and the constant social climbing in society that people engaged in. **2** *The Mikado* was set in Japan and **satirized** politics and government bureaucracies. **3** Other common themes in Gilbert and Sullivan's works were romance, mistaken identities, plot twists, and the division of classes, most of which appear in *The Gondoliers*. **4**

The attacks on social norms came from Gilbert's natural wit and sarcasm and his desire to poke fun at the upper levels of British society. Sullivan, on the other hand, came from a serious musical background and longed to be a part of upper society. These differences often caused strains in their working relationship. In 1890, the pair had a falling out over financial issues. They soon reconciled and worked on two more comic operas, both of which were failures. After 1896, they parted ways and hardly saw each other before Sullivan died in 1900.

*topsy-turvy: upside down; confused
*satirize: to make fun of; to ridicule

Vocabulary

- _____ = to disobey or break a law or accepted type of behavior
- _____ = to write; to author
- _____ = to work together
- _____ = to add

1   In paragraph 2, why does the author mention "*Thespis*"?

   Ⓐ To point out that it was more successful than *HMS Pinafore*

   Ⓑ To claim it was the work that brought Gilbert and Sullivan great fame

   Ⓒ To argue that it was a well-written comic opera

   Ⓓ To name the first piece Gilbert and Sullivan worked on

2   In stating that "they once again struck gold with *The Mikado*," the author means that they

   Ⓐ created a successful work

   Ⓑ got their work published

   Ⓒ received praise from critics

   Ⓓ worked together again

3   Look at the four squares [▮] that indicate where the following sentence could be added to the passage.

   Audiences saw through the foreign setting and understood that the opera was actually making fun of England's political system.

4   An introductory sentence for a brief summary of the passage is provided below. Complete the summary by selecting the THREE answer choices that express the most important ideas of the passage. Some sentences do not belong because they express ideas that are not presented in the passage or are minor ideas in the passage.

   The collaborations of Gilbert and Sullivan were mostly well received and made fun of the society in which they lived.

   ANSWER CHOICES

   1   Some of their most successful works ridiculed organizations such as the Royal Navy and government bureaucracies.

   2   Even though their works mocked modern society, Sullivan had a strong desire to be accepted by members of the upper class.

   3   Among the most popular of their works were *The Mikado, The Pirates of Penzance*, and *HMS Pinafore*.

   4   *The Gondoliers* was the last major success that the two men had while working together.

   5   Some of their works, such as *The Sorcerer*, were much less successful than other works, such as *Trial by Jury*.

   6   The Victorian society of the time was extremely strict, and their sarcastic and humorous works satirized it.

🎧 CH08_4A

The Republic of Genoa

The Italian city of Genoa existed as an independent state from the eleventh to the eighteenth century and developed its power thanks to trade and its large navy. At one time, it possessed a gigantic empire throughout the Mediterranean Sea. The territory it controlled included large parts of the northwest Italian mainland, regions on France's southern coast, and the islands of Corsica and Sardinia. For a time, the Genoese even extended their power into the Aegean and Black seas, where they established trading colonies. In later times, however, wars with Venice and Ottoman expansion reduced Genoa's power. It went into a long period of decline, and the city's independence came to an end during the Napoleonic Wars in 1797.

Genoa rose to prominence in the eleventh century during a series of clashes with pirates from North Africa. Genoa and Pisa, a nearby city-state, formed an alliance to defeat them. After this success, Genoese traders began expanding their reach across the western part of the Mediterranean Sea. ■ Their efforts were assisted by the Genoese navy. ■ They soon fought their former ally Pisa since both coveted the islands of Corsica and Sardinia. ■ At the Battle of Meloria in 1284, the Genoese navy defeated the Pisan navy, so Pisa posed no threat to Genoa afterward. ■

Genoese traders then began looking for new markets in the eastern Mediterranean world. This brought them into conflict with Venice. In 1204, the Venetians challenged the power of the waning Byzantine Empire and helped Western Crusaders sack its capital of Constantinople. The victors then divided Byzantine possessions amongst themselves. Genoa took the opportunity to ally itself with the remaining Byzantines. As they recovered some of their lost land with the help of the Genoese, the Byzantines granted them some trading rights and colonies on islands in the Aegean Sea. The Byzantines also granted the Genoese access to the Black Sea. There, they established more trading colonies.

The conflict with Venice continued intermittently until well into the fourteenth century. The long decline of Genoa's Byzantine allies at the hands of the Ottoman Turks weakened the position of the Genoese. The wars with Venice finally ended after the Venetians triumphed at sea at the Battle of Chiogga in 1380. This initiated the long decline of the Genoese Empire. It slowly lost territory and, eventually, its independence. It came under the thumb of the French and, later, the city of Milan. It also had Corsica and Sardinia taken from it. Gradually, all of its colonies in the eastern Mediterranean Sea and the Black Sea were lost due to Ottoman expansion. Yet this was eventually halted at the Battle of Lepanto in 1571. In that battle, the Genoese navy allied itself with Western European forces, including its old enemy, Venice.

The sixteenth century saw Genoa regain some standing as a satellite of the powerful Spanish Empire after 1528. The city's wealth was still intact. Many of its residents served as bankers for the Spanish rulers as well. Then, Spain's decline in the following century saw a change in the fortunes of Genoa since the country's bankruptcy ruined many wealthy Genoese families. The city was later subjected to various invasions and internal revolts. In addition, a deadly plague killed large numbers of its residents in 1656. The final blow to Genoese independence came in 1797 when Napoleon's army occupied the city. He established a popular republic to replace the powerful ruling families. France then annexed Genoa in 1805. Later, after Napoleon's defeat, Genoa was bestowed upon the Kingdom of Sardinia at the Congress of Vienna in 1815.

*Glossary

Crusader: a person who participated in any of the Crusades to the Middle East that took place during the Middle Ages

plague: a disease that affects a large number of people

1   In paragraph 1, the author's description of Genoa mentions all of the following EXCEPT:

    (A) some of the lands that its empire possessed at times

    (B) the year during which it lost its freedom

    (C) the reasons why it became a strong republic

    (D) the person most responsible for increasing its power

2   The word "coveted" in the passage is closest in meaning to

    (A) desired

    (B) revered

    (C) occupied

    (D) invaded

3   Which of the sentences below best expresses the essential information in the highlighted sentence in the passage? Incorrect answer choices change the meaning in important ways or leave out essential information.

As they recovered some of their lost land with the help of the Genoese, the Byzantines granted them some trading rights and colonies on islands in the Aegean Sea.

    (A) Genoa gave some trading rights to the Byzantines in addition to helping them recover some of their colonies in the Aegean Sea.

    (B) The Byzantines gave Genoa various rights and colonies for helping them get back some of the land they had lost.

    (C) Because some of their colonies and trading rights had been lost, the Byzantines joined forces with the Genoese.

    (D) The Byzantines worked together with Genoa to recapture some of the colonies in the Aegean Sea which had been lost.

4 In stating that the conflict with Venice "continued intermittently," the author means that the fighting

Ⓐ never stopped

Ⓑ happened from time to time

Ⓒ came to a sudden end

Ⓓ was violent at times

5 In paragraph 4, why does the author mention "the Battle of Chiogga"?

Ⓐ To argue that Genoa should have been able to win it

Ⓑ To explain the strategy used by the Venetians

Ⓒ To claim that the Ottoman Empire fought in it

Ⓓ To point out the way in which it affected Genoa

6 In paragraph 5, the author implies that Genoa

Ⓐ played a major role in the eventual defeat of Napoleon

Ⓑ lost its independence due to the weakness of its navy

Ⓒ was influenced by a foreign power in the sixteenth century

Ⓓ saw its power increase when it was ruled by the French

7 According to paragraph 5, what happened to Genoa when Spain went bankrupt?

Ⓐ Many families there that were rich lost most of their money.

Ⓑ The ruling families were replaced by a popular republic.

Ⓒ Genoese bankers demanded that their loans be repaid.

Ⓓ Genoa lost a great deal of power and ceased being independent.

8 Look at the four squares [■] that indicate where the following sentence could be added to the passage.

In fact, Pisa went into a rapid decline and was completely defeated in a war with Florence two decades later.

Where would the sentence best fit?

Click on a square [■] to add the sentence to the passage.

9 Directions: An introductory sentence for a brief summary of the passage is provided below. Complete the summary by selecting the THREE answer choices that express the most important ideas of the passage. Some sentences do not belong because they express ideas that are not presented in the passage or are minor ideas in the passage. **This question is worth 2 points.**

Drag your answer choices to the spaces where they belong. To remove an answer choice, click on it. To review the passage, click on VIEW TEXT.

Thanks in part to its navy, Genoa became powerful during the Middle Ages, but it eventually declined due to the actions of other powers in Europe.

-
-
-

ANSWER CHOICES

1 At various times, Genoa found itself both allied and fighting against Italian city-states such as Pisa and Venice.

2 From the 1500s to 1800s, Genoa was influenced by both Spain and France, and it lost its independence during the wars of Napoleon.

3 Genoa allied itself with the Byzantine Empire, but that brought it into conflict with Venice, which caused it to lose power.

4 Over time, Genoa established an empire that controlled land in both the western and eastern parts of the Mediterranean Sea.

5 The Battle of Chiogga was of great importance to both the history of Genoa and the Venetian Republic.

6 The Genoese navy joined with the Venetians and others to fight the Ottoman Turks at the Battle of Lepanto.

The Feline Sense of Smell

Like most mammals, felines such as the domestic cat have the five senses of hearing, sight, touch, taste, and smell. They utilize these senses to interpret their environment and, especially, to hunt and kill prey. While the primary senses employed by felines are hearing and sight, smell also plays a crucial role. In fact, cats' sense of smell is a major one and plays a giant role in their daily lives.

Cats have a superior sense of smell than humans. Whereas humans have approximately five million olfactory receptor cells in their noses, cats have around 200 million. Additionally, cats have a smell organ in the roofs of their mouths. Called the vomeronasal organ, or, more commonly, Jacobsen's organ, it is located between the hard upper roof of the mouth and the nasal region. When a cat opens its mouth and draws its lips back in something of a grimace, it is actually pulling air into its Jacobson's organ, which has tiny ducts that draw in air. It then interprets any scents it detects and sends signals to the brain that the cat can comprehend. The primary purpose of Jacobsen's organ is to employ the cat's sense of smell to locate prey, to avoid predators, and to find mates.

Cats mark their territory by using urine and feces, which other felines can easily smell. By knowing where territorial boundaries exist, cats can avoid enemies and conflicts. They also release pheromones, chemical signals employed by numerous animals, to communicate and to attract mates to produce offspring. A male cat's Jacobsen's organ allows it to understand which pheromones come from female cats that may be in heat and are therefore ready to mate. Cats use pheromones to identify friends as well. When a pet cat rubs up against its owner, it normally releases pheromones on that individual to indicate that the two are friends.

Cats are carnivores, and even housecats hunt for food. Hunting appears to be an innate function of a cat's life, and its senses are attuned to help it catch prey. When searching for prey, a cat's sense of smell plays a more secondary role behind sight and hearing. Nevertheless, its heightened sense of smell helps it identify prey at a distance. More importantly, hunting stimulates a cat's appetite. Felines have a very poor sense of taste, mainly because they lack many taste buds in their mouths and cannot taste sugars very well. Fortunately, a cat's sense of smell arouses its hunger response. This then prompts it to hunt for prey to sate its hunger. In many cases, a cat that becomes ill with a blocked nose or respiratory system infection may lose its sense of smell and thereby lose its appetite, too.

There is one main drawback to a cat's strong sense of smell. It usually becomes upset when it smells something unfamiliar, particularly a strong odor. ■1 A new perfume or air freshener may make a cat wrinkle its nose in distaste and flee the area. ■2 Scented cat litter in the home is also not recommended since it may drive a cat away from its litterbox. ■3 Foods such as citrus fruit may offend a cat's sense of smell, too. ■4 It is therefore advisable to avoid having strong odors around cats lest they become upset or uncomfortable.

*Glossary

taste buds: small bodies found mostly on the tongue that provide animals with their sense of taste

feces: solid waste matter that comes from the anus

10 According to paragraph 1, which of the following is true about felines' sense of smell?

   Ⓐ It is the most useful for them when they are trying to hide from predators.

   Ⓑ It is of less importance to cats than their senses of hearing and sight.

   Ⓒ It is something that some cats are able to improve during their lifetimes.

   Ⓓ It is the most vital of all of the five senses that cats make use of.

11 The author discusses "Jacobsen's organ" in paragraph 2 in order to

   Ⓐ focus on the importance of its location in the bodies of cats

   Ⓑ mention that zoologists are not exactly sure what its purpose is

   Ⓒ argue that it is more important to cats' sense of smell than the nose is

   Ⓓ go into detail on the manner in which it helps cats smell things

12 In paragraph 2, the author implies that cats

   Ⓐ have a sense of smell that is a hundred times better than that of humans

   Ⓑ are both hunters of animals and sometimes animals that are hunted themselves

   Ⓒ rely on their sense of smell when they are both awake and asleep

   Ⓓ cannot function properly when their sense of smell is impaired in any way

13 According to paragraph 3, which of the following is NOT true about pheromones?

   Ⓐ Some cats mark their owners with pheromones to show that they are on good terms.

   Ⓑ A cat's Jacobsen's organ allows it to interpret what some pheromones mean.

   Ⓒ It is possible for cats to use pheromones to show that they are no longer willing to mate.

   Ⓓ They can be used as a way for animals to communicate with other ones.

14 The word "heightened" in the passage is closest in meaning to

- (A) sensitive
- (B) concentrated
- (C) effective
- (D) apparent

15 The word "sate" in the passage is closest in meaning to

- (A) approve of
- (B) satisfy
- (C) improve
- (D) ignore

16 According to paragraph 5, how do cats respond to certain strong odors?

- (A) They depart from the places where they can smell them very quickly.
- (B) They attempt to find the odors in order to smell them more closely.
- (C) They remember the smells so that they can avoid them in the future.
- (D) They become angry and may even attack the sources of the smells.

17 Look at the four squares [■] that indicate where the following sentence could be added to the passage.

In addition, they dislike the smells of other foods such as bananas as well as strong spices, including pepper and curry.

Where would the sentence best fit?

Click on a square [■] to add the sentence to the passage.

18 **Directions**: An introductory sentence for a brief summary of the passage is provided below. Complete the summary by selecting the THREE answer choices that express the most important ideas of the passage. Some sentences do not belong because they express ideas that are not presented in the passage or are minor ideas in the passage. **This question is worth 2 points.**

Cats' sense of smell is important to them for several reasons.

-
-
-

ANSWER CHOICES

1 Cats use their sense of smell to improve their appetites, which helps because of their poor sense of taste.

2 Jacobsen's organ allows cats to have a very sensitive sense of smell as well as to detect pheromones.

3 Cats do not always need to use their sense of smell when they are hunting small animals.

4 Since cats have such a good sense of smell, certain strong odors can have negative effects on them

5 Because cats are mammals, they have five senses, including heightened senses of sight, smell, and hearing.

6 Domestic cats usually have a stronger sense of smell than other felines, such as lions, tigers, and panthers.

◾ Vocabulary Review

A Complete each sentence with the appropriate word from the box.

gap   swamp   extends   juvenile   drag

1 It can be difficult to move through a _____ since the ground is so wet.

2 Due to the effects of _____, some planes must have powerful engines to get into the air.

3 The cows escaped from the farm because there was a _____ in the fence.

4 _____ animals have not yet become mature so are not considered adults.

5 Lewis bought more property, so now his land _____ all the way to the lake.

B Complete each sentence with the correct answer.

1 An animal which is **gigantic** is _____ than most other animals.

   a. more dangerous   b. larger

2 The lion became **upset** when there was a smell that it _____.

   a. disliked   b. enjoyed

3 Because Jane and Mark will **collaborate**, they plan to _____.

   a. work together   b. conduct research

4 Irene gave an **insufficient** effort during the race by _____.

   a. not trying hard enough   b. running as fast as she could

5 **Waterfowl** are basically _____.

   a. birds that live in wetlands   b. mammals that live near ponds

6 Because the **colony** began to succeed, more and more people moved to the _____.

   a. military base   b. settlement

7 When the doctor **injects** the patient with medicine, the doctor gives the patient _____.

   a. some pills   b. a shot

8 Jeff was asked to **interpret** some data because he was able to _____ the information well.

   a. understand   b. record

9 When an eagle **soars**, it flies _____ the ground.

   a. high above   b. close to

10 A **superior** piece of equipment is much _____ than anything else.

   a. more expensive   b. better

Chapter **09**

Prose Summary

Question Type | Prose Summary

◢ About the Question

Prose Summary questions focus on the main theme or idea of the passage. First, you must read a thesis sentence that covers the main points in the passage. Then, you must read six sentences that cover parts of the passage and choose the three sentences that describe the main theme or idea of the passage the closest. These questions always appear last, but they do not always appear. When there is a Fill in a Table question, there is not a Prose Summary question. However, Prose Summary questions are much more common than Fill in a Table questions. Almost every passage now has 1 Prose Summary question.

Recognizing Prose Summary questions:

Directions: An introductory sentence for a brief summary of the passage is provided below. Complete the summary by selecting the THREE answer choices that express the most important ideas of the passage. Some sentences do not belong because they express ideas that are not presented in the passage or are minor ideas in the passage. This question is worth 2 points.

[You will see an introductory sentence and six answer choices.]

Helpful hints for answering the questions correctly:

- Try to understand the main theme or idea of the passage as you are reading it.

- Only select answer choices that focus on the main theme. Ignore answer choices that focus on minor themes.

- Do not select answer choices that contain incorrect information. In addition, ignore answer choices that contain information which is correct but which is not mentioned in the passage.

Strip Mining

In some cases, various ores or mineral deposits are located relatively close to the surface. When that happens, a process known as strip mining is typically utilized to extract the ore or minerals. Essentially, the top part of the land, called the overburden, is removed by bulldozers. Then, holes are dug into the ground, and explosives are placed in them. Once they are detonated, the ground can quickly be removed by earthmoving equipment. This gives miners easy access to whatever they are removing. Coal is frequently mined through this method. Unfortunately, there are several disadvantages to strip mining. The first is that the land which is mined is utterly destroyed as trees, rocks, and everything on the ground are removed. While there are attempts to restore the land after the mining is complete, the land almost never returns to its prior condition. The animals that live in the mined areas also lose their homes and must seek new places to live. The land on many sites become polluted, and waterways also become dirtied. Sometimes poisonous chemicals such as arsenic are introduced into streams and rivers, and the end result is that fish and other aquatic animals die.

Directions: An introductory sentence for a brief summary of the passage is provided below. Complete the summary by selecting the THREE answer choices that express the most important ideas of the passage. Some sentences do not belong because they express ideas that are not presented in the passage or are minor ideas in the passage. **This question is worth 2 points.**

Strip mining is an effective method of getting ore and minerals that has several disadvantages.

ANSWER CHOICES

1 Animals on land and in the water are often killed or must get new homes as a result of strip mining.

2 Using strip mining lets miners easily remove their objective from the ground.

3 Strip mining is a much cheaper method than other types of mining.

4 Coal is a frequent objective of miners who utilize strip mining.

5 Much of the land that is strip mined is destroyed after the mining is complete.

6 Explosives are used to loosen the land for earthmoving machines before strip mining begins.

| Answer Explanation |

Choices 1, 2, and 5 are the correct answers. The passage reads, "The animals that live in the mined areas also lose their homes and must seek new places to live," and, "Sometimes poisonous chemicals such as arsenic are introduced into streams and rivers, and the end result is that fish and other aquatic animals die." In addition, the author writes, "Once they are detonated, the ground can quickly be removed by earthmoving equipment. This gives miners easy access to whatever they are removing." Finally, the author points out, "The first is that the land which is mined is utterly destroyed as trees, rocks, and everything on the ground are removed. While there are attempts to restore the land after the mining is complete, the land almost never returns to its prior condition." Choice 3 is not mentioned in the passage, so it is incorrect. And choices 4 and 6 are minor points, so they are wrong as well.

A | **Land Bridges**

🎧 CH09_2A

 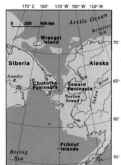

A land bridge is a strip of land that connects two larger pieces of land to each other. Throughout history, they have served as highways for human and animal migrations to new lands. During past ice ages, water levels in the world's oceans fell. This created several land bridges. The most important land bridges for past migrations were the one connecting Asia and North America and those connecting Australia with New Guinea and Tasmania.

About 15,000 years ago, a new ice age caused water levels in the Bering Sea to drop. This <u>exposed</u> the seabed between Siberia in Asia and Alaska in North America. Both humans and animals promptly migrated eastward from Asia to America. No written proof for this theory exists. Yet modern DNA testing of Native Americans proves they are descendants of Siberians living in Northeast Asia. In addition, no human settlements in North America have been found dated prior to that time. This shows that the continent had no human <u>inhabitants</u> prior to the exposure of the land bridge.

The Aboriginal people of Australia likely migrated from Asia to Australia 40,000 years ago. They island-hopped across land bridges close to Asia. At that time, an ice age made sea levels 100 meters lower than they are today. Australia, New Guinea, and Tasmania were united as a single continent. Asian migrants were able to walk to all three lands until the water levels rose again 8,000 years ago.

*expose: to reveal; to show
*inhabitant: a person who lives in a certain place

An introductory sentence for a brief summary of the passage is provided below. Complete the summary by selecting the THREE answer choices that express the most important ideas of the passage. Some sentences do not belong because they express ideas that are not presented in the passage or are minor ideas in the passage.

In the past, land bridges connected several lands to one another and permitted both human and animal migrations to occur.

ANSWER CHOICES

1. Ice ages have caused sea levels to lower, which resulted in some land bridges being formed.

2. People have been living in Australia for 40,000 years since they arrived there from Asia.

3. The people of the Americas arrived there from Asia by crossing a land bridge.

4. Australia, New Guinea, and Tasmania were connected by land bridges that people crossed.

5. The last ice age that revealed numerous land bridges took place around 15,000 years ago.

6. Land connecting Asia to Australia was exposed thousands of years ago.

Vocabulary

• _____ = a time when the Earth was very cold
• _____ = the bottom of a sea

• _____ = at once; immediately
• _____ = to move by traveling from island to island

B | Mold

Mold is a general term used to describe thousands of forms of fungi. It is commonly found where there is a source of moisture. It can grow from a single spore into a multicellular colony of filaments known as hyphae. As a mold colony increases in size, it typically appears as white or greenish fuzz. Mold obtains its nourishment from the organic matter upon which it grows, which is why it is normally found on food, plant matter, or dead organisms. It secretes enzymes, which break down the organic matter for the mold to use as energy.

It is possible for mold to benefit people. For instance, it is used in many food processes, including the making of some types of cheese, such as brie. Some types of it also have medicinal properties. Alexander Fleming used a form of the *Penicillium* mold to create one of the first antibiotics, penicillin, in 1928. Other forms of mold have cholesterol-reducing properties and are therefore used in medicines which treat high cholesterol.

Conversely, some molds are harmful to humans. These toxic molds typically grow on food and in homes with excessive moisture problems. They may grow in wet areas, such as in bathrooms, under kitchen sinks where pipes are leaking, and in storage areas with poor ventilation. Toxic molds can produce allergic reactions and lead to coughing, sneezing, watery red eyes, and rashes. They are particularly dangerous to individuals with asthma as they can cause death in some instances.

*spore: a tiny reproductive body of an organism that can produce more of its type
*secrete: to release; to discharge

An introductory sentence for a brief summary of the passage is provided below. Complete the summary by selecting the THREE answer choices that express the most important ideas of the passage. Some sentences do not belong because they express ideas that are not presented in the passage or are minor ideas in the passage.

Mold is a type of fungi which has both positive and negative effects on humans.

ANSWER CHOICES

1. In general, mold appears white or green in color and grows on organic material.

2. There are some molds that can be used by people for medicinal purposes.

3. The majority of mold is found growing in dark places with plenty of moisture.

4. Mold of a toxic nature can cause people to suffer various health problems.

5. People utilize some kinds of mold in order to make certain kinds of food.

6. Mold is capable of reproducing at very swift rates when it has ideal conditions.

Vocabulary

- _____ = a very thin thread
- _____ = a type of fluffy matter

- _____ = a type of substance that can kill bacteria
- _____ = poisonous; having the effects of poison

C | Red Blood Cells

Red blood cells are vital components of the human body whose main task is to transport oxygen from the lungs to places throughout the body and then to take carbon dioxide back to the lungs. They carry oxygen in a protein called hemoglobin, which is what gives them their reddish appearance. As red blood cells move through small blood vessels called capillaries, oxygen is filtered out to cells while carbon dioxide filters into them.

Having the appearance of a small, round disc with an inverted center, red blood cells constantly circulate throughout the body for the 100 to 120 days that they live for. When they die, **bone marrow** produces new red blood cells to replace them. It takes roughly seven days for this process of creation to occur. Red blood cells are the largest part of the blood as they comprise around seventy percent of its volume.

Nutrition plays an integral role in maintaining the health of red blood cells. Eating foods with vitamin E and vitamin B is essential for people to have healthy red blood cells. This is necessary since several diseases, the most common of which is anemia, can affect them. Anemia results when there are not enough red blood cells in the body to transport oxygen everywhere it is needed. It is caused by an insufficient amount of iron in a person's diet. It can also result when red blood cells have **abnormal** shapes or are larger or smaller than normal.

*bone marrow: tissue in the interiors of bones that produces red blood cells
*abnormal: irregular; odd

An introductory sentence for a brief summary of the passage is provided below. Complete the summary by selecting the THREE answer choices that express the most important ideas of the passage. Some sentences do not belong because they express ideas that are not presented in the passage or are minor ideas in the passage.

Red blood cells have important roles in the human body and need to be kept healthy to avoid getting various diseases.

ANSWER CHOICES

1. Red blood cells look like small discs and can stay alive for more than 100 days.

2. A person can suffer from anemia when red blood cells in the body fail to get enough iron.

3. Carbon dioxide is transported from the body back to the lungs by red blood cells.

4. One role of red blood cells is to take oxygen from the lungs and to spread it throughout the body.

5. It is the hemoglobin that is found in red blood cells that makes them appear red in color.

6. Bone marrow can produce new red blood cells in about a week's time.

Vocabulary

- _____ = the organ that provides oxygen to the body
- _____ = turned upside down or inside out
- _____ = important; crucial
- _____ = not enough; lacking something, often of importance

◾ Mapping

The following chart shows the structure of the passage. Fill in the blanks with the appropriate words.

Red Blood Cells

Are vital components of human body

– transport ❶ _____ through body and take
  ❷ _____ to lungs

– have protein called ❸ _____

Are small, round discs with inverted center

– ❹ _____ through body for 100-120 days

– new ones made by bone ❺ _____

– take ❻ _____ days to make

– make up ❼ _____% of volume of blood

Need good ❽ _____ to stay healthy

– vitamins B and E necessary

– can be affected by ❾ _____

– not enough red blood cells in body to transport oxygen

– caused by insufficient amount of ❿ _____, red blood cells with abnormal shapes, or red bloods cells larger or small than normal

◾ Summary

The following is a summary of the passage. Fill in the blanks with the appropriate words.

Red blood cells ❶ _____ oxygen from the lungs and take carbon dioxide to the lungs. They contain hemoglobin, making them appear ❷ _____. They look like small, round ❸ _____ with inverted centers and circulate for up to ❹ _____ days. New ones are made by bone marrow when old ones die. A person who consumes vitamins E and B can have ❺ _____ red blood cells. Anemia, which is caused by an ❻ _____ amount of iron, can affect them. This results in red blood cells not transporting ❼ _____ everywhere it is needed.

A | Ann Radcliffe and Gothic Literature

CH09_3A

English writer Ann Radcliffe is noted for being one of the creators of the Gothic novel. Radcliffe was born in 1764 and died in 1823, but not much is known about her life due to her intense privacy and the few surviving letters and manuscripts about her. What is known is that she was born Ann Ward in London and married journalist William Radcliffe in 1787. As her husband frequently worked late, Radcliffe began writing stories to pass the time. Ultimately, she published six novels, which are now revered as classics of Gothic literature.

Radcliffe wrote during a time when her genre, Gothic fiction, was considered a low form of literature. Horace Walpole's 1764 work *The Castle of Otranto* is widely considered the first Gothic novel, but the genre was not looked upon kindly by the members of the literary establishment. They viewed it as **tawdry** entertainment on account of its dark castles, supernatural elements, ladies in distress, and romantic heroes. However, this changed after Radcliffe published her works. Sir Walter Scott commented in 1824 that Radcliffe's skill as a writer had enabled her to elevate the genre to respectability.

Radcliffe's works shared similar themes. She thrust a beautiful heroine into a perilous situation, and there were often gloomy surroundings and a villain intent upon doing harm to her. She spiced up her novels with long descriptive passages of travels and the places that the heroine found herself in. She had to solve a mystery to survive and often found herself in suspenseful situations while doing so. She additionally dealt with events that seemed supernatural but had sensible explanations in the end. Romance was a primary feature of Radcliffe's works as the heroine always fell in love by the conclusion of the story.

Her first novel was *The Castles of Athlin and Dunbayne*, which was published in 1789. It was set in the Scottish highlands and involved feuding clans, romance, and mystery. Her later works often featured European settings, particularly France and Italy. They included *A Sicilian Romance* (1790), *The Romance of the Forest* (1791), *The Mysteries of Udolpho* (1794), and *The Italian* (1797). Publisher paid Radcliffe huge sums for her later works, including 800 pounds, an astronomical number at the time, for the rights to *The Italian*. She died while working on another novel, *Gaston de Blondville*, which was published **posthumously** in 1826.

Radcliffe's works were enormously popular during her lifetime despite the fact that she did not embrace fame and shunned the public eye. Her writing had a major influence on many writers, including Jane Austen, Edgar Allen Poe, Sir Walter Scott, Victor Hugo, and Fyodor Dostoyevsky.

*tawdry: tasteless; showy
*posthumously: after death

Vocabulary

- _____ = a type or kind
- _____ = relating to something that is not natural
- _____ = very dangerous
- _____ = a bad or evil person

1 In paragraph 2, the author uses "*The Castle of Otranto*" as an example of

  Ⓐ the most popular work that was written by Horace Walpole

  Ⓑ a Gothic novel which Sir Walter Scott approved of

  Ⓒ a book that is from the same genre which Radcliffe wrote in

  Ⓓ one of the first novels to include supernatural elements

2 According to paragraph 3, which of the following is NOT true about the works of Ann Radcliffe?

  Ⓐ They included stories that had supernatural villains in them.

  Ⓑ They each had a woman who was the main character of the story.

  Ⓒ There were aspects of both love and adventure found in them.

  Ⓓ There were parts of the books that had very long descriptions.

3 The word "astronomical" in the passage is closest in meaning to

  Ⓐ surprising

  Ⓑ enormous

  Ⓒ stellar

  Ⓓ wealthy

4 An introductory sentence for a brief summary of the passage is provided below. Complete the summary by selecting the THREE answer choices that express the most important ideas of the passage. Some sentences do not belong because they express ideas that are not presented in the passage or are minor ideas in the passage.

Ann Radcliffe was a writer of Gothic novels whose works had similar themes and both influenced other writers and made the genre respected by others.

ANSWER CHOICES

☐1 Many individuals, including Sir Walter Scott, praised Radcliffe's works, which affected the writing of numerous other authors.

☐2 Most of Radcliffe's works centered on a character who had to solve a mystery and was put into dangerous situations.

☐3 Radcliffe's first novel was published in 1789, and the last one she wrote was published in 1826, which was after she died.

☐4 Radcliffe based her novels up the works of Horace Walpole, whom she had long admired for his writing ability.

☐5 It was not until Radcliffe began publishing her own novels that the genre she wrote in gained respect from others.

☐6 Some of the advances that Radcliffe received for her novels were much higher than those offered to other authors.

Flashfloods and the Environment

Flashfloods are the sudden movement of a mass of water, often over a low-lying area. They occur quickly and with little warning, and they can cause extensive damage and take many lives. The major causes of flashfloods are sudden, intense rainfall over a short amount of time, the collapse of a dam or levee, the rapid melting of snow or ice, tidal waves, and storm surges caused by tropical storms such as hurricanes. They have also been associated with volcanic activity. An eruption can melt large amounts of ice and snow, sending a wall of water and mud down a volcano's slopes.

Flashfloods are characterized by the rapid movement of water. This begins at the source of the flood, such as a dam breach or a volcanic eruption, or it may be a gathering of water in a river channel from several sources, including rainfall and snowmelt accumulation. Along shorelines, storm surges and tidal waves come from the ocean and flood the land inland for long distances. In nearly every case, the water gathers speed, and, at the front, a wall of water appears along with **debris** as it rushes forward and destroys everything in its path.

When the floodwaters pass through, they change the nature of the land. They uproot trees, sweep away crops, kill animals, and destroy habitats. The land is left **gouged**, and new channels in rivers may appear. Coastlines often get changed after a flashflood from the sea. The influx of salty seawater can also make inland croplands infertile for a long time. An additional hazard is that the environment gets contaminated by flashfloods. Oil and gas spills are common during them as they destroy fuel facilities and then dump the fuel onto the land. Chemicals may enter the environment in a similar manner. After the floodwaters recede, huge amounts of polluted mud and silt remain.

Despite these negative aspects, there are some benefits to flashfloods. In desert environments, many plants and animals have adapted so that they become active only after heavy rainfall brings sudden flashfloods with life-giving water. The water seeps into the earth and renews groundwater supplies. Wetlands also benefit from flashfloods as the floodwaters carry nutrient-rich soil, which helps the wetlands by letting plants grow and animals thrive.

Flashfloods can revitalize soil on floodplains, too. Throughout history, civilizations survived on floodplains due to yearly floods that brought silt rich with nutrients. These floods were sometimes gentle but could also be flashfloods. By carefully managing the floodwaters with dams and canals, people in civilizations such as Mesopotamia and Egypt prevented flashfloods from destroying their land and ensured they would have rich soil and abundant amounts of water for their crops.

*debris: rubble; the remains of something that has been destroyed
*gouge: to cut grooves or notches into

Vocabulary

- _____ = a sudden move forward
- _____ = a break or hole in something solid
- _____ = to move back
- _____ = a flat area of land around a body of water that often floods

1　The word "it" in the passage refers to

   Ⓐ　the rapid movement of water

   Ⓑ　the source of the flood

   Ⓒ　a dam breach

   Ⓓ　a volcanic eruption

2　In paragraph 3, the passage implies that flashfloods

   Ⓐ　are deadlier when they come from the ocean rather than from rivers

   Ⓑ　are responsible for most of the worst chemical spills in recent years

   Ⓒ　can make the growing of plants in certain places impossible at times

   Ⓓ　can result in the forming of lakes in low-lying lands

3　Which of the sentences below best expresses the essential information in the highlighted sentence in the passage? Incorrect answer choices change the meaning in important ways or leave out essential information.

In desert environments, many plants and animals have adapted so that they become active only after heavy rainfall brings sudden flashfloods with life-giving water.

   Ⓐ　Unless plants and animals in the desert get water from flashfloods, most of them will die.

   Ⓑ　Flashfloods that happen in deserts can provide some advantages and disadvantages for the plants and animals living in them.

   Ⓒ　Nearly all of the plants and animals found in desert environments need flashfloods to occur with regularity.

   Ⓓ　Some plants and animals in deserts have changed so that they rely upon the water provided by flashfloods.

4　An introductory sentence for a brief summary of the passage is provided below. Complete the summary by selecting the THREE answer choices that express the most important ideas of the passage. Some sentences do not belong because they express ideas that are not presented in the passage or are minor ideas in the passage.

Flashfloods can have both positive and negative effects.

ANSWER CHOICES

☐1 People in ancient Egypt and Mesopotamia learned to predict when the yearly flashfloods that they relied upon would happen.

☐2 In some cases, the eruptions of volcanoes have caused flashfloods to occur along the sides of mountains.

☐3 People living in past civilizations relied upon flashfloods to bring water that they could use to grow their crops.

☐4 When flashfloods occur, they can change the way that the land looks and also deposit large amounts of debris on it.

☐5 Chemicals, oil, and other pollutants may be spilled by flashfloods and thus contaminate large areas of land.

☐6 When large amounts of snow or ice melt at once, it is possible for flashfloods to occur in some places.

CH09_4A

Humphry Davy

A portrait of Humphry Davy © Wellcome Collection

Humphry Davy was a British chemist who lived from 1778 to 1829. He is renowned for his discoveries of several elements and was a pioneer in the field of electrochemistry. Davy also invented a safety lamp for use in mines and was a gifted poet and writer. He was born into a middle-class family and received a good education, which was compounded by his natural intelligence and curious nature. At the age of sixteen, he became an apprentice to a doctor. This sparked an interest in chemistry as he studied in the doctor's well-equipped laboratory. This would result in chemistry becoming his life's work.

Most of Davy's early experiments were with gases. These included nitrous oxide—laughing gas—to which Davy later became addicted. In 1800, he published a book entitled *Researches, Chemical and Philosophical*, which enhanced his reputation in the field of chemistry. In 1801, the Royal Institution of Great Britain appointed Davy a professor of chemistry. He soon delved into electricity and produced the first well-known instance of using an electric current to create light. He was also famed for his highly entertaining lectures and demonstrations at the Royal Institution, most of which drew large crowds.

Davy's experiments with electricity led him to use electrolysis with a voltaic pile, an early type of electric battery, in order to split compounds. These experiments enabled him to discover several new elements. The first two he found were potassium and sodium in 1807. He used electricity to isolate the elements from compounds that contained them. Employing the same methods, he proceeded to discover calcium, strontium, barium, and magnesium the following year. **1** Davy is also credited with showing that chlorine could exist by itself. **2** Later, he proved that the alkaline earth metals react with oxygen. **3** He also challenged the prevailing theory that all acids contain oxygen, a notion which was incorrect. **4**

In 1815, after getting married and taking a European tour, Davy became interested in developing a safety lamp for miners. At that time, lamps using open flames caused countless accidental explosions. These took place when the flames came into contact with methane gas in mines. The lamp Davy developed used wire gauze, a mesh material, to surround the wick and flames. Tiny perforations in the material allowed gases into the lamp but did not permit the flames to escape. Therefore, if methane entered the lamp, it would only burn inside the lamp and not ignite a large mass of the gas inside the mine. The lamp also acted as a warning device since methane burns with a bluish color. Whenever a lamp's flame burned bright blue, miners became aware that methane was present.

Davy, however, had the misfortune to invent his safety lamp at the same time that a British engineer, George Stephenson, created a similar lamp. Stephenson was not a professional scientist, so many people believed he had stolen Davy's idea. Yet Stephenson successfully proved he had invented his lamp independent of Davy and had even shown it to Davy before he had made his own lamp. Various scientific committees credited both men with the invention. Yet Davy was never satisfied with this outcome. For the remainder of his life, he bitterly resented having to share credit with Stephenson. Today, the outcome remains the same as both men are said to have invented it.

*Glossary

electrolysis: the passage of an electrical current through an electrolyte
alkaline: a base

1. The word "gifted" in the passage is closest in meaning to

(A) presented

(B) aware

(C) talented

(D) productive

2. According to paragraph 1, Humphry Davy decided to study chemistry when

(A) he apprenticed with a doctor as a teenager

(B) he chose not to become a writer of poetry

(C) he discovered a new element in a laboratory

(D) he received lessons from a tutor at his home

3. In paragraph 2, why does the author mention "*Researches, Chemical and Philosophical*"?

(A) To claim that it was the first book written by Davy after he became a professor

(B) To point out how Davy became more prominent in his field of study

(C) To state that it describes the research Davy conducted on nitrous oxide

(D) To give the title of the book that influenced Davy's study of chemistry

4. The phrase "delved into" in the passage is closest in meaning to

(A) covered

(B) wrote about

(C) discussed

(D) investigated

5 According to paragraph 3, which of the following is NOT true about the elements Humphry Davy discovered?

Ⓐ Barium was discovered by him when he separated it from a compound.

Ⓑ He was the first person to discover oxygen existing by itself.

Ⓒ He discovered several elements in a period that lasted two years.

Ⓓ One of the first elements that he discovered was sodium.

6 Which of the following can be inferred from paragraph 4 about the safety lamp?

Ⓐ It helped decrease the amount of danger that was involved in mining.

Ⓑ It was initially too expensive for most English miners to afford.

Ⓒ It sometimes failed to work properly and therefore caused some deaths.

Ⓓ It was used by some people in professions other than mining.

7 Which of the sentences below best expresses the essential information in the highlighted sentence in the passage? Incorrect answer choices change the meaning in important ways or leave out essential information.

Yet Stephenson successfully proved he had invented his lamp independent of Davy and had even shown it to Davy before he had made his own lamp.

Ⓐ Stephenson believed that an independent investigation would show that he had made a lamp by himself and not with Davy's help.

Ⓑ Stephenson claimed that he assisted Davy in making a lamp and that he had previously made a lamp of his own.

Ⓒ Stephenson stated that he worked together with Davy to create a lamp but that Davy wanted credit for making it himself.

Ⓓ Stephenson was able to show that he made his lamp without input from Davy and before Davy made his own.

8 Look at the four squares [■] that indicate where the following sentence could be added to the passage.

Previously, many scientists had thought it could only exist as a compound with oxygen.

Where would the sentence best fit?

Click on a square [■] to add the sentence to the passage.

9 **Directions:** An introductory sentence for a brief summary of the passage is provided below. Complete the summary by selecting the THREE answer choices that express the most important ideas of the passage. Some sentences do not belong because they express ideas that are not presented in the passage or are minor ideas in the passage. **This question is worth 2 points.**

> Drag your answer choices to the spaces where they belong. To remove an answer choice, click on it. To review the passage, click on VIEW TEXT.

Humphry Davy was a scientist known for his accomplishments in chemistry as well as for an invention he made.

-
-
-

ANSWER CHOICES

1. Davy conducted some experiments on oxygen and the elements that it was able to combine with to form compounds.

2. The safety lamp that Davy made enabled miners to know when dangerous methane was in an area that they were working.

3. Davy became a professor of chemistry and was known for giving lectures that were enlightening and entertaining.

4. There was a minor controversy between Davy and a man named George Stephenson regarding the safety lamp.

5. Davy utilized electrolysis to enable him to discover a large number of elements in a short period of time.

6. Davy conducted many experiments with electricity and based a great deal of his research upon it.

The Sika Deer

Sika deer in Nara, Japan

The sika deer is a species native to East Asia but has been introduced to numerous other places around the world by humans. It is sometimes called the Japanese deer or the spotted deer due to the white spots on its brown hide. The name sika is taken from the Japanese word for deer. There are twelve known subspecies of sika deer, each coming from a distinct geographical region in East Asia. While it was once abundant throughout East Asia, today, the majority of sika deer reside in Japan.

The deer is easily recognizable by the distinctive color pattern on its hide. Although the fur on its belly and rump is white, most of its legs and upper body are orange-brown with the aforementioned white spots. The orange-brown fur grows darker in winter but becomes lighter in summer. The sika deer has a small head and short legs when compared to other deer species. Male sika deer are called stags while females are called hinds. Males are distinguished from females by a short set of antlers whereas females merely have two small black bumps on their heads. Like many species of deer, males' antlers grow and fall off annually. Males are larger than females as they average ninety centimeters in height at the shoulder and weigh between thirty and forty-five kilograms.

The sika deer has a lifespan ranging between twelve and twenty-five years with approximately eighteen being the most common maximum age. For most of the year, it lives a solitary life, coming together only to mate and to give birth. Its breeding season is between September and November. During this time, stags frequently mark their territory by using their hooves and antlers to dig shallow holes on its boundaries. Upon completion, they attempt to attract a small herd of hinds, called a harem, by making a wide range of vocalizations. Once impregnated, a hind carries a single offspring during a gestation period lasting seven and a half months. In the birthing season, small groups of hinds and their offspring establish herds. Sika deer offspring are called fawns and normally remain with their mothers for a year, during which time they consume milk produced by their mothers. For the first few weeks of their lives, fawns are hidden in dense brush by their mothers to protect them. Afterward, they emerge to join other fawns in the herd and then reach adulthood at eighteen months of age.

The sika deer is primarily nocturnal yet is known to be active during daylight hours at times. It is an herbivore and acquires most of its nutrition from grasses, small plants, tree bark, and leaves. Those sika deer living near human populations are known to invade gardens to eat crops which are growing. They particularly relish soybeans and corn.

Historically, in East Asia, the main predators of sika deer have been tigers, leopards, bears, and wolves. Some people have reported seeing large birds of prey attacking newborn fawns as well. Centuries of human encroachment in forests as well as hunting have reduced sika deer numbers in mainland Asian countries to just a few thousand individual animals. In Taiwan, it was hunted to extinction. It is only in Japan that it is still thriving, and that has happened mainly due to the demise of its major predator, the wolf, which went extinct in Japan more than one century ago. Today, experts estimate that hundreds of thousands of sika deer reside in Japan.

*Glossary

rump: the hind part, or buttocks, of an animal

gestation period: the time it takes for a baby to develop inside its mother's womb

10 In paragraph 1, the author's description of the sika deer mentions all of the following EXCEPT:

A the name of the place in East Asia where it is the most common

B the various countries in East Asia where it can currently be found living

C the number of subspecies of the deer that exist in East Asia

D the reason that it can be found residing in places other than East Asia

11 Which of the following can be inferred from paragraph 2 about the sika deer?

A It is simple for people to differentiate it from other types of deer.

B It has a lot of fur on its body because of the cold weather in Japan.

C It is known for being able to live in areas with large human populations.

D It sometimes has orange and black spots on various parts of its body.

12 According to paragraph 2, which of the following is true about sika hinds?

A They have orange-brown fur on their upper bodies for the entire year.

B They are capable of weighing up to forty-five kilograms and may be ninety centimeters high.

C They have bumps on their heads rather than antlers like male sika deer have.

D They have small heads as well as legs that are longer than males of their species.

13 In paragraph 3, why does the author mention "a harem"?

A To say that it is established when a stag and a hind mate with each other

B To describe how it operates when formed with hinds and fawns

C To point out that not all stags are capable of establishing one

D To give the name of a group of females that are attracted to a stag

14 Which of the sentences below best expresses the essential information in the highlighted sentence in the passage? Incorrect answer choices change the meaning in important ways or leave out essential information.

Sika deer offspring are called fawns and normally remain with their mothers for a year, during which time they consume milk produced by their mothers.

- (A) Sika deer fawns are unable to survive by themselves for the first year of their lives, so they stay with their mothers.
- (B) Sika deer mothers produce milk, which is what their babies, called fawns, consume in order to survive.
- (C) Fawns, which are baby sika deer, stay with their mothers for a year and drink their mothers' milk.
- (D) Baby sika deer are called fawns, and they are only able to live by drinking milk produced by their mothers.

15 The word "relish" in the passage is closest in meaning to

- (A) enjoy
- (B) search for
- (C) avoid
- (D) require

16 The word "encroachment" in the passage is closest in meaning to

- (A) destruction
- (B) trapping
- (C) poisoning
- (D) invasion

17 According to paragraph 5, the sika deer does well in Japan because

- (A) humans have set aside numerous game preserves for the animal to live in
- (B) the main animal that hunted it no longer lives anywhere in the country
- (C) tigers, leopards, bears, and wolves are presently extinct in Japan
- (D) laws designed to protect it have been passed by the Japanese government

18 **Directions**: An introductory sentence for a brief summary of the passage is provided below. Complete the summary by selecting the THREE answer choices that express the most important ideas of the passage. Some sentences do not belong because they express ideas that are not presented in the passage or are minor ideas in the passage. **This question is worth 2 points.**

The sika deer mostly lives in East Asia and is distinct for a number of reasons.

-

-

-

ANSWER CHOICES

1. It takes around seven and a half months for a pregnant sika deer to give birth to a fawn.

2. The orange-brown coloring on the sika deer makes it easy to tell it apart from other deer.

3. The sika deer normally lives alone, but during the breeding season, large groups of hinds attracted to a stag may form.

4. The sika deer's numbers have been reduced greatly in East Asia, but there are still many deer in Japan.

5. There are more than ten subspecies of sika deer, and each has unique differences from the others.

6. The sika deer enjoys eating various types of vegetation and avoids going to places where humans live.

◼ Vocabulary Review

A Complete each sentence with the appropriate word from the box.

integral	surge	fuzz	seabed	lungs

1 Doug is considered a(n) _____ member of the sales team.

2 You use your _____ in order to take air in and out of your body.

3 That green _____ on the loaf of bread is mold growing on it.

4 There was a storm _____ that sent water far inland during the hurricane.

5 All kinds of animals, including lobsters and crabs, live on the _____.

B Complete each sentence with the correct answer.

1 By fulfilling the request _____, Beth was praised for acting **promptly**.
   a. quickly   b. properly

2 Animals that only eat _____ are known as **herbivores**.
   a. meat   b. vegetation

3 When floodwaters **recede**, then they _____.
   a. go back   b. move forward

4 Do not drink any **toxic** liquids because they are _____ to people.
   a. poisonous   b. fattening

5 The concert is held **annually**, so it takes place _____.
   a. once a month   b. once a year

6 If you succeed at **igniting** a building, then you have _____.
   a. renovated it   b. set it on fire

7 The _____ in a movie or novel is said to be the **villain**.
   a. bad guy   b. hero

8 Patients with the virus must be **isolated**, so they should spend time _____.
   a. in a hospital   b. alone

9 Animals that _____ in underground areas **reside** in subterranean ecosystems.
   a. hunt   b. live

10 Few people visit the _____ mountain since climbing it can be **perilous**.
   a. dangerous   b. steep

Chapter **10**

Fill in a Table

Question Type | Fill in a Table

◢ About the Question

Fill in a Table questions focus on the entire passage. You are asked to answer a question that breaks down the passage into two or three major theme or topics. There will be a number of sentences about these themes. You have to determine which theme each of the sentences you read refers to. These questions may ask about cause and effect, problem and solution, and compare and contrast, or they may focus on other themes. These questions always appear last, but they do not always appear. When there is a Prose Summary question, there is not a Fill in a Table question. Fill in a Table questions rarely appear anymore. Prose Summary questions are much more common than Fill in a Table questions.

Recognizing Fill in a Table questions:

- **Directions:** Select the appropriate statements from the answer choices and match them to X to which they relate. TWO of the answer choices will NOT be used. **This question is worth 3 points.**

  [You will see seven statements.]

- **Directions:** Select the appropriate statements from the answer choices and match them to X to which they relate. TWO of the answer choices will NOT be used. **This question is worth 4 points.**

  [You will see nine statements.]

Helpful hints for answering the questions correctly:

- These questions only ask about the major themes or topics in the passage.

- Passages that have two or three major themes or topics frequently have this type of question.

- Ignore any minor themes or topics in the passage. These are not covered on this type of question.

- There are always two answer choices that are incorrect. They may have irrelevant information, incorrect information, or information that is correct but which does not appear in the passage.

The Cretaceous Period

The final period of the Mesozoic Era was the Cretaceous Period. It began with the extinction event that ended the Jurassic Period. That happened around 145 million years ago. It ended with another extinction event about 65 million years ago. The Cretaceous Period has been divided into two parts. They are the Early Cretaceous Period (145-100 million years ago) and the Late Cretaceous Period (100-65 million years ago). The Earth's geology underwent vast changes during these two eras. During the Early Cretaceous Period, Pangaea, the supercontinent, began to split up. Water levels then were much higher than they were today. When the Cretaceous Period ended, the continents were close to their modern-day appearances. Still, Australia and Antarctica had not separated by then. But South America and Africa had already taken their distinctive shapes. As for plant and animal life, flowering plants—called angiosperms—began to appear roughly 125 million years ago. Dinosaurs thrived at the beginning of the period and lived all throughout it. Smaller animals, including insects, birds, and mammals, also developed during this time. At the end of the Cretaceous Period, an asteroid struck the planet. This caused a mass-extinction event. It resulted in the disappearance of the dinosaurs and enabled other animals, such as mammals, to dominate.

Directions: Select the appropriate statements from the answer choices and match them to the period to which they relate. TWO of the answer choices will NOT be used. **This question is worth 3 points.**

STATEMENTS

① Was the time when flowering plants started growing

② Saw the water rise to the level it is at today

③ Was when the dinosaurs went extinct

④ Was when the division of Australia and Antarctica happened

⑤ Started with an extinction event

⑥ Was the time when South America assumed its shape

⑦ Saw Pangaea begin to divide

PERIOD

Early Cretaceous (Select 3)

-
-
-

Late Cretaceous (Select 2)

-
-

| Answer Explanation |

The Early Cretaceous Period is choices ①, ⑤, and ⑦. About it, the author writes, "Flowering plants—called angiosperms—began to appear roughly 125 million years ago." (①) The author also points out, "It began with the extinction event that ended the Jurassic Period. That happened around 145 million years ago," (⑤) and, "During the Early Cretaceous Period, Pangaea, the supercontinent, began to split up." (⑦) The Late Cretaceous Period is choices ③ and ⑥. Regarding it, the author points out, "At the end of the Cretaceous Period, an asteroid struck the planet. This caused a mass-extinction event. It resulted in the disappearance of the dinosaurs," (③) and, "When the Cretaceous Period ended . . . South America and Africa had already taken their distinctive shapes." (⑥)

A | **Early Space Stations**

CH10_2A

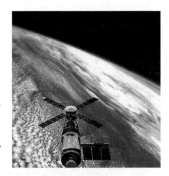

In the 1970s, the United States and the Soviet Union desired a permanent presence in outer space, so they put space stations into low-Earth orbit. Their purposes were to examine how humans would react to spending long periods of time in zero-gravity conditions and to serve as platforms for experiments and sensitive information-gathering equipment.

The first to attain orbit was *Salyut 1*, which the Soviets launched on April 19, 1971. Overall, nine *Salyut* stations were launched, but two never managed to achieve orbit. The most successful were *Salyut 6*, launched in 1977, and *Salyut 7*, which blasted into space in 1982. Together, they hosted twenty-five different crews. The longest stay was made by three <u>cosmonauts</u> on *Salyut 7*, who remained in space for 237 days in 1984. *Salyut 7* spent the longest amount of time—nearly ten years—in space before being consumed by the Earth's atmosphere in 1991.

The only early American space station was *Skylab*, which was launched by NASA in 1973 and <u>plummeted</u> to the Earth in 1979. *Skylab* was larger than the *Salyut* stations, with roughly four times the mass and more than three times the interior space. It was designed for a crew of three to reside for long amounts of time, yet only three crews totaling nine astronauts visited it. The longest stay was eighty-four days. While the Americans planned more manned missions and stations, they lacked the funding to do so.

*cosmonaut: a Russian or Soviet astronaut

*plummet: to fall far at a great speed

Select the appropriate statements from the answer choices and match them to the country to which they relate. TWO of the answer choices will NOT be used.

Soviet Union (Select 3)	United States (Select 2)
•	•
•	•
•	

STATEMENTS

1. Suffered losses of life on some occasions
2. Had the largest space station
3. Launched the first space station into orbit
4. Hosted nine men on its space station
5. Had a space station stay in orbit for a decade
6. Suffered a failure the first time a space station was launched
7. Was responsible for the *Salyut* program

Vocabulary

• _____ = a condition where there is no gravity		• _____ = to reach	
• _____ = a structure		• _____ = to destroy completely	

Cell Division

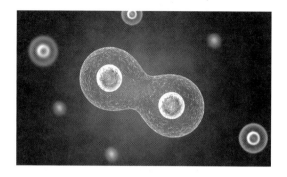

There are approximately thirty-seven trillion cells in an adult human's body. Each day, some die and are replaced, and the body additionally grows by making new cells. New cells are created by dividing old ones in two primary ways: mitosis and meiosis.

Mitosis occurs in non-reproductive cells, which constitute the majority of cells in the body. When it takes place, the parent cell easily divides into two daughter cells, both of which are exact **replicas** of the parent cell and contain the same DNA as it. Prior to dividing, the DNA in the parent cell is copied, so it contains two sets of DNA for a short period of time.

As for meiosis, it occurs in reproductive cells, such as male sperm and female eggs. A parent cell for either of them starts with forty-six **chromosomes**. During the division process, the number of chromosomes is halved. When sperm and egg meet, they combine to create a complete set of forty-six chromosomes. Meiosis happens in two stages. First, two daughter cells are made from a parent cell, and then each daughter cell divides to produce a total of four second stage daughter cells. While this happens, a small part of each chromosome breaks off and reattaches to another chromosome. The genetic information in the four daughter cells is different from that of the original parent cell, and every daughter cell is different as well. This is what enables genetic variety to children born to the same parents.

*replica: a duplicate; an exact copy
*chromosome: a threadlike body which carries genes

Select the appropriate statements from the answer choices and match them to the type of cell division to which they relate. TWO of the answer choices will NOT be used.

Mitosis (Select 3)	Meiosis (Select 2)
•	•
•	•
	•

STATEMENTS

1. Requires a process that takes hours to complete
2. Enables children with the same parents to have different genes
3. Takes place in most of the body's cells
4. Is responsible for twins being born to some parents
5. Occurs in reproductive cells
6. Requires two different steps for it to occur
7. Happens when the parent cell divides into two exact daughter cells

Vocabulary

• _____ = to make up
• _____ = the bulk of something; most of something
• _____ = to cut into half
• _____ = to become connected to again

C | Roman Architecture

In classical Greek and Roman architecture, there are five orders, or design styles, that are based primarily on columns. The Greeks created the Doric, Ionic, and Corinthian orders. While the Romans often copied the three Greek orders, they produced two styles which were uniquely Roman. They are the Tuscan and Composite orders.

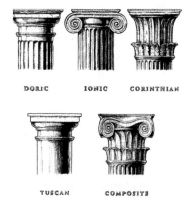

Modern architects regularly describe the Tuscan order as being a simplified Doric style. Tuscan columns **bear** some resemblance to Doric columns since both are shorter than the other styles and have no elaborate designs at their tops. However, Doric friezes, which are the horizontal structures at the tops of columns, have many designs. In contrast, Tuscan friezes are plain. Additionally, Tuscan columns are slender and smooth and lack the **grooves** that Doric columns possess. Due to its simplicity, the Tuscan style was frequently used by the Romans to make military structures.

As for the Composite order, it is a mixture of the Ionic and Corinthian styles. Composite columns are slender and grooved and are similar in height to Corinthian columns. They are the two tallest of all five styles of columns. Composite columns have ornate leaf-like designs at their tops, making them like Corinthian columns, but they also have the spiral scroll-like designs of Ionic columns. The scrolls on Composite columns are larger than those on Ionic ones though. Finally, the friezes on Composite columns are decorative, which enabled these columns to be used on a wide variety of structures.

*bear: to have; to possess
*groove: a long, narrow cut in a surface

Select the appropriate statements from the answer choices and match them to the Roman architectural style to which they relate. TWO of the answer choices will NOT be used.

Tuscan (Select 3)	Composite (Select 2)
•	•
•	•
•	

STATEMENTS

1 Has a simple style that the military used

2 Combines the styles of two Greek orders

3 Possesses friezes that have ornate designs

4 Is similar in nature to the Greek Doric style

5 Has scrolls which are shorter than Ionic ones

6 Has columns that have designs at their tops

7 Has friezes that do not have any designs

Vocabulary

- _____ = distinctively
- _____ = basic; easy
- _____ = thin
- _____ = a combination of two or more things

216

▰ Mapping

The following chart shows the structure of the passage. Fill in the blanks with the appropriate words.

Roman Architecture

Romans used orders like the Greeks

– often copied the Greeks

– came up with two orders of their own

Tuscan order: simplified ❶ _____ style

– short ❷ _____ with no elaborate structures at tops

– ❸ _____ have no designs

– columns are slender and smooth and lack ❹ _____

– order was popular with the military due to ❺ _____

Composite order: ❻ _____ of Ionic and Corinthian orders

– columns are slender and grooved and similar in height to ❼ _____ ones

– columns have ❽ _____ designs at tops and scroll-like designs

– have ❾ _____ friezes

▰ Summary

The following is a summary of the passage. Fill in the blanks with the appropriate words.

The Greeks created the Doric, ❶ _____, and Corinthian orders of architecture. The Romans ❷ _____ the Greeks but also came up with the Tuscan and Composite orders. The ❸ _____ order is like a simplified Doric style. It has ❹ _____ columns with no elaborate designs at the tops. Tuscan friezes are ❺ _____ while the columns are slender and smooth. The Romans made ❻ _____ structures with it. The ❼ _____ order combines the Ionic and Corinthian styles. The columns are tall, have ornate designs at their tops, and have ❽ _____ scroll-like designs. They also have decorative friezes.

A | The Peloponnesian War

🎧 CH10_3A

The Peloponnesian War took place from 431 B.C. to 404 B.C. and was fought between Sparta and Athens and their allied states. For years, the war was a stalemate because of the Spartans' supremacy on land and the Athenians' control of the seas. The Athenians, however, made several costly mistakes which gave the Spartans the advantage and ultimately led to their emerging from the war triumphant.

Prior to the outbreak of fighting, Sparta and Athens had become the most powerful city-states in Greece. Athens defeated a Persian invasion in 480 B.C. and led a coalition of Greek city-states, the Delian League, in attacking Persian possessions in the Aegean and Ionian seas. That conflict established Athens as an empire and the preeminent state in Greece. Furthermore, it enabled Athens to dominate the other Greek city-states, with the exception of Sparta and its allies. The two sides clashed off and on between 460 B.C. and 446 B.C. Despite continuing tensions, Athens and Sparta signed a peace treaty in 446 B.C. which was supposed to last for thirty years.

A war between Corinth, a Spartan ally, and the city-state of Corcyra on the island of Corfu resulted in renewed hostilities. In 435 B.C., Corcyra defeated Corinth, but the Corinthians recovered and began building a large navy. Corcyra sought an alliance with Athens. Then, timely Athenian naval intervention prevented Corinth from defeating Corcyra. Afterward, Athenian attempts to control two other city-states, Potidaea and Megara, resulted in further fighting with Corinth in 433 B.C. Corinth subsequently called upon Sparta, the leader of the Peloponnesian League, to act with regard to Athenian dominance. A great assemblage of the league's members took place in Sparta in 432 B.C., and, after extensive debate, the members established that Athens had violated the peace treaty, prompting Sparta to declare war on Athens.

What would eventually be called the Peloponnesian War began in 431 B.C. when a large Spartan army invaded Attica, the Athenian homeland. The first part of the war lasted until 421 B.C. Neither side could gain a significant advantage and therefore attain total victory. There was peace for six years, but fighting began again when Athens attacked Syracuse in Sicily in 415 B.C. Syracuse requested assistance from Sparta, which was provided. The Athenians suffered a total defeat in Sicily, giving the Spartans the advantage, which resulted in their victory over Athens in 404 B.C.

The initial consequence of the war was a shift from Athenian dominance of Greece to Spartan supremacy. However, Athens was not crushed, so it soon recovered. Tensions still existed, and fighting between various city-states and coalitions plagued Greece for decades. This would leave the region exhausted and ripe for the Macedonian invasion and victory in 338 B.C.

*stalemate: a situation in which neither side is able to win
*hostility: warfare; fighting

Vocabulary

- _____ = power; dominance
- _____ = an alliance between two or more groups
- _____ = relating to the navy or sea
- _____ = to cause huge problems

1   The word "preeminent" in the passage is closest in meaning to

(A) oldest   (B) largest

(C) dominant   (D) democratic

2   Which of the sentences below best expresses the essential information in the highlighted sentence in the passage? Incorrect answer choices change the meaning in important ways or leave out essential information.

A great assemblage of the league's members took place in Sparta in 432 B.C., and, after extensive debate, the members established that Athens had violated the peace treaty, prompting Sparta to declare war on Athens.

(A) Out of a desire to declare war on Athens, the Spartans and members of the league met to have a debate on the current events.

(B) The members met in Sparta and determined that the peace treaty had been broken, so war on Athens was declared by Sparta.

(C) Sparta went to war against Athens because it felt that the Athenians were about to violate the peace treaty against the league.

(D) The Spartans called together the members of the league to determine whether the Athenians had broken the treaty or not.

3   Which of the following can be inferred from paragraph 3 about the Peloponnesian League?

(A) All of the leading city-states in Greece were members of it.

(B) It was comprised of Sparta and the city-states it allied with.

(C) The league formed as a result of Sparta's concerns about Athens.

(D) Some of its members quit when they were pressured by Sparta.

4   Select the appropriate statements from the answer choices and match them to the causes and effects of the Peloponnesian War to which they relate. TWO of the answer choices will NOT be used.

Cause (Select 3)	Effect (Select 2)
●	●
●	●
●	

STATEMENTS

1   The Delian League defeated the Persian Empire in battle.

2   Sparta became the most powerful city-state in Greece.

3   A treaty was violated when Athens attacked Corinth.

4   Athens found itself in an alliance with Corcyra.

5   Alexander the Great defeated an alliance of Greek city-states.

6   Greece was invaded and defeated by the Macedonians.

7   City-states in Greece were worried about the power of Athens.

The Structures of Flowering Plants

Flowering plants are those which grow flowers to reproduce and have four main parts: roots, the stem, leaves, and flowers. Each of these parts plays a crucial role in the survival of flowering plants.

The first part of a flowering plant to grow is its roots, which sprout from a seed underground. The primary functions of roots are to absorb water and nutrients from the soil and to anchor the plant to the soil to prevent it from getting uprooted. There are fibrous root systems and taproot systems. Fibrous root systems, which many types of grasses have, possess slender roots that are mostly the same size and spread out in various directions to find and absorb water and nutrients. Conversely, taproot systems, which are what carrots and radishes have, produce one large root and many small ones. The large root, called the taproot, sinks deeply straight underground in search of water.

The stem grows upward from the ground and provides the main trunk for the other parts of the plant. Water and nutrients flow from the roots to the leaves and flowers by traveling through the stem. It additionally provides a solid structure that prevents the plant from collapsing due to the weight of its leaves and flowers. Stems such as the trunks of trees are long and solid whereas others, such as those of cabbages, are short. Stems are classified as woody or herbaceous. The former are found in trees and shrubs and possess strong structures because they contain large amounts of woody xylem tissue. Herbaceous stems have less xylem tissue and are accordingly softer and greener in nature.

Leaves produce energy for flowering plants. Green chlorophyll in leaves absorbs sunlight and manufactures energy through the process of photosynthesis, which happens through the combining of water with carbon dioxide. This process produces two products: glucose and oxygen. The glucose is used by the plant for energy while it releases the oxygen into the atmosphere, where it can be breathed by various organisms, including humans.

The flowers of a flowering plant constitute its main reproductive system. Inside a flower are male and female organs. The female organ contains the ovary, the style, and the stigma. The flower's seeds are in the ovary while the style is a thin tube leading from the ovary to the stigma, which is the receptacle that receives the pollen used to fertilize the seeds. The male organ has two parts: the anther and the filament. The anther sits on top of the filament and has sacs containing pollen, which is normally transferred to the stigma through the action of the wind, birds, or insects.

*herbaceous: having the texture and characteristics of a leaf
*xylem tissue: a compound tissue in a plant that provides support for it and also transports water and nutrients from the roots

Vocabulary

- _____ = to take a plant out of the ground
- _____ = being made of many fibers
- _____ = to fall down
- _____ = a container; a vessel

1 In paragraph 2, why does the author mention "the taproot"?

  Ⓐ To point out that it is found in fibrous root systems

  Ⓑ To explain the role it plays in the survival of a plant

  Ⓒ To claim it is more efficient than small roots that spread out

  Ⓓ To note the manner in which it grows underground

2 The word "others" in the passage refers to

  Ⓐ leaves

  Ⓑ flowers

  Ⓒ stems

  Ⓓ the trunks of trees

3 In paragraph 4, the author's description of photosynthesis mentions which of the following?

  Ⓐ The time of day when it occurs the most efficiently

  Ⓑ What is provided by the leaves to enable it to occur

  Ⓒ The amount of water that is necessary for it to take place

  Ⓓ The chemical formula that describes what happens

4 Select the appropriate statements from the answer choices and match them to the part of flowering plants to which they relate. TWO of the answer choices will NOT be used.

Roots (Select 3)	Stems (Select 2)	Flowers (Select 2)
•		
•	•	•
•	•	•

STATEMENTS

1 Absorb sunlight to help photosynthesis take place

2 Are responsible for extracting water from the soil

3 Provide support to let plants remain upright

4 Contain the chlorophyll needed to create energy

5 Have both male and female parts

6 May descend deep underground

7 Contain parts such as the stigma and anther

8 Help keep plants from being pulled out of the ground

9 May be long and hard like those of trees

Primates

Ring-tailed lemurs

Primates are species of mammals that include humans, apes, lemurs, and monkeys. Aside from humans, most primates reside in the tropical regions of Africa, Asia, and the Americas. Primates are classified into two main groups: prosimians and simians. Prosimians include lemurs, bushbabies, and lorises while simians include humans, apes, and monkeys. One type of primate, tarsiers, has characteristics of both groups. All primates share some features. For instance, they reproduce slowly compared to other mammals, have binocular vision, and depend more on vision than smell to find food. Primates also have nails on their digits instead of claws. They mainly live in trees although some species spend copious amounts of time on the ground.

Prosimian lemurs are from the island of Madagascar and are among the smallest primates. One species, the mouse lemur, weighs only around thirty grams. Lemurs have close-set and protruding teeth on their lower jaw. They use their teeth to chew plant matter and also as combs, which they utilize to clean their fur. Lemurs mostly consume plant matter, but some eat insects and small animals if the opportunity arises. Bushbabies, also called galagos, live mainly in West African jungles. They weigh no more than one kilogram and have a diet consisting of fruits and insects. They hunt at night by using their large eyes and sensitive hearing to detect insects in the darkness. Bushbabies have strong limbs and a tail for climbing and are capable of leaping long distances. Like lemurs, they have a comb-like lower set of teeth.

Lorises are similar to bushbabies in some ways. They are small, nocturnal primates that mostly feed on vegetation and insects and have similar types of lower teeth. Lorises are found mostly in India, Sri Lanka, and Southeast Asia. As for tarsiers, they also dwell in Southeast Asia and are tiny, with an average weight of around 100 grams. They reside in trees and have strong limbs for climbing. Their main diet is insects and small vertebrates. While they appear mostly prosimian, they have skull structures similar to those of simians and may have shared a common ancestor.

Simian apes can be divided into great apes and lesser apes. Great apes include gorillas, orangutans, chimpanzees, and bonobos whereas lesser apes include gibbons and their larger cousins, called siamangs. **1** Apes, which are found mostly in Africa and Southeast Asia, are the largest primates and live in highly organized social groups. **2** The diets of different ape species vary, but they mainly eat plant matter and insects; however, some species have been observed hunting and eating small mammals. **3** Their highly developed brains allow some apes to utilize tools, such as long sticks, which they use to dig out insects from the ground and trees. **4**

There are two subgroups of monkeys: New World monkeys and Old World monkeys. New World monkeys live in the Americas while the others live in Africa and Asia. It is speculated that New World monkeys originated in the Old World and somehow made their way to the Americas millions of years ago. There are a large number of species in both groups. Most live on diets of plants, fruits, and insects. Many New World monkeys, including spider monkeys and capuchin monkeys, have a long prehensile tail which aids them while climbing. Old World monkeys have been subdivided into those that mainly eat leaves and those that consume all types of plant matter and insects. They are distinguished by their teeth and digestive systems, which have adapted to their diets. Leaf eaters include colobuses and langur monkeys, and the other group contains macaques and baboons.

*Glossary

digit: a finger or toe

prehensile: adapted for grabbing or grasping things

1 The word "copious" in the passage is closest in meaning to

- (A) plentiful
- (B) vital
- (C) apparent
- (D) tiny

2 According to paragraph 1, which of the following is true about primates?

- (A) They prefer to live in trees rather than on the ground.
- (B) They are reliant mostly upon their eyes to locate food.
- (C) They only live on three of the Earth's continents.
- (D) They all have characteristics of simians and prosimians.

3 In paragraph 2, the author's description of lemurs mentions all of the following EXCEPT:

- (A) the types of food that they normally consume each day
- (B) how their teeth look and what activities they are used for
- (C) the area in which they can be found living in the wild
- (D) the number of species that there are and their sizes

4 According to paragraphs 2 and 3, which of the following can be inferred about the teeth of lorises?

- (A) They are close to one another and stick out.
- (B) They are effective at tearing into flesh.
- (C) They can be displayed to threaten other animals.
- (D) They are useful for chewing hard food.

5 According to paragraph 3, tarsiers are similar to simians because of

- (A) their large sizes
- (B) their ability to walk on two legs
- (C) the shape of their heads
- (D) the diet that they eat

6   Which of the sentences below best expresses the essential information in the highlighted sentence in the passage? Incorrect answer choices change the meaning in important ways or leave out essential information.

It is speculated that New World monkeys originated in the Old World and somehow made their way to the Americas millions of years ago.

Ⓐ   Nobody knows exactly how monkeys went from the Old World to the New World millions of years ago.

Ⓑ   New World monkeys may be the descendants of Old World monkeys that visited the Americas in the past.

Ⓒ   A long time ago, New World monkeys visited the Old World and became the ancestors of the monkeys there.

Ⓓ   Old World monkeys and New World monkeys are thought to have evolved together millions of years ago.

7   The word "those" in the passage refers to

Ⓐ   many New World monkeys

Ⓑ   spider monkeys and capuchin monkeys

Ⓒ   Old World monkeys

Ⓓ   leaves

8   Look at the four squares [■] that indicate where the following sentence could be added to the passage.

Some are also intelligent enough to have learned sign language, which they use to communicate with humans.

Where would the sentence best fit?

Click on a square [■] to add the sentence to the passage.

9 **Directions**: Select the appropriate statements from the answer choices and match them to the type of primate to which they relate. TWO of the answer choices will NOT be used. **This question is worth 3 points.**

Drag your answer choices to the spaces where they belong. To remove an answer choice, click on it. To review the passage, click on VIEW TEXT.

STATEMENTS

1 Has teeth that are used like combs

2 Tends to be smaller than the other

3 Is the group to which tarsiers belong

4 Is capable of using some types of tools

5 Lives on all of the continents on the planet

6 Includes both bushbabies and lorises

7 Is the group which includes humans

TYPE OF PRIMATE

Prosimian (Select 3)

-
-
-

Simian (Select 2)

-
-

Plant Root Systems

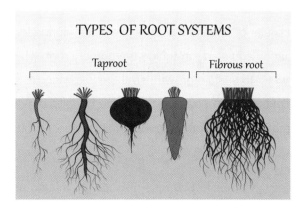

TYPES OF ROOT SYSTEMS

Taproot   Fibrous root

Plants acquire nourishment in the form of water and nutrients through the utilization of complex root systems. Plant roots come in many forms, but most have similar characteristics. They are positively geotropic, meaning that they grow down into the soil since gravity pushes them downward. Roots are additionally hydrotropic, so they grow toward water. They are negatively phototropic as well, which causes them to grow away from light. Finally, roots lack chlorophyll, so they are not green, and they have no buds, leaves, or flowering parts. There are two main root systems: taproots and fibrous roots. Many root systems also have a primary root, secondary roots, and tertiary roots.

Taproot systems are formed from a large primary root, such as that found in turnips and carrots. Stemming from the main taproot are numerous secondary and smaller tertiary roots, whose main duty is to absorb water and nutrients from the soil. These are both subsequently stored in the main taproot. One advantage of a taproot system is that it provides a strong anchor for the plant in the soil. **1** As for fibrous root systems, they begin with a small primary root, and then a number of secondary and tertiary roots branch off, thereby forming a large web of small roots underground. **2** Many grasses and cereal grains such as wheat have fibrous root systems. **3** The primary disadvantage of this type of root system is that plants with it are not strongly anchored in the soil, so they can be uprooted effortlessly. **4**

Most primary roots grow from a section of a plant seed embryo called the radicle. It is the first part of a plant to begin growing from the seed. From this beginning, the root develops into four major sections. At the tip is the primary rootcap, which is like a thimble protecting the root as it pushes down into the soil. The rootcap secretes a lubricant called mucilage, so it does not dry out as it pushes through the soil; however, the rootcap frequently suffers damage during the growing process so must be replaced through constant growth. The primary rootcap covers the area of the root called the zone of cellular division. There, rectangular-shaped cells called apical meristem continuously grow through the actions of mitosis, or division.

Alongside the zone of cellular division is the zone of cellular elongation. There, the growing cells begin forming hexagonal shapes and start stretching the primary root, which gives it length. The root then begins to require water to sustain growth, so there is a vascular structure in the center of this region. Above the zone of cellular elongation is the zone of cellular maturation. In that area, the primary root cells begin to mature and to form secondary and tertiary roots which expand from the primary root.

In taproot systems, these new roots bear a resemblance to hair and are usually thin as they extend from the primary root. In fibrous systems, the primary root is gradually replaced by roots of equal size that spread from the base of the plant. In turn, these roots may branch out into smaller secondary and tertiary roots. The primary function of these new roots is to absorb water and nutrients from the soil. In many plants, the primary root continues growing even as it develops more roots. This secondary growth serves to strengthen the primary root by giving it an outer structure that is tough like the bark of a tree.

*Glossary

cereal grain: a type of grass such as rye, barley, rice, oats, and wheat that is grown for its edible grain

embryo: the basic part of a plant that is found in a seed

10 According to paragraph 1, which of the following is true about plant roots?

Ⓐ They grow away from sources of light but in the direction of water.

Ⓑ They are known to grow upward at times when minerals are nearby.

Ⓒ They may sometimes have chlorophyll so can be green in color.

Ⓓ They have tertiary roots which are more extensive than their secondary ones.

11 The phrase "branch off" in the passage is closest in meaning to

Ⓐ spread out

Ⓑ combine

Ⓒ shrink

Ⓓ swell up

12 In paragraph 2, the author implies that wheat

Ⓐ has only secondary roots that are able to absorb water and minerals

Ⓑ has a taproot system that enables it to acquire enough water to survive

Ⓒ lacks a primary root that can help anchor it to the fields it grows in

Ⓓ can be pulled out of the ground easily because of its root system

13 In paragraph 3, the author mentions "a thimble" in order to

Ⓐ show what allows the rootcap to push down through the soil as the roots grow

Ⓑ make a comparison in order to describe the role of the rootcap in the roots

Ⓒ explain the manner in which the lubricant mucilage is secreted by the rootcap

Ⓓ show how strong the rootcap must be in order for it to grow larger

14 According to paragraph 3, the rootcap is constantly replaced because

(A) it dries out and dies when it fails to produce enough mucilage

(B) the actions of mitosis cause the cells in it to reproduce constantly

(C) it gets damaged a great deal as the root gets bigger

(D) plant seed embryos in the radicle continually provide new cells

15 In paragraph 4, all of the following questions are answered EXCEPT:

(A) How do the hexagonal shapes of cells benefit the roots of their plants?

(B) Where in the roots is the zone of cellular maturation located?

(C) What does a plant root need in order for it to continue to grow?

(D) What happens in the zone of cellular elongation in roots?

16 In stating that the new roots "bear a resemblance to hair," the author means that the new roots

(A) get longer as fast as hair

(B) grow in the same way as hair

(C) look similar to hair

(D) function like hair does

17 Look at the four squares [■] that indicate where the following sentence could be added to the passage.

For instance, the taproots of some conifers can be several meters long, which prevents them from being uprooted during violent storms.

Where would the sentence best fit?

Click on a square [■] to add the sentence to the passage.

18 **Directions:** Select the appropriate statements from the answer choices and match them to the type of root system to which they relate. TWO of the answer choices will NOT be used. **This question is worth 3 points.**

> Drag your answer choices to the spaces where they belong. To remove an answer choice, click on it. To review the passage, click on VIEW TEXT.

STATEMENTS

1. Does not have either a zone of cellular elongation or a rootcap

2. Is the type of root system that carrots and turnips both have

3. Is capable of helping a plant become strongly attached to the ground

4. Is the kind of system that a large number of cereals and grasses have

5. May grow new thin, hair-like roots from the main root

6. Has secondary roots that make the outer structure of a primary root hard

7. Begins to grow even while a plant is just an embryo still in a seed

TYPE OF ROOT SYSTEM

Taproot System (Select 3)

-
-
-

Fibrous Root System (Select 2)

-
-

A   Complete each sentence with the appropriate word from the box.

secrete	plagued	supremacy	strengthen	characteristics

1   One of Cindy's most appealing _____ is her ability to listen to others.

2   The illness _____ the people of the village for more than six months.

3   He hopes to _____ his muscles by lifting weights five times a week.

4   Some frogs _____ dangerous poison on their backs.

5   The country's strong military has allowed it to gain _____ over its neighbors.

B   Complete each sentence with the correct answer.

1   _____ of the people must vote in favor of the proposal for there to be a **majority**.

a. More than half   b. A few

2   When the bridge **collapsed** and _____ the water, there was nobody on it.

a. fell down into   b. was built over

3   **Nocturnal** animals are those which are active _____.

a. during the day   b. at night

4   This **mixture** is basically _____ of several herbs and spices.

a. an aroma   b. a combination

5   The fire **consumed** three houses and _____ them.

a. destroyed   b. damaged

6   Marcia gave a **simplified** answer, so her solution to the problem was _____.

a. detailed   b. not complex

7   During the storm, several trees were **uprooted**, so they _____ due to the wind.

a. lost many of their branches   b. were pulled out of the ground

8   A person who can **distinguish** between two things can _____.

a. recognize which one is which   b. understand what they are made of

9   When a person **attains** fame, that person _____ well known.

a. becomes   b. wishes to be

10 David **halved** the large rock by _____ with a laser.

a. cutting to the inside   b. cutting it into two pieces

Actual Test

Reading Section Directions

This section measures your ability to understand academic passages in English. You will have **54 minutes** to read and answer questions about **3 passages**. A clock at the top of the screen will show you how much time is remaining.

Most questions are worth 1 point but the last question for each passage is worth more than 1 point. The directions for the last question indicate how many points you may receive.

Some passages include a word or phrase that is underlined. Click on the word or phrase to see a definition or an explanation.

When you want to move to the next question, click on **NEXT**. You may skip questions and go back to them later. If you want to return to previous questions, click on **BACK**. You can click on **REVIEW** at any time, and the review screen will show you which questions you have answered and which you have not answered. From this review screen, you may go directly to any question you have already seen in the Reading section.

Click on **CONTINUE** to go on.

Fault Lines

San Andreas Fault in California, USA

Among the most destructive forces of nature are earthquakes, which occur suddenly with little or no warning and frequently cause widespread death and destruction. Many earthquakes happen in the same regions, such as Japan, Turkey, and the western part of North America. This happens mainly because of plate tectonics, which involves the colliding or separating of the large plates comprising the Earth's crust and which are in constant motion. In zones where the plates meet, there is a great deal of stress. It causes the crust to move, thereby resulting in earthquakes when the energy realized is strong and violent. In some places where plates meet, fault lines may actually appear on the surface.

A fault is a place where stress on the rock causes it to fracture in noticeable lines. Both vertical and horizontal motion can cause fault lines to form. These lines vary in size; some are as tiny as the width of a hair whereas others, such as the San Andreas Fault in California, USA, and the North Anatolian Fault in Turkey, are large enough to be visible from space. Faults are particularly obvious in layers of sedimentary rock. This type of rock contains a distinctive separation of the visible bands of different layers, and it can clearly show the presence of a fault line. There are three main types of fractures which can occur: strike-slip faults, normal faults, and reverse faults.

Each fault is categorized based upon the type of motion causing the fraction. A strike-slip fault occurs when the separation in the rock happens in the horizontal plane and involves little or no vertical motion. The fault line itself is vertical—straight up and down—but the blocks of rock move past one another horizontally. The two most visible faults on the planet, the San Andreas and

North Anatolian fault lines, are both classified as strike-slip fault lines. Normal fault lines occur when there is vertical movement of the rock as one side of the fracture becomes lower than the normal surface level of the crust. The blocks of rock are additionally pulled apart, creating space between them along the fault line. Over time, extensive normal fault lines can create wide valleys such as the Rift Valley in East Africa. The third type is the reverse fault line. It also involves vertical motion but happens when two places collide. In this situation, one region of rock is thrust upward higher than the opposite region. Due to this motion, this kind of fault is sometimes called a thrust fault.

Arguably the world's most famous and extensively studied fault line is the San Andreas Fault. First noticed in 1895, it begins near San Francisco and runs in a southeasterly direction around 1,300 kilometers to a location east of Los Angeles. From afar, it appears to be a single fissure in the crust, but a closer inspection reveals there are numerous fault lines in the same area. A region like this is called a fault zone. This zone is the result of the Pacific Plate sliding northwest while the adjoining North American Plate slides southeast at the same time. The movement rate is roughly thirty to forty centimeters a year. Countless earthquakes have occurred in the area abutting the San Andreas Fault. The strongest one known to happen near the fault zone was the 1906 San Francisco earthquake, which measured an estimated 7.8 on the Richter Scale.

A second large and well-studied fault line is the North Anatolian Fault. It runs along the boundary between the large Eurasian Plate and the smaller Anatolian Plate. Like the San Andreas Fault, it is not a single fault but is instead composed of a series of fault lines, therefore forming a fault zone. Extending from east to west for around 1,500 kilometers, it starts near Istanbul, Turkey, and goes to the far eastern region of the country. The North Anatolian Fault is a strike-slip fault as the Anatolian Plate moves mostly westward and slightly to the southwest while the Eurasian Plate moves eastward. It moves slowly at around 25 millimeters a year. This fault zone has had its share of destructive earthquakes. The strongest in modern times happened in 1939 and measured 7.9 on the Richter Scale.

*Glossary

sedimentary rock: rock that forms in layers after sediment is deposited and hardens

Richter Scale: a measurement from 1 to 10 of the intensity an earthquake

Beginning

Fault Lines

➡ Among the most destructive forces of nature are earthquakes, which occur suddenly with little or no warning and frequently cause widespread death and destruction. Many earthquakes happen in the same regions, such as Japan, Turkey, and the western part of North America. This happens mainly because of plate tectonics, which involves the colliding or separating of the large plates comprising the Earth's crust and which are in constant motion. In zones where the plates meet, there is a great deal of stress. It causes the crust to move, thereby resulting in earthquakes when the energy realized is strong and violent. In some places where plates meet, fault lines may actually appear on the surface.

⇨ A fault is a place where stress on the rock causes it to fracture in noticeable lines. Both vertical and horizontal motion can cause fault lines to form. These lines vary in size; some are as tiny as the width of a hair whereas others, such as the San Andreas Fault in California, USA, and the North Anatolian Fault in Turkey, are large enough to be visible from space. Faults are particularly obvious in layers of sedimentary rock. This type of rock contains a distinctive separation of the visible bands of different layers, and it can clearly show the presence of a fault line. There are three main types of fractures which can occur: strike-slip faults, normal faults, and reverse faults.

1   In paragraph 1, the author uses "the western part of North America" as an example of

Ⓐ a place where two tectonic plates have combined to form a single plate

Ⓑ the area on the Earth that has the greatest number of tremors

Ⓒ a region where earthquakes commonly take place

Ⓓ the zone where powerful earthquakes are known to happen

Paragraph 1 is marked with an arrow (➡).

2   The word "noticeable" in the passage is closest in meaning to

Ⓐ clear

Ⓑ jagged

Ⓒ straight

Ⓓ large

3   According to paragraph 2, which of the following is NOT true about faults?

Ⓐ They are clearly evident when they happen in sedimentary rock.

Ⓑ Reverse faults are more common than the other two types of faults.

Ⓒ They can be caused through motion that moves vertically or horizontally.

Ⓓ Some are difficult to see whereas others are easily observable.

Paragraph 2 is marked with an arrow (⇨).

*Glossary

sedimentary rock: rock that forms in layers after sediment is deposited and hardens

4   According to paragraph 3, what causes a strike-slip fault to form?

(A) Two plates move away from each other horizontally.

(B) There is motion up and down but not any movement to the side.

(C) Two plates move vertically as one moves above the other.

(D) There is no motion up or down but only movement to the side.

Paragraph 3 is marked with an arrow (➡).

➡ Each fault is categorized based upon the type of motion causing the fraction. A strike-slip fault occurs when the separation in the rock happens in the horizontal plane and involves little or no vertical motion. The fault line itself is vertical—straight up and down—but the blocks of rock move past one another horizontally. The two most visible faults on the planet, the San Andreas and North Anatolian fault lines, are both classified as strike-slip fault lines. Normal fault lines occur when there is vertical movement of the rock as one side of the fracture becomes lower than the normal surface level of the crust. The blocks of rock are additionally pulled apart, creating space between them along the fault line. Over time, extensive normal fault lines can create wide valleys such as the Rift Valley in East Africa. The third type is the reverse fault line. It also involves vertical motion but happens when two places collide. In this situation, one region of rock is thrust upward higher than the opposite region. Due to this motion, this kind of fault is sometimes called a thrust fault.

5 The word "fissure" in the passage is closest in meaning to

Ⓐ line

Ⓑ area

Ⓒ crack

Ⓓ cliff

6 According to paragraph 4, what is a fault zone?

Ⓐ An area that has a large number of faults in it

Ⓑ A watery place in which fault lines may appear

Ⓒ A place where new faults form with regularity

Ⓓ A region which gets numerous earthquakes each year

Paragraph 4 is marked with an arrow (➡).

➡ Arguably the world's most famous and extensively studied fault line is the San Andreas Fault. First noticed in 1895, it begins near San Francisco and runs in a southeasterly direction around 1,300 kilometers to a location east of Los Angeles. From afar, it appears to be a single fissure in the crust, but a closer inspection reveals there are numerous fault lines in the same area. A region like this is called a fault zone. This zone is the result of the Pacific Plate sliding northwest while the adjoining North American Plate slides southeast at the same time. The movement rate is roughly thirty to forty centimeters a year. Countless earthquakes have occurred in the area abutting the San Andreas Fault. The strongest one known to happen near the fault zone was the 1906 San Francisco earthquake, which measured an estimated 7.8 on the Richter Scale.

*Glossary

Richter Scale: a measurement from 1 to 10 of the intensity an earthquake

7   The author discusses "the North Anatolian Fault" in paragraph 5 in order to

Ⓐ compare it with some of the world's other large faults

Ⓑ establish that the worlds' most powerful earthquakes happen there

Ⓒ describe its characteristics and the reason that it formed

Ⓓ argue that it is not really a fault line but is instead a fault zone

Paragraph 5 is marked with an arrow (➡).

8   Which of the sentences below best expresses the essential information in the highlighted sentence in the passage? Incorrect answer choices change the meaning in important ways or leave out essential information.

The North Anatolian Fault is a strike-slip fault as the Anatolian Plate moves mostly westward and slightly to the southwest while the Eurasian Plate moves eastward.

Ⓐ The North Anatolian Fault was formed when the Anatolian Plate and Eurasian Plate moved away from each other.

Ⓑ The movements of the two plates comprising the North Anatolian Fault result in it being a strike-slip fault.

Ⓒ When the Eurasian plate and the Anatolian Plate move in different directions, they can cause a strike-slip fault to form.

Ⓓ The world's largest strike-slip fault is the North Anatolian Fault, which is created by the Anatolian and Eurasian plates.

➡ A second large and well-studied fault line is the North Anatolian Fault. It runs along the boundary between the large Eurasian Plate and the smaller Anatolian Plate. Like the San Andreas Fault, it is not a single fault but is instead composed of a series of fault lines, therefore forming a fault zone. Extending from east to west for around 1,500 kilometers, it starts near Istanbul, Turkey, and goes to the far eastern region of the country. The North Anatolian Fault is a strike-slip fault as the Anatolian Plate moves mostly westward and slightly to the southwest while the Eurasian Plate moves eastward. It moves slowly at around 25 millimeters a year. This fault zone has had its share of destructive earthquakes. The strongest in modern times happened in 1939 and measured 7.9 on the Richter Scale.

9 Look at the four squares [■] that indicate where the following sentence could be added to the passage.

It is more than 6,400 kilometers long and can be more than sixty kilometers wide, too.

Where would the sentence best fit?

Click on a square [■] to add the sentence to the passage.

Each fault is categorized based upon the type of motion causing the fraction. A strike-slip fault occurs when the separation in the rock happens in the horizontal plane and involves little or no vertical motion. The fault line itself is vertical—straight up and down—but the blocks of rock move past one another horizontally. The two most visible faults on the planet, the San Andreas and North Anatolian fault lines, are both classified as strike-slip fault lines. Normal fault lines occur when there is vertical movement of the rock as one side of the fracture becomes lower than the normal surface level of the crust. The blocks of rock are additionally pulled apart, creating space between them along the fault line. ■ Over time, extensive normal fault lines can create wide valleys such as the Rift Valley in East Africa. ■ The third type is the reverse fault line. ■ It also involves vertical motion but happens when two places collide. ■ In this situation, one region of rock is thrust upward higher than the opposite region. Due to this motion, this kind of fault is sometimes called a thrust fault.

10 **Directions:** An introductory sentence for a brief summary of the passage is provided below. Complete the summary by selecting the THREE answer choices that express the most important ideas of the passage. Some sentences do not belong because they express ideas that are not presented in the passage or are minor ideas in the passage. **This question is worth 2 points.**

Drag your answer choices to the spaces where they belong. To remove an answer choice, click on it. To review the passage, click on **VIEW TEXT**.

There are three main types of fault lines, all of which are formed by plate tectonics.

-
-
-

ANSWER CHOICES

1. Earthquakes happen all the time around the world, but most of them are not strong enough to be noticed.

2. A strike-slip fault involves horizontal movement, so it often results in the faults being highly noticeable.

3. When rock fractures due to the action of plate tectonics, a fault, which can be thousands of kilometers long, forms.

4. Sometimes two plates moving away from each other can create a valley, like at the African Rift Valley.

5. Both normal faults and reverse faults are formed based upon the way that two or more plates underground interact.

6. Fault zones are created when a large number of faults occur in an area.

Filter Feeders

Baleen of a gray whale

Animals obtain food in various ways, typically by either eating plants or by hunting and killing other animals. Another manner in which they obtain food is through filter feeding. Filter feeders take in large amounts of water and mud, which then passes through a special filtering part in their bodies, where food is extracted. Most filter feeders are marine animals, such as some species of whales and sharks as well as many kinds of shellfish. However, filter feeding is not restricted to marine life as several types of aquatic birds are also filter feeders.

The mechanism of filter feeding varies from species to species, but each operates on the same basic principles. Within water, whether it be a vast ocean, river, or lake, there are minute marine lifeforms and tiny particles of suspended matter which can be consumed as food. A filter feeder draws water into its filtering part, and the food particles get stuck there while water merely passes through. The food particles are then taken into the body to be digested. The process is often equated with straining boiled foods such as pasta or vegetables in a <u>sieve</u>. In animals, the sieve-like body part varies depending on the species. Filter-feeding whales, for instance, have baleen rather than teeth. These are similar to stiff bristles, and they line the mouth, enabling whales to trap food as water passes through them. As for filter-feeding sharks, they have wide mouths and special structures in their gills and throats which trap food floating in the water. Another method is used by several species of shellfish, which capture food in their gills as they draw in water to breathe.

Filter feeders are either stationary or active while eating. Stationary filter feeders do not move and therefore draw water into their bodies. One example of a stationary filter feeder is the class of

bivalve shellfish including oysters, mussels, and scallops. They suck in water to breathe, and food particles simultaneously get stuck in their gills. On the gills are tiny hairs called cilia that trap the food and then move it past the gills for the shellfish to consume. Active filter feeders such as whales and sharks, conversely, must move through the water to feed. Whales with baleen, which include the blue whale and the humpback whale, open their wide mouths as they swim, so tons of water pass through their baleen and then go out the sides of their mouths. By using this method, they can capture enormous amounts of small plankton, their primary source of nutrition.

Aquatic birds are also active filter feeders. They usually swim on the surface of the water or walk around in shallow water while feeding. Then, they dip their beaks into the water, thereby collecting large quantities of water and mud in their mouths. They hold their heads up and strain the water and mud to acquire food. The flamingo, which lives in tropical and subtropical environments, is a filter feeder. The diet of flamingoes consists mainly of brine shrimp and blue-green algae, which they find in mud in shallow water. They dip their heads into the water and scoop up large amounts of mud and water into their mouths. Inside a flamingo's mouth are special hairs called lamellae. They separate the food from the mud and water as it drains out of the bird's mouth.

Filter feeders are considered essential components of a healthy marine ecosystem. They help other species survive by removing pollution from water and by keeping the water clean in general. Clean water allows more sunlight to reach deeper depths, enabling marine plants to survive at those levels. Filter feeders also remove excess nitrogen from the water. Nitrogen is responsible for large algae blooms that deplete the oxygen level in water. It is estimated that a single oyster can cleanse up to fifty-five liters of water on a daily basis. A large shellfish population in a small region can therefore clean millions of liters per day. The impact of the loss of such filter feeders can be seen in Chesapeake Bay in the eastern United States. There, the decline of its oyster population due to overfishing in recent years has led to mounting ecological problems in the bay area.

*Glossary

sieve: an instrument used to separate solids from liquids

algae bloom: a condition when a large amount of algae suddenly grows in an area

Filter Feeders

➡ Animals obtain food in various ways, typically by either eating plants or by hunting and killing other animals. Another manner in which they obtain food is through filter feeding. Filter feeders take in large amounts of water and mud, which then passes through a special filtering part in their bodies, where food is extracted. Most filter feeders are marine animals, such as some species of whales and sharks as well as many kinds of shellfish. However, filter feeding is not restricted to marine life as several types of aquatic birds are also filter feeders.

⇨ The mechanism of filter feeding varies from species to species, but each operates on the same basic principles. Within water, whether it be a vast ocean, river, or lake, there are minute marine lifeforms and tiny particles of suspended matter which can be consumed as food. A filter feeder draws water into its filtering part, and the food particles get stuck there while water merely passes through. The food particles are then taken into the body to be digested. The process is often equated with straining boiled foods such as pasta or vegetables in a sieve. In animals, the sieve-like body part varies depending on the species. Filter-feeding whales, for instance, have baleen rather than teeth. These are similar to stiff bristles, and they line the mouth, enabling whales to trap food as water passes through them. As for filter-feeding sharks, they have wide mouths and special structures in their gills and throats which trap food floating in the water. Another method is used by several species of shellfish, which capture food in their gills as they draw in water to breathe.

*Glossary

sieve: an instrument used to separate solids from liquids

11 In paragraph 1, all of the following questions are answered EXCEPT:

    Ⓐ What are some animals that obtain their nutrients by engaging in filter feeding?

    Ⓑ Which species of birds regularly make use of filter feeding to get food?

    Ⓒ What is the process through which filter feeders obtain food?

    Ⓓ How do animals usually acquire the food that they need to survive?

Paragraph 1 is marked with an arrow (➡).

12 According to paragraph 2, whales can engage in filter feeding because

    Ⓐ their gills have special structures that let them extract food from water

    Ⓑ they can remove food from water thanks to baleen in their mouths

    Ⓒ their wide mouths allow them to scoop up organisms in the water

    Ⓓ they have sharp teeth which help filter out the nutrients they require

Paragraph 2 is marked with an arrow (⇨).

13 Why does the author mention "cilia"?

 Ⓐ To show their role in capturing food from water for shellfish

 Ⓑ To detail their importance to active filter feeders

 Ⓒ To describe how they form in shellfish

 Ⓓ To argue that they are more important than gills for filter feeders

14 Which of the sentences below best expresses the essential information in the highlighted sentence in the passage? Incorrect answer choices change the meaning in important ways or leave out essential information.

Whales with baleen, which include the blue whale and the humpback whale, open their wide mouths as they swim, so tons of water pass through their baleen and then go out the sides of their mouths.

 Ⓐ Most whales are like the blue whale and humpback whale in that they get food when water passes through their baleen.

 Ⓑ When whales open their mouths, water enters their baleen and is then expelled from their mouths.

 Ⓒ The baleen of whales are useful when water passes into and out of their mouths so that they can get food.

 Ⓓ The blue whale and the humpback whale are two species of whales that use baleen to extract nutrients from the water.

15 According to paragraph 3, which of the following is true about stationary filter feeders?

 Ⓐ They include shellfish such as mollusks as well as fish such as sharks.

 Ⓑ They can use gills, to obtain food from water.

 Ⓒ They cannot move a large majority of the time.

 Ⓓ They eat at the same time that they breathe with their gills.

Paragraph 3 is marked with an arrow (➡).

➡ Filter feeders are either stationary or active while eating. Stationary filter feeders do not move and therefore draw water into their bodies. One example of a stationary filter feeder is the class of bivalve shellfish including oysters, mussels, and scallops. They suck in water to breathe, and food particles simultaneously get stuck in their gills. On the gills are tiny hairs called cilia that trap the food and then move it past the gills for the shellfish to consume. Active filter feeders such as whales and sharks, conversely, must move through the water to feed. Whales with baleen, which include the blue whale and the humpback whale, open their wide mouths as they swim, so tons of water pass through their baleen and then go out the sides of their mouths. By using this method, they can capture enormous amounts of small plankton, their primary source of nutrition.

End ▲

16 According to paragraph 4, flamingoes use lamellae to

Ⓐ avoid picking up food particles that are too large

Ⓑ determine where there may be food in mud and water

Ⓒ remove food particles from mud and water

Ⓓ scoop up large amounts of mud and water

Paragraph 4 is marked with an arrow (➡).

17 The word "deplete" in the passage is closest in meaning to

Ⓐ utilize

Ⓑ plummet

Ⓒ sacrifice

Ⓓ exhaust

18 In paragraph 5, the author implies that oysters

Ⓐ could be useful at removing pollution from Chesapeake Bay

Ⓑ are able to absorb nitrogen and turn it into oxygen

Ⓒ will not live in large numbers if there is polluted water

Ⓓ can reproduce quickly even in conditions that are less than ideal

Paragraph 5 is marked with an arrow (⇨).

➡ Aquatic birds are also active filter feeders. They usually swim on the surface of the water or walk around in shallow water while feeding. Then, they dip their beaks into the water, thereby collecting large quantities of water and mud in their mouths. They hold their heads up and strain the water and mud to acquire food. The flamingo, which lives in tropical and subtropical environments, is a filter feeder. The diet of flamingoes consists mainly of brine shrimp and blue-green algae, which they find in mud in shallow water. They dip their heads into the water and scoop up large amounts of mud and water into their mouths. Inside a flamingo's mouth are special hairs called lamellae. They separate the food from the mud and water as it drains out of the bird's mouth.

⇨ Filter feeders are considered essential components of a healthy marine ecosystem. They help other species survive by removing pollution from water and by keeping the water clean in general. Clean water allows more sunlight to reach deeper depths, enabling marine plants to survive at those levels. Filter feeders also remove excess nitrogen from the water. Nitrogen is responsible for large algae blooms that deplete the oxygen level in water. It is estimated that a single oyster can cleanse up to fifty-five liters of water on a daily basis. A large shellfish population in a small region can therefore clean millions of liters per day. The impact of the loss of such filter feeders can be seen in Chesapeake Bay in the eastern United States. There, the decline of its oyster population due to overfishing in recent years has led to mounting ecological problems in the bay area.

*Glossary

algae bloom: a condition when a large amount of algae suddenly grows in an area

19 Look at the four squares [■] that indicate where the following sentence could be added to the passage.

For instance, there are several species of ducks that get their sustenance through filter feeding.

Where would the sentence best fit?

Click on a square [■] to add the sentence to the passage.

Aquatic birds are also active filter feeders. **1** They usually swim on the surface of the water or walk around in shallow water while feeding. **2** Then, they dip their beaks into the water, thereby collecting large quantities of water and mud in their mouths. **3** They hold their heads up and strain the water and mud to acquire food. **4** The flamingo, which lives in tropical and subtropical environments, is a filter feeder. The diet of flamingoes consists mainly of brine shrimp and blue-green algae, which they find in mud in shallow water. They dip their heads into the water and scoop up large amounts of mud and water into their mouths. Inside a flamingo's mouth are special hairs called lamellae. They separate the food from the mud and water as it drains out of the bird's mouth

VIEW TEXT

REVIEW

HELP

BACK

NEXT

HIDE TIME 00:54:00

20 **Directions:** Select the appropriate statements from the answer choices and match them to the type of filter feeder to which they relate. TWO of the answer choices will NOT be used. **This question is worth 3 points.**

Drag your answer choices to the spaces where they belong. To remove an answer choice, click on it. To review the passage, click on **VIEW TEXT**.

STATEMENTS

1. Are capable of polluting large amounts of water

2. Can include both stationary and active feeders

3. Take mud and water into their mouths while feeding

4. May take in tons of water on a daily basis

5. May sometimes cause algae blooms to appear in water

6. Typically hunt for food in water that is very shallow

7. Can rely upon baleen to extract food particles

TYPE OF FILTER FEEDER

Marine Animals (Select 3)

-
-
-

Aquatic Birds (Select 2)

-
-

The Dusseldorf School of Painting

Washington Crossing the Delaware by Emanuel Leutze (1851)

During the early to mid-nineteenth century, the city of Dusseldorf, Germany, was the center of an art movement based at the Prussian Royal Academy of Fine Arts. The academy had been founded in the late eighteenth century and was initially simply a local art school. But the academy soon developed an enhanced reputation. In 1819, after the Kingdom of Prussia took over Dusseldorf following the end of the Napoleonic Wars, the school was renamed. For the next hundred years, thousands of art students from around Europe and the Americas studied at the Prussian Royal Academy of Fine Arts. This laid the foundations for what would later become known as the Dusseldorf School of Painting. Most of its students eventually returned to their home countries or immigrated overseas. This enabled them to spread the ideas of the school far and wide. Prominent artists in the Dusseldorf School include Karl Friedrich Lessing, Johann Wilhelm Schirmer, the brothers Andreas and Oswald Achenbach, and Emanuel Leutze.

The Prussian Royal Academy of Fine Arts reached its peak from the 1820s to the 1850s. For most of that time, Friedrich Wilhelm von Schadow was its director. Schadow was a Romantic painter from the Nazarene School who had spent time in Rome as a young man. Religious themes influenced Schadow's works. He continued using them when he became the director of the academy in 1826. For the next three decades, the academy's students and teachers transmitted his ideas across the European and American art world. Eventually, new ideas on naturalism in art led to a struggle, during which Schadow was forced to resign from his post in 1859.

The academy produced a number of impressive fresco painters. Many were commissioned to create detailed religious works inside churches throughout Europe. However, the academy became

famous for the landscape paintings which its artists produced and which formed the core of the Dusseldorf School. The landscape artists worked primarily with oil on canvas. Their works were noted for the subdued coloring that gave them a somewhat drab appearance. The landscape paintings they produced vary in subject matter, but forests and mountains stand out as regular themes. Artists were encouraged to create landscapes in the open air by taking their easels and palettes to the countryside to paint what they saw. They also attempted to infuse moods into their landscapes. To accomplish that, they painted dramatic scenes with religious themes, stormy cloud-filled skies, high mountains, and dramatically posed people.

One famous example of this type of work is Emanuel Leutze's dramatic 1851 painting *Washington Crossing the Delaware*. It depicts American General George Washington crossing the ice-filled Delaware River in a small rowboat on a December night in 1776. This was an attempt to recreate an actual historical event from the American Revolutionary War. The scene takes place at dawn with Washington posed in a dramatic stance as he stands upright in the boat. He seems an almost godlike figure as he leads his men toward battle and stares off at the far riverbank, where the enemy may be lying in wait. A soldier behind Washington holds the American flag in a dramatic pose. The rest of the boat's occupants row and push aside the ice floes impeding the boat's progress. More boats filled with soldiers occupy the background while a muted dawn light floods over the scene from a cloudy sky.

All of the elements in *Washington Crossing the Delaware* were intended to evoke emotions and a sense of patriotism in viewers. While later criticized for its numerous historical inaccuracies, Leutze's work has stood the test of time as a representative example of the Dusseldorf School. Emanuel Leutze himself also exemplified the international flavor and influence of the school. He was born in the German state of Wurttemberg and moved to the United States as a child. He later moved to Dusseldorf to study at the academy and came under the influence of Schadow and Lessing. In time, he became a prime aide to many American students attending the school as he helped them adapt to life in a foreign land. Several of those artists he assisted later went on to become members of the Hudson River School of landscape artists in the United States.

*Glossary

fresco: a type of art that involves painting on plaster

palette: a board which painters use to keep paints and to mix colors

21 The author discusses "the Prussian Royal Academy of Fine Arts" in paragraph 1 in order to

   Ⓐ focus on its importance to an influential school of painting

   Ⓑ note that its name was changed during the early 1800s

   Ⓒ name some of the artists who served as its director

   Ⓓ describe the curriculum that was commonly taught there

Paragraph 1 is marked with an arrow (➡).

22 Select the TWO answer choices from paragraph 1 that identify characteristics of the Dusseldorf School of Painting. *To receive credit, you must select TWO answers.*

   Ⓐ It was important only in countries in Europe.

   Ⓑ It developed at a school located in Prussia.

   Ⓒ It was based on the school of abstract art.

   Ⓓ It influenced students from countries around the world.

Paragraph 1 is marked with an arrow (➡).

The Dusseldorf School of Painting

➡ During the early to mid-nineteenth century, the city of Dusseldorf, Germany, was the center of an art movement based at the Prussian Royal Academy of Fine Arts. The academy had been founded in the late eighteenth century and was initially simply a local art school. But the academy soon developed an enhanced reputation. In 1819, after the Kingdom of Prussia took over Dusseldorf following the end of the Napoleonic Wars, the school was renamed. For the next hundred years, thousands of art students from around Europe and the Americas studied at the Prussian Royal Academy of Fine Arts. This laid the foundations for what would later become known as the Dusseldorf School of Painting. Most of its students eventually returned to their home countries or immigrated overseas. This enabled them to spread the ideas of the school far and wide. Prominent artists in the Dusseldorf School include Karl Friedrich Lessing, Johann Wilhelm Schirmer, the brothers Andreas and Oswald Achenbach, and Emanuel Leutze.

23 Which of the following can be inferred from paragraph 2 about the Prussian Royal Academy of Fine Arts?

    Ⓐ It imported a number of instructors from the Nazarene School.

    Ⓑ It was prominent only when being led by Friedrich Wilhelm von Schadow.

    Ⓒ Religious themes were taught at it during its highest point.

    Ⓓ Several different types of art were taught to its students.

Paragraph 2 is marked with an arrow (➡).

24 According to paragraph 2, which of the following is NOT true about Friedrich Wilhelm von Schadow?

    Ⓐ He lost his position at the academy as the result of a power struggle.

    Ⓑ He began creating works of art while he was the director of the academy.

    Ⓒ He painted similar themes before working at the academy and while he was there.

    Ⓓ He served as the director of the academy for around thirty years.

Paragraph 2 is marked with an arrow (➡).

➡ The Prussian Royal Academy of Fine Arts reached its peak from the 1820s to the 1850s. For most of that time, Friedrich Wilhelm von Schadow was its director. Schadow was a Romantic painter from the Nazarene School who had spent time in Rome as a young man. Religious themes influenced Schadow's works. He continued using them when he became the director of the academy in 1826. For the next three decades, the academy's students and teachers transmitted his ideas across the European and American art world. Eventually, new ideas on naturalism in art led to a struggle, during which Schadow was forced to resign from his post in 1859.

PASSAGE 3

REVIEW

HELP
BACK
NEXT

HIDE TIME 00:54:00

More Available ▲

25 The word "subdued" in the passage is closest in meaning to

Ⓐ silent

Ⓑ dull

Ⓒ matching

Ⓓ vibrant

26 According to paragraph 3, students at the academy often painted by

Ⓐ making drawings on canvas first and then painting over them

Ⓑ visiting places outdoors and painting pictures while they were at them

Ⓒ taking photographs of places and then painting pictures that looked similar

Ⓓ using pictures painted in the past as their primary models

Paragraph 3 is marked with an arrow (➡).

➡ The academy produced a number of impressive fresco painters. Many were commissioned to create detailed religious works inside churches throughout Europe. However, the academy became famous for the landscape paintings which its artists produced and which formed the core of the Dusseldorf School. The landscape artists worked primarily with oil on canvas. Their works were noted for the subdued coloring that gave them a somewhat drab appearance. The landscape paintings they produced vary in subject matter, but forests and mountains stand out as regular themes. Artists were encouraged to create landscapes in the open air by taking their easels and palettes to the countryside to paint what they saw. They also attempted to infuse moods into their landscapes. To accomplish that, they painted dramatic scenes with religious themes, stormy cloud-filled skies, high mountains, and dramatically posed people.

*Glossary

fresco: a type of art that involves painting on plaster
palette: a board which painters use to keep paints and to mix colors

27 The word "impeding" in the passage is closest in meaning to

Ⓐ propelling

Ⓑ abstracting

Ⓒ compelling

Ⓓ hindering

28 According to paragraph 5, which of the following is true about Emanuel Leutze?

Ⓐ He was one of the founders of the Hudson River School.

Ⓑ He provided help to a lot of foreign students in Prussia.

Ⓒ He was praised for the historical accuracy of his paintings.

Ⓓ He moved to the United States after attending the academy.

Paragraph 5 is marked with an arrow (➡).

One famous example of this type of work is Emanuel Leutze's dramatic 1851 painting *Washington Crossing the Delaware*. It depicts American General George Washington crossing the ice-filled Delaware River in a small rowboat on a December night in 1776. This was an attempt to recreate an actual historical event from the American Revolutionary War. The scene takes place at dawn with Washington posed in a dramatic stance as he stands upright in the boat. He seems an almost godlike figure as he leads his men toward battle and stares off at the far riverbank, where the enemy may be lying in wait. A soldier behind Washington holds the American flag in a dramatic pose. The rest of the boat's occupants row and push aside the ice floes impeding the boat's progress. More boats filled with soldiers occupy the background while a muted dawn light floods over the scene from a cloudy sky.

➡ All of the elements in *Washington Crossing the Delaware* were intended to evoke emotions and a sense of patriotism in viewers. While later criticized for its numerous historical inaccuracies, Leutze's work has stood the test of time as a representative example of the Dusseldorf School. Emanuel Leutze himself also exemplified the international flavor and influence of the school. He was born in the German state of Wurttemberg and moved to the United States as a child. He later moved to Dusseldorf to study at the academy and came under the influence of Schadow and Lessing. In time, he became a prime aide to many American students attending the school as he helped them adapt to life in a foreign land. Several of those artists he assisted later went on to become members of the Hudson River School of landscape artists in the United States.

29 Look at the four squares [■] that indicate where the following sentence could be added to the passage.

American soldiers led by Washington won a crucial victory in the battle they fought as the war was just beginning.

Where would the sentence best fit?

Click on a square [ ] to add the sentence to the passage.

One famous example of this type of work is Emanuel Leutze's dramatic 1851 painting *Washington Crossing the Delaware*. ■ It depicts American General George Washington crossing the ice-filled Delaware River in a small rowboat on a December night in 1776. ■ This was an attempt to recreate an actual historical event from the American Revolutionary War. ■ The scene takes place at dawn with Washington posed in a dramatic stance as he stands upright in the boat. ■ He seems an almost godlike figure as he leads his men toward battle and stares off at the far riverbank, where the enemy may be lying in wait. A soldier behind Washington holds the American flag in a dramatic pose. The rest of the boat's occupants row and push aside the ice floes impeding the boat's progress. More boats filled with soldiers occupy the background while a muted dawn light floods over the scene from a cloudy sky.

30 **Directions:** An introductory sentence for a brief summary of the passage is provided below. Complete the summary by selecting the THREE answer choices that express the most important ideas of the passage. Some sentences do not belong because they express ideas that are not presented in the passage or are minor ideas in the passage. **This question is worth 2 points.**

> Drag your answer choices to the spaces where they belong. To remove an answer choice, click on it. To review the passage, click on **VIEW TEXT**.

The Dusseldorf School of Painting was an influential art movement based at the Prussian Royal Academy of Fine Arts.

-

-

-

ANSWER CHOICES

1 Friedrich Wilhelm von Schadow was one of the longest-lasting directors at the academy as he served there for three decades.

2 Many of the artists in the movement painted landscapes that had dark colors and religious themes.

3 The academy had its name changed in the early 1800s, which was around the time that it became important.

4 Artists at the academy, such as Friedrich Wilhelm von Schadow and Emanuel Leutze, influenced numerous other painters.

5 Almost none of the artists who studied at the school returned to the United States to found a new art movement of their own.

6 *Washington Crossing the Delaware* is a notable example of the school of painting on account of the images it presents.

Authors

Michael A. Putlack

- MA in History, Tufts University, Medford, MA, USA
- Expert test developer of TOEFL, TOEIC, and TEPS
- Main author of the Darakwon *How to Master Skills for the TOEFL® iBT* series and *TOEFL® MAP* series

Stephen Poirier

- Candidate for PhD in History, University of Western Ontario, Canada
- Certificate of Professional Technical Writing, Carleton University, Canada
- Co-author of the Darakwon *How to Master Skills for the TOEFL® iBT* series and *TOEFL® MAP* series

Allen C. Jacobs

- BS in Physics, Presbyterian College, Clinton, SC, USA
- BCE in Civil Engineering, Auburn University, Auburn, AL, USA
- MS in Civil Engineering, University of Alabama, Tuscaloosa, AL, USA

Decoding the TOEFL® iBT
READING Intermediate NEW TOEFL® EDITION

Publisher Chung Kyudo
Editor Kim Minju
Authors Michael A. Putlack, Stephen Poirier, Allen C. Jacobs
Proofreader Michael A. Putlack
Designers Koo Soojung, Park Sunyoung

First published in October 2020
By Darakwon, Inc.
Darakwon Bldg., 211, Munbal-ro, Paju-si, Gyeonggi-do 10881
Republic of Korea
Tel: 82-2-736-2031 (Ext. 250)
Fax: 82-2-732-2037

ISBN 978-89-277-0880-3 14740
978-89-277-0875-9 14740 (set)

www.darakwon.co.kr

Photo Credits
p. 29 Tony Hisgett / Wikimedia Commons
https://commons.wikimedia.org/wiki/File:Engine_House_ (3452966818).jpg
p. 95 Therina Groenewald / Shutterstock.com
p. 200 Wellcome Collection https://wellcomecollection.org/works/ f48jat3q

Components Student Book / Answer Book
12 11 10 9 8 7 6   24 25 26 27 28